HYDROFICTIONS

HYDROFICTIONS

Water, Power and Politics in Israeli and Palestinian Literature

Hannah Boast

EDINBURGH
University Press

Edinburgh University Press is one of the leading university presses in the UK. We publish academic books and journals in our selected subject areas across the humanities and social sciences, combining cutting-edge scholarship with high editorial and production values to produce academic works of lasting importance. For more information visit our website: edinburghuniversitypress.com

© Hannah Boast, 2020, 2022

Edinburgh University Press Ltd
The Tun – Holyrood Road
12(2f) Jackson's Entry
Edinburgh EH8 8PJ

First published in hardback by Edinburgh University Press 2020

Typeset in 11/15 Adobe Garamond by
IDSUK (DataConnection) Ltd,

A CIP record for this book is available from the British Library

ISBN 978 1 4744 4380 7 (hardback)
ISBN 978 1 4744 4381 4 (paperback)
ISBN 978 1 4744 4382 1 (webready PDF)
ISBN 978 1 4744 4383 8 (epub)

The right of Hannah Boast to be identified as the author of this work has been asserted in accordance with the Copyright, Designs and Patents Act 1988, and the Copyright and Related Rights Regulations 2003 (SI No. 2498).

CONTENTS

Acknowledgements		vi
Introduction		1
1	Crossing the River: Home and Exile at the River Jordan	31
2	'The dense, murky water of the past': Swamps, Nostalgia and Settlement Myth in Meir Shalev's *The Blue Mountain*	69
3	'Current Liquidisations Ltd.': Israel's 'Mediterranean' Identity in Amos Oz's *The Same Sea*	108
4	Water Wars: Infrastructures of Violence in Sayed Kashua's *Let It Be Morning*	148
Conclusion		189
Bibliography		198
Index		233

ACKNOWLEDGEMENTS

Many people helped with this project and without them it would never have been completed. This book started life as a doctoral thesis in English and Geography at the Universities of York and Sheffield, and I would like to thank the White Rose Universities Consortium for funding my research. I am grateful to Jessica Dubow and Ziad Elmarsafy for their confidence in me and for conversations that always left me with a renewed sense of why research is worthwhile. Anna Bernard first introduced me to Israeli and Palestinian literature when I was an MA student at York and has been a constant source of guidance and inspiration since, including as a model of politically committed scholarship. Claire Westall offered incisive readings of early drafts that prompted me to think more deeply, invariably for the better. Claire and Pablo Mukherjee gave invaluable comments on the final thesis that helped it to become a book. Helen Smith gave me the opportunity to work on the Imagining Jerusalem network, through which I encountered people and ideas that expanded my understanding immeasurably. I would like to thank Sharae Deckard, Graham Huggan and the late Anthony Carrigan for treating me as an equal contributor to a shared intellectual project from the early stages of my time in academia. Dorothy Butchard, Asha Rogers and Rachel Sykes kept me afloat as a teaching fellow at the University of Birmingham and I miss them a lot. Mike Niblett brightened the final stages of this project with his support for my Leverhulme application at Warwick.

Helen Battison and Cecy Marden have stuck with me in spite of occasionally extreme neglect on my side of the friendship. Stef Lambert, Cat Oakley and Lucy Potter have been intellectual co-conspirators, confidantes, and providers of solidarity and delicious food. I was lucky enough to be able to make Sheffield my home while writing much of this project. Many people there contributed to my intellectual and political development and were also a lot of fun. Particular thanks go to Charlotte Jones, Seán McCorry and Gabby Patterson, who have challenged me to think more deeply about the world, offered serious emotional support and kept me aware that there is more to life than academia. I benefited greatly from conversations with Christine Gilmore and Will Wright and it was a pleasure to see our work grow together. Tom Langley helped to set me on this course by urging me to read Raja Shehadeh's *Palestinian Walks* a long time ago. Thanks to Geoffrey Humble for kindness and a place to stay in Jerusalem, and to Jo Bridger and Murad Alkhufash for showing me environmental resistance in practice and introducing me to *knafeh*. Assaf Gavron generously shared unpublished work and took the time to talk hydropolitics with me in ways that informed this project. Guy Davidi helped out by sharing with me his and Alexandre Goetschmann's documentary, *Interrupted Streams*.

My parents, Paul and Kathryn, have supported me in many ways. My mum helped me to pursue educational opportunities that she did not have access to and I am so proud of her for graduating from the Open University in 2015 with a 2:1 degree in History. My aunt and uncle, Dianne and Kevin Leahy, similarly deserve thanks for their support and for sharing their boundless love of learning. My grandparents, Gordon and Margaret Boast, and Tim and Rosemary Leahy, nurtured my environmental interests and my Leahy grandparents helped to develop my political ones. Tom O'Shea has helped me to think in new ways and with new ideas, while being a constant source of love and care.

Material from Chapter 1 was previously published as '"A River without Water": Hydropolitics and the River Jordan in Palestinian Literature', *Journal of Commonwealth Literature*, 51(2), pp. 275–86. I am grateful to the journal for permission to reproduce it.

INTRODUCTION

In his 2008 eco-thriller *Hydromania*, Israeli novelist Assaf Gavron imagines a future Israel/Palestine in the aftermath of dramatic climate change.[1] Set in the worryingly close year of 2067, *Hydromania* presents a drastically altered political scenario in which Palestinians have won the conflict, claimed Jerusalem as their capital and become the regional power. In a reversal of the current territorial situation, Israelis have been left with a narrow coastal strip comprising the two now overcrowded cities of Caesarea and Tiberias. The novel's main theme, however, is water scarcity, with Gavron producing an Israeli version of the emerging genre of climate fiction, or 'cli-fi'.[2] The world of *Hydromania* is effectively governed by corporations from three countries – China, Japan and, more surprisingly, Ukraine – who exercise control over every aspect of Israeli citizens' lives through their monopoly on the scarce commodity of water, now known by its brand names of 'Ohiya Water' or 'Gobogobo Water'. Rainfall is rare, with each event timed using sophisticated technologies, and citizens are prevented from collecting their own water, leaving them constantly thirsty. This state of affairs is policed through heavy surveillance, including tracking and identification chips in every person's arm. In Gavron's novel the loss of easy access to water alters every aspect of Israeli existence.

Reviewing *Hydromania* for the Israeli newspaper *Haaretz*, Inbal Malka described it as tapping into contemporary Israeli fears. She cautioned that '[t]he future that Assaf Gavron depicts in *Hydromania* is a prospect familiar to every anxious Israeli'.[3] Yet in an age in which talk of 'climate emergency' has belatedly entered the mainstream, Gavron's dystopian scenario now speaks to many more than just Israelis. Recent years have seen frenzied reporting in the Anglophone media of 'Day Zero' in Cape Town, California's near-constant state of drought and the UK's increasingly regular heatwaves, with attention (if rather less of it) focused at the time of writing on water shortages in Chennai. Gavron's novel, however, does more than merely anticipate this trend: its specific national context is crucial to how we understand the concept of water crisis in the present. Israel/Palestine has become the site at which twenty-first-century anxieties and hopes about our water supply coalesce.

Israel/Palestine is well known as the archetypal 'water war'. Past, present and possible future conflict in the region is regularly framed by academics, politicians and the media as motivated by the need to secure scarce resources. This supposed phenomenon appears to exemplify a coming crisis according to which, as then World Bank Vice-President Ismail Serageldin famously predicted in 1995, 'many of the wars of this century were about oil, but wars of the next century will be over water'.[4] The Syrian Civil War and the war in Yemen are often presented as exacerbated or even caused by water shortages, seeming to show Serageldin's prediction coming true (the reality, as ever, is more complicated).[5] Curiously, Israel is described as vulnerable to water wars yet promoted at the same time as having 'solved' its water crisis and even having a 'water surplus' due to advances in desalination, drip irrigation and wastewater recycling. Lauded as the 'Start-up Nation' and the 'Silicon Valley of water technology', Israel seems to tell us that we might entirely circumvent the problem of limited supply (that is, if we can afford it).[6]

Israel's 'water miracle' may be bringing relief to parched California, but it is one that has not been shared with its immediate neighbours, the Palestinians. If Gavron's novel imagines water scarcity as a frightening Israeli future, in many ways it reflects a Palestinian reality: 97 per cent of Gaza's groundwater is contaminated by fertilisers, saltwater and sewage, and the United Nations has declared that lack of clean water will render Gaza unliveable by 2020. Worryingly for Israel, this is not a problem that can be contained. A recent report by EcoPeace Middle East predicted thousands of Gazan refugees fleeing across Israel's borders to escape disease, echoing fears in the countries of the world's core about the potential for our offshoring of capitalism's environmental costs to come back to haunt us in a massive refugee crisis.[7] Palestinians, however, are active agents in resisting this phenomenon. The Palestinian struggle for water justice is at the centre of a growing global movement led by Black and Indigenous communities from Flint, Michigan, to Standing Rock, North Dakota, to Australia and New Zealand that is forging new models of transnational resistance. If Israel has become the putative 'saviour' of the water-intensive lifestyles of the global core, Palestine's longstanding status as 'the emblematic solidarity movement of our time' has transformed it today into the emblematic movement for water justice.[8]

This book turns to Israeli and Palestinian literature to unpack the dynamics of Israeli and Palestinian water politics. In doing so, it aims to deepen our understanding of the world's water crisis. I develop an analysis of Israeli and Palestinian literature as 'hydrofiction', a category I propose as a new literary critical tool. In using this term I ask what literary texts might tell us about what political ecologists call 'hydrosocial relations', or the ways that water is not simply acted on by humans but 'is both shaped by, and shapes, social relations, structures and subjectivities'.[9] Hydrofiction is a literary category for our era of 'hydromodernity' in which vast hydraulic engineering schemes – including dams, regularised rivers and drinking water infrastructures – have been used around the world to 'conquer' nonhuman nature and power nations into the modern era, with profoundly mixed consequences.[10] Hydromodernist thinking persists in responses to climate change that see the answers solely in the next 'technological fix'.[11] Taking its cue from the emerging field of 'petrofiction', this book asks what it might mean to 'read' the resource of water in literature. This approach offers a new direction in environmental literary criticism by focusing on a substance which is crucial to life but which has too often been overlooked.

The relevance of literature to Israeli and Palestinian hydropolitics may not seem immediately obvious outside literary studies. Indeed, to some in the climate movement any academic work is a misdirection of energy from the urgent task at hand. In Israel/Palestine there seem to be certain objective hydrological facts that are beyond dispute and that render literary perspectives superfluous. Israel/Palestine, namely, belongs to a water-scarce region in which shortages are inevitable and conflict likely. As such, equitable water distribution would seem to be a matter for engineers, scientists and politicians, not critics, novelists and poets. Yet Ramallah has a higher annual rainfall than London and Jerusalem's is higher than that of Berlin.[12] Our sense of Israel/Palestine as a naturally arid environment and home of 'water wars' is just one narrative that can be told about this place. What is more, it is a narrative that plays into an Orientalist and environmentally determinist narrative of the Middle East as a land of 'barren deserts and dangerous Arab dictators' that reaffirms the need for Israel to control Israel/Palestine's resources in an era of intensifying climate crisis.[13] Turning to literature can allow us to see that different stories about water in Israel/Palestine have been told over time and that the most important factor in whether water is constructed as scarce or abundant is dominant forms of political power.[14] This tells us that the current situation is not an unalterable 'fact of nature', but a product of political decisions: as Samer Alatout writes, 'water scarcity is not a fixed object, nor are relations of power that sustain it'.[15] Palestine's water inequalities may be severe, but they need not be permanent. In this context the notion of 'hydrofictions' reminds us of the extent to which 'natural' hydropolitical realities are socially and politically produced.

Literary studies has a vital role to play in deepening and critiquing the existing political, scientific and increasingly corporate dialogue on Israeli and Palestinian water. It contains the potential to unearth and complicate a range of widespread and influential assumptions, notably around water 'scarcity' and the 'proper' quantities and behaviours of water, typically derived from observation of Northern European environments.[16] By starting with the early Zionist hydromodernist projects at the start of the twentieth century and concluding with the infrastructural warfare of the present, this book offers an account of the role of water in changing ways of imagining the Israeli and Palestinian nations, of waging war and of practising resistance that has not previously been given. Reading key moments in Israeli and Palestinian history from a literary perspective draws attention to practices often taken for granted, telling us how hydropolitics shapes Israeli and Palestinian lives and giving insight into what Terje Tvedt and Terje Oestigaard call our 'lifeworlds', or 'worlds of water'.[17] Finally, a literary approach complements and extends the work of activists and political ecologists by allowing us to see the present situation as contingent, and encouraging us to imagine, and work for, an alternative. I hope this book will be a contribution to that project.

This book also seeks to make a distinct addition to the study of Israeli and Palestinian literature. Its goals are threefold. First, by foregrounding Israeli and Palestinian literature as environmental literature – something that has, amazingly, rarely been done – I aim to bring this writing to new audiences in the Anglophone world, where it has an unjustifiably low profile.[18] Second, I show that a move away from the dominant framework of conflict over land brings a new metaphorical and formal register into play, with a foregrounding of connectivity and flow over fixity and rootedness leading to new and perhaps surprising ways of encountering Israeli and Palestinian literatures. This hydrological imaginary does not, however, take us as far away from the politics of the land as we might expect. Instead, practices of nation-building, occupation and war re-emerge through watery contexts and tropes, with representations of water complementing more familiar Israeli and Palestinian environmental imaginaries. Finally, a turn to water brings neglected texts to light and shows us familiar authors in new ways.

I begin in Chapter 1 with the 1910 short story 'Hawaja Nazar' by the Hebrew writer and farmer Moshe Smilansky, reading his representation of a Jewish immigrant's feverish attachment to the River Jordan alongside better-known works on the river by the contemporary Palestinian poets Mahmoud Darwish and Mourid Barghouti to show the role of the Jordan in imagining home and exile and envisioning national futures. Chapter 2 examines Israeli novelist Meir Shalev's reappraisal of the Zionist movement and later Israel's swamp drainage programmes in *The Blue Mountain* (1988), bringing together the post-Zionist critique of Israel's national narratives in the 1980s with the parallel emergence of Israel's environmental movement. Chapter 3 turns to Amos Oz's vision of Israel's 'Mediterranean' identity in his novel *The Same Sea* (1999), a notion that appeared to hold peacemaking promise in the optimistic Oslo era. In the final chapter I read Sayed Kashua's novel *Let It Be Morning* (2004) in relation to the strategies of infrastructural warfare used by Israel against Palestinians with increasing frequency since Operation Defensive Shield in 2002, strategies that marked the definitive end of the false hopes of the Oslo period and take us to the present day. This book proposes that Israeli and Palestinian cultures, so long seen as defined by their conflict over land, are in fact equally defined by water.

In bringing a literary approach to bear on issues typically seen as essentially techno-scientific, this book forms part of the disciplines of ecocriticism and the wider Environmental Humanities. It contributes to the 'hydrological turn' in the Environmental Humanities known as the 'Blue Humanities' and to a 'turn' to resources most visible in work on 'petrofiction', a topic to which I return at the end of this introduction. As an examination of literatures from a context of ongoing, if disputed, settler colonialism, this book is situated within postcolonial studies and postcolonial ecocriticism.[19] It also draws on and contributes to cultural geography and political ecology, with a particular debt to Erik Swyngedouw's work on hydropolitics and the state.[20] I bring together insights from anthropology, science and technology studies, and inevitably, politics, notably the work of Jan Selby, whose foundational *Water, Power and Politics in the Middle East: The Other Israeli-Palestinian Conflict* (2003) I acknowledge in my title.[21] This excursion into multiple disciplines reflects the paucity of literary critical work on water until recently. At the same time, it indicates the necessity of interdisciplinary thinking on water, a substance which intersects with our lives in a multiplicity of ways: biophysical, cultural, religious and geopolitical, to name just a few. This work pushes against conventional disciplinary boundaries of academic research, which restrict our ability to understand and respond to environmental crisis.

In spite of the rapprochement of environmental and postcolonial studies in recent years and the 'turns' to water and resources noted above, there has been little engagement with water or environmental politics in Israeli and Palestinian literature. This book corrects this significant absence, which can be traced to core characteristics of both postcolonial studies and ecocriticism. Israel/Palestine has long been a glaring absence in postcolonial studies, in spite of the founding influence of the Palestinian scholar Edward Said. Israel/Palestine is of course not yet strictly 'post-colonial'; Palestinians remain subject to the ongoing violence of Israeli settler colonialism, while Israel's non-white citizens endure institutionalised discrimination and state violence.[22] Yet the 'post' in 'postcolonial' has never simply been about historical periodisation. A more pertinent issue, as Patrick Williams and Anna Ball rightly note, may be the significant professional risks of appearing to criticise Israel.[23] Postcolonialists, perhaps unsurprisingly, may not be willing to enter an area of debate which might lead to attacks from pro-Israel lobby groups that could endanger their careers and livelihoods. The same explanation seems transferable to ecocriticism, which remains most well-established in American literature departments and, as Rob Nixon has pointed out, has been largely reluctant to engage with the impact of US foreign policy.[24] Unconditional support for Israel remains a key pillar of US Middle East policy, more than ever under the Trump administration. As such, it seems predictable that there has been little ecocritical work on Israel/Palestine. It is the context in which the stakes for an American academic are highest.

The historical preference of both postcolonial studies and ecocriticism for land has also, until recently, mitigated against studies of water. The postcolonial preoccupation with land derives from the centrality of the issue of land sovereignty in anticolonial movements, which developed as an outcome of the land dispossession and expropriation initiated by colonial regimes and formed, in part, the origins of postcolonialism.[25] Postcolonialism's foundational concerns with national resource sovereignty and national cultures seem an awkward fit with the study of water, a substance which crosses national borders and seems as a result to necessitate transnational ways of thinking and different conceptions of resource ownership. A similar point applies in the case of ecocriticism and its sister discipline of the Environmental Humanities, with its roots in Romantic and Heideggerian philosophies of 'dwelling', bioregions and national environments, and insular fantasies of a self-sufficient 'return to the soil'. The Blue Humanities have brought water onto arts and humanities agendas in recent years, yet have focused primarily on the sea, specifically the culture, literature and history of the Anglo-American Atlantic world. Water itself, of course, moves constantly between salty and fresh states in the water cycle and the desalination technologies likely to play an increasing part in our future, while focusing on Britain and the United States misses out many countries already bearing the brunt of water shortages and replicates the parochialism of earlier environmental criticism. I hope this book will encourage future Blue Humanities work in new world-literary contexts, making the field better equipped to map correspondences between harms to water, practices of resistance and modes of representation across different geographies.[26]

The Anthropocene would seem an obvious context for a project on a substance fundamental to the continuation of human, and much nonhuman, life. This term was first proposed in 2000 by scientists Paul J. Crutzen and Eugene F. Stoermer as a name for the current geological era in which, they argue, human activities have become the primary influence on geological processes.²⁷ Advocates of the term such as Dipesh Chakrabarty argue that the impact of human practices on the planet is now so great as to threaten our own survival.²⁸ It has since become widely used, generating a great deal of literary and cultural criticism, and is being considered by the Anthropocene Working Group for formal adoption as the name of our present geological era. In this book I offer an analysis of Israeli and Palestinian writing as evidence against the notion of the Anthropocene, showing that the idea of 'humanity' as responsible for ecological devastation elides unequal accountability, unequally borne consequences, and the origins and persistence of these effects in colonial histories and what Derek Gregory calls our 'colonial present'.²⁹ I am inspired by Kathryn Yusoff's call to think more deeply about the 'anthropos' of the Anthropocene and the extent to which categorisations as 'inhuman' serve to justify manifold forms of extractive colonial violence.³⁰ In Israel/Palestine these include Israel's enclosure of Palestinian water resources and, as discussed in Chapter 4, its repeated destruction of Palestinian water infrastructure.

Rethinking Israeli and Palestinian Environments

While the notion of 'water wars' appears frequently in political and social sciences discourse, in cultural and historical contexts it is the land that dominates. When we think about Israeli and Palestinian environments we think of maps, soil, trees and the struggle for territory, with its emblem in Israel's separation wall snaking across the West Bank. We might remember the map of Palestine worn by Palestinian women as a necklace, or the Palestine Solidarity Movement's 'Disappearing Palestine' timeline. We might call to mind the soil from home villages treasured by Palestinian refugees, or sold from stalls outside the Church of the Holy Sepulchre as a tourist souvenir. In an Israeli context we may recall the kibbutz, with its role in 'redeeming' the land of Israel/Palestine and the Jewish people from their 'degraded' condition during Jewish exile. The Zionist movement developed extensive cultural practices aimed at cultivating and performing Jewish attachment to and ownership of the land, including the revival of the Jewish tree-planting festival of Tu B'shvat, teaching of the subject called 'knowing the land' (*yediat ha'aretz*) and youth movement hiking trips. Those who grew up with them in their homes may remember the Jewish National Fund's 'Blue Box', which allowed the Jewish Diaspora to contribute to the 'rebuilding' of the homeland through funding the planting of trees as 'proxy immigrants'.[31]

This preoccupation with the land is certainly widespread in Israeli and Palestinian literature. In Palestinian writing, for instance, the Palestinian village is often portrayed as a 'lost paradise' from which Palestinians have been unnaturally separated by Israel, imagined as an 'alien' and ecologically damaging intruder. In 'The Path of Affection' Layla 'Allush writes:

> The land is still the old land
> despite pawned trees on the hillsides
> despite green clouds and fertilized plants
> and water sprinklers spinning so efficiently
> On the startling road seized from the throat of new accounts
> the trees were smiling at me with Arab affection
> In the land I felt an apology for my father's wounds
> and on all the bridges
> the shape of my Arab face
> echoed there in the tall poplar trees,
> in the winding rings of smoke.
>
> Everything is Arabic still, despite the change of language
> despite the huge trucks, and foreign tractors.
> Each poplar and the orange grove of my ancestors
> laughed to me, my God, with Arab affection.[32]

'Allush contrasts efficient, mechanised Israeli agriculture with her own intimate, ancestral connection with the land, which remains 'Arab' and waits for her inevitable return. Her reference to the orange tree evokes another Palestinian symbol, found most famously in Ghassan Kanafani's short story 'Land of Sad Oranges' (1958), that would seem to affirm what we might call Palestinian literature's 'terrestrocentrism'.[33] The olive tree, too, is a recurring image.[34] Both are features of traditional Mediterranean economies, with the orange a reminder of Palestine's historic, now lost, centrality in the citrus industry as the home of the Jaffa orange. In Palestinian literature and art trees possess a greater significance as metonym for the rootedness of the Palestinians themselves and a reminder of the virtue of *sumud*, or steadfastness. This terrestrial focus is, as Liisa Malkki notes, characteristic of nationalist writing, art and rhetoric, with trees projecting the duration and 'natural' belonging of the nation itself.[35] A desire to project these qualities seems unsurprising in two national communities concerned with articulating a relationship between a diaspora and a longed-for homeland. Yet as 'Allush's references to sprinklers suggests, water is crucial for the health of the soil and for agriculture. In this sense water is fundamental to the more familiar nationalist imagery of land and trees, even if its importance is not apparent on the surface.

Water may not be the primary focus of Israeli and Palestinian literature in such an overt way as the land, yet it appears in many more places than may be expected. To continue with Palestinian examples: the most immediate way in which water appears in Palestinian writing is as a metaphor for dispersal and dispossession. Clouds, drops of rain and tears proliferate in Palestinian poetry, as in Darwish's line 'And I cry so that a returning cloud might carry my tears' in his 1986 poem 'I Belong There', or Nathalie Handal's poem 'The Lives of Rain' in her 2005 collection of the same name, in which rain becomes a moment of connection between the narrator and 'an old Chinese man/in the health food shop/at 98th and Broadway'.[36] Handal writes:

> Rain, he tells me, carries rumors of the dead,
> of those with suitcases and epidemics.
> Rain carries the memory of droughts,
> of houses gone, rain like lovers
> comes and goes, like soldiers go
> and sometimes return to a life
> no longer standing.
> The Chinese man waits for me to ask—
> Who really knows how many lives to come.

In Darwish's poem the global movement of the water cycle provides a way to imagine an intimate connection to the land even in exile, with his tears over its loss still irrigating the land when he is unable to care for it directly. For Handal, the experience of rain in different places prompts reflection on reasons for migration – disease, drought, war – writing Palestinian experiences into a broader history of displacement including, perhaps, climate migration. The renewal of the water cycle provides a metaphor for the lives lived by migrants in different places, while the concluding line hints at the end of the 'lives of rain' and suggests the potential for more forced beginnings of human lives anew after climate-induced displacement. Turning to water in these poems offers a new perspective on the familiar and sometime hackneyed Palestinian tropes of exile and displacement, allowing us to read Darwish's well-known work in a new light and to draw attention to Handal, a writer who deserves to be more widely read. Water's appearance as a subject for technical, managerial and political calculations rather than one that inspires deep attachment and literary reflection has led to its cultural significance for Israelis and Palestinians being overlooked.

Israeli and Palestinian Water

Readers of this book may not be familiar with the region's hydrography, so I will provide a brief sketch as context for what follows. These should not, however, be taken as 'natural' limits, since, as I discuss in greater detail below, 'nature' and 'culture' are inseparable and 'culture' determines the quantities of a 'natural' resource available to us at a given time. As Erich Zimmerman famously wrote, '[r]esources are not, they become'.[37] Israel/Palestine has two transboundary aquifers which are subject to ongoing contestations over their ownership. The Mountain Aquifer extends from north to south through central Israel and the West Bank, while the Coastal Aquifer is located beneath Gaza, Israel and the Sinai Peninsula and is Gaza's only freshwater source. Both aquifers, particularly the Coastal Aquifer, are threatened by over-extraction and contamination. The volume of the River Jordan, historically a major source of water for drinking and agriculture in Israel/Palestine, is vastly diminished, with a loss of 95 per cent of its flow since the 1950s. The river is heavily contaminated by saline spring water, sewage and agricultural chemicals.

The Jordan's reduced flow is a result of the diversion of much of its water into Israel's National Water Carrier, a network of pipes, tunnels, canals and reservoirs that redistributes the country's water to its populated coastal cities and arid south. The Carrier was completed by Israel's national water company, Mekorot, in 1964 after a ten-year construction period and was the new state's largest and most expensive environmental undertaking at the time. It redirects water from Israel's largest freshwater reservoir Lake Kinneret (also known as Lake Tiberias and the Sea of Galilee), before it reaches the southern section of the Jordan. In 2017 the Kinneret dwindled to its lowest level in a century, leading *Haaretz* to report that 'it's no longer that hard to walk on water at the Sea of Galilee'.[38] Overuse of the Jordan's water continues to have a dramatic impact downstream in the rapid shrinking of the Dead Sea, which in recent years has developed a shoreline pockmarked with alarming sinkholes. The hypersaline Dead Sea is not, of course, drinkable, but it is a unique ecosystem, tourist destination and source of mineral wealth; currently for Israel, but potentially in future for Palestinians too. The water levels of the Kinneret and the Dead Sea have been watched nervously by Israelis during recent years of drought, with the Israel Water Authority reviving its 'Israel is Drying Out' public information campaign in 2018.[39] Both the Kinneret and Dead Sea are also the target of mega-hydraulic development projects: in 2018 the Israeli government proposed 'topping up' the Kinneret with desalinated water, while the long-stalled 'Red-Dead Canal' project has recently re-emerged. These may yet alleviate the problems, or, as the history of mega-hydraulic development suggests, they may not.

Water management trends in Israel nevertheless indicate less cause for concern about supply in the immediate term than we might assume from the above – for Israelis, at least. Israel, like many countries, saves on local supplies by importing what geographer Tony Allan calls 'virtual water' embedded in food.[40] It also recycles 82 per cent of wastewater, mostly in agricultural irrigation.[41] Israeli innovations in drip irrigation, which feeds plants directly at the roots, have increased agricultural water efficiency, while cloud seeding is used on a small scale. However, the most significant development in Israeli water management is unquestionably desalination. As in many arid countries, most famously the Gulf, desalination has become an increasing priority for Israel. Israel has undertaken desalination research since the early 1950s, but the use of desalination did not become widespread until the early 2000s when a severe drought caused the Knesset to override Treasury fears.[42] The first seawater desalination plant was completed in Ashkelon in 2005 and today eighty-five per cent of the country's drinking water and forty per cent of its total water comes from desalination.[43]

Desalination is often promoted as an answer to the world water crisis. It is, however, energy-intensive and discharges hypersaline effluent and chemicals used in the desalination process back into the ocean. The effects of this discharge on coastal ecosystems are not yet clear, while the process of removing dissolved salts also removes magnesium and calcium, minerals crucial to human health. Desalination on the Mediterranean coast is regularly disrupted by contaminated seawater and, intriguingly, by jellyfish, one of the few species likely to flourish in a warming, acidified and overfished ocean. Israel's desalination plants are also threatened by its own military policies. The combined effect of Israel's bombing and blockade has meant that Gazans are unable to effectively process the region's sewage, so over 100 million litres flow into the ocean every day, including down the coast to Israel's Zikim beach and Ashkelon plant.[44] Israeli politicians including Ariel Sharon and Effi Eitan have described this as a 'sewage intifada' or 'water intifada'.[45] As this suggests, Israel's self-image as an ecologically responsible country is undermined by its treatment of Palestinians.

Palestinians in Israel/Palestine (as opposed to in the significant Palestinian diaspora) often endure such difficulties accessing water that living in conditions of scarcity shapes 'the experience and idea of being Palestinian'.[46] There is not, however, one 'Palestinian experience' of water shortage. Experiences vary widely, influenced by the different experiences of occupation and Israeli rule in the West Bank, Gaza and East Jerusalem, and within what became Israel after 1948, including Bedouin populations living in 'unrecognised' villages. The most immediately apparent division is between Gaza and the West Bank. As I discuss in Chapter 4, Palestinian access to water in Gaza is heavily affected by the devastation caused to water and electricity infrastructure by periodic Israeli bombardment. Electricity shortages mean sewage cannot be processed; neither can water be pumped to homes. Most Gazans buy their water from unregulated private water sellers because the water from their taps is contaminated and irregular, but this water is expensive and rarely much cleaner. The ongoing blockade means that Palestinian engineers are unable to access materials needed to repair the damage to infrastructure, which are classified by Israel as being of 'dual use' for military and civilian ends. Gaza's only power plant still operates at dramatically reduced capacity since being bombed by Israel in 2006, with the damage further compounded in the 2014 war. Feuds between Hamas and Fatah have exacerbated Gaza's electricity shortages, while US President Donald Trump's removal of funding for the UN Relief and Works Agency (UNRWA) in 2018 is likely to worsen the situation.

In the West Bank there are legal and bureaucratic obstacles to navigate. The Joint Water Committee, for instance, was created in the Oslo Accords (1993–5) to encourage 'cooperation' over water management between Palestinians and their settler neighbours. In reality, it perpetuates unequal access by giving settlers effective veto over Palestinian development.[47] Local water infrastructure is degraded, causing heavy leakage, and any installations built without a permit are demolished. As a result of their inability to access local groundwater (which is largely drinkable) the Palestinian Authority is forced to buy water at inflated prices from Mekorot, accumulating massive debts that intensify the colonial relationship between Israel and Palestine. Even within a West Bank community, lack of water pressure causes vast differences in access between homes at the top or bottom of hills, or on different floors of a tower block.[48]

As a rule, Palestinian water is costlier, less reliable and lower in quality, leading to the widespread occurrence of water-associated disease. This is notoriously the case in Gaza, where 26 per cent of disease is water-related.[49] Water shortages are also a major constraint on the Palestinian economy, restricting the economic potential of Palestinian agriculture. This can be seen as an example of what Sara Roy has called Israel's strategy of 'de-development', in which Palestinian development is not just delayed, but reversed.[50] Desalination is regularly mooted as a solution to Palestine's water shortages and to disputes between Israel and Palestine over water, providing a 'scalar fix' that has been backed financially by international institutions and NGOs including the EU and UNICEF.[51] Palestinians have rightly been sceptical of this approach because of its potential to leave them even more vulnerable to Israeli-induced electricity shortages and dependent on aid. Crucially, however, desalination skirts the question of Palestinian rights to water from the aquifers, lakes and rivers of their own land.

Understanding Israeli and Palestinian water politics today requires understanding some of the longer history of Zionist attitudes to water and the environment. As noted above, fears of dramatic water shortages coexist today in Israel with apparently contradictory expectations of limitless supply. The only constraint to the perpetual manufacturing of 'new' water seems financial. Israeli environmental engineering professor Hillel Shuval declares: 'Of course there is so much water, water is an endless resource. You can have all the water of the sea, if you can afford it, that is.'[52] Shuval's comment reflects the wider discourse on desalination in which the sea, as Swyngedouw notes, is portrayed as a 'seemingly endless, free, and uncontested source of unlimited supplies of water', with halting climate change requiring no need for a change in the way our world is organised.[53] At the same time, it recalls the rhetoric of Israel's first Prime Minister, David Ben-Gurion, who initiated the country's early 1950s experiments with desalination. Ben-Gurion saw desalination as a crucial element in Israel's attempts, in the famous Zionist slogan, to 'make the desert bloom', opening up the space needed to accommodate large numbers of new Jewish immigrants, accessing the Negev's potential mineral 'treasures', providing 'defensive depth' and showing Israel's success in 'redeeming' the land and the Jewish people to the world.[54] Ben-Gurion made grand pronouncements, asking: 'Should Israel be afraid of dreams that can transform the natural order by science, imagination and pioneering? Of course not, for that is our vocation'.[55] In 1953 he moved to the small Negev kibbutz Sde Boker to participate directly in the 'redemption' of the desert.

Like every political project, Zionism was also an environmental project.[56] Ben-Gurion's enthusiasm for dramatic alterations of the environment recalls a wider nineteenth- and twentieth-century enthusiasm for large-scale national engineering projects characterised by James C. Scott as 'high modernism'.[57] This was founded on 'a supreme self-confidence about continued linear progress' and faith in 'the development of scientific and technical knowledge, the expansion of production, the rational design of social order, the growing satisfaction of human needs, and, not least, an increasing control over nature (including human nature)'.[58] Water took on a central role in 'high modernist' projects as part of modernity's 'hydraulic mission', a topic I return to in relation to the discussion of Israel's swamp drainage programmes in Chapter 2 and the politics of infrastructure in Chapter 4.[59] The most famous examples of high modernist projects may be the dams and irrigation infrastructures of the American West, precursors to the global megadam craze of the 1950s and 1960s, while massive hydraulic engineering and irrigation works were frequent projects of European late-nineteenth-century colonialism in countries including Egypt, India and Sudan.[60] In postcolonial contexts dams functioned as 'a kind of national performance art' that showed a country's independence from colonial masters.[61] The Zionist movement and Israel's mega-hydraulic projects can to some extent be situated in this context as part of Israel's complex status as a '"post-colonial" colony'.[62] At the same time as instantiating a wider high modernist ideology, Ben-Gurion's faith in technology represented a specifically Zionist utopianism, embodied in Theodor Herzl's mantra '[i]f you will it, it is no longer a dream', a famous phrase that appeared on the title page of Herzl's 1902 utopian novel *Altneuland*.[63] The crucial role of a utopian novel in the early Zionist canon underscores the importance of a literary perspective in understanding Zionism's environmental politics, in which limits to what can be done have often been understood as imposed only by the imagination.

If in earlier years the Zionist movement and Israeli state sought more often to dominate nonhuman nature and bend it to their will, Israel has more recently aligned itself with environmental causes. Israel is a major developer and exporter of desalination and water conservation technologies, assisted by significant government support for water start-ups. In government promotional materials encouraging investment in Israeli 'cleantech' and 'bluetech' we find Ben-Gurion's ostensibly socialist nation-building discourse repurposed to serve capitalist ends, providing Israel's tech exporters with a compelling heritage narrative which authenticates their claims of expertise.[64] Water scarcity has changed since the founding of the state from an issue primarily associated with territorial expansion, statebuilding and the display of national technological ability to one with which neoliberal economics and globalisation are now intertwined.[65] Water may be, as Karen Bakker notes, an 'uncooperative commodity', with a degree of resistance to being privatised and commercialised inherent in its fluid materiality.[66] Nevertheless, Israel's government and start-ups are trying and, so far, succeeding, with exports of water technology and expertise contributing over 2 billion dollars to the economy a year.[67]

It is worth noting, however, that the historical link between water and Israeli territorial expansion has not gone away. Desalination is seen as having a key future role to play in Israel's attempt to construct new towns in its spacious but arid south as part of the Jewish National Fund's 'Blueprint Negev' programme. Yet the Negev, like early-twentieth-century Palestine, is not empty. It is home to Bedouin communities who suffer repeated eviction in order to produce this 'emptiness', including the al-Turi residents of the village of al-ʿAraqib.[68] Today, as in the past, assumptions that Palestine is unsettled and uncultivated by a neglectful and itinerant Arab population serve as justification for the capacity of Jewish 'return' to restore Palestine to a 'natural' state of biblical 'milk and honey'.[69] This mirrors a broader European colonial discourse of environmental ruination in which perceived desertification and overgrazing by indigenous people justified European land expropriation around the world, itself replicated in modern international conservation projects initiated without local consultation or consent.[70] In Israel it is part of a wider use of environmental policy for territorial ends, as in the designation of areas of East Jerusalem and the West Bank as 'national parks' and 'nature reserves', hiding the histories of these areas as Palestinian villages depopulated in 1948 and restricting Palestinian recreation and urban growth in the present.[71] Here, as elsewhere, the apparent 'universalism' of environmental causes covers up the ease with which these can easily align with capitalist and colonial ends.

The Israeli government's emphasis on Israel as the home of sustainable water management practices might be read as an example of 'greenwashing', or the use of environmental claims by countries or corporations to disguise more dubious practices. Along with gay rights, Israel's 'green' credentials have been at the forefront of its attempt to reframe itself internationally since 2006 through the 'Brand Israel' campaign.[72] 'Brand Israel' is an attempt to portray Israel as a country which shares European and North American values, encouraging political and military support and economic investment. Environmental concern works to smooth over acts of Israeli violence against Palestinians which might dent already waning support for Israel in Europe and North America, particularly among young American Jews (the Israel Defense Forces (IDF) now has vegan combat boots). At the same time, these claims disguise the environmental harms caused by Israel's occupation, which include the use of West Bank 'sacrifice zones' for disposal and treatment of hazardous wastes.[73] Palestinians, by contrast, are portrayed as causing environmental harm, as in the 'sewage intifada' or criticisms of the burning of tyres during Gaza's 'Great March of Return' in 2018, which Gazan protesters used to block the view of Israeli snipers. This rhetoric serves to present Palestinians as distant from European and American concerns even when Israel bears significant responsibility for environmental harm in Palestine.

Concern for water in particular seems to suggest an especially praiseworthy lack of national self-interest on the part of Israel, given its nature as a mobile substance which is globally shared and universally needed.

The environmental costs of the occupation are, however, clear from Israeli and Palestinian literature, particularly writing on refugee camps. Sewage and mud are inescapable features of these texts, highlighting the impact of Palestine's improvised, ineffective and overloaded urban water infrastructures and evoking the use of sewage as an instrument of settler violence. This can be seen in Lena Khalaf Tuffaha's 2017 poem 'Abu Nasser'.[74] Tuffaha describes the life of a refugee widower who 'nurses arthritis and longing' as he looks out of his door, 'beyond the road outside and past the thin stream of sewage trickling down the road, stench hanging low in July heat, flies buzzing overhead in thick clouds'. Significantly, we do not know whether this sewage is Palestinian or Israeli; villagers in the West Bank village of Salfit regularly endure the pollution of their land and streets by sewage released from the Israeli settlement Ariel, which sits directly above it.[75] Tuffaha's poem indicates that the origin of the sewage does not matter, since both flows are caused by Israel's occupation. Her widower, even so, maintains his dignity and *sumud* in the face of degradation by Israel, looking 'beyond' and 'past' the stream.

Representations of sewage in Israeli writing also prompt sympathy and self-criticism. This can be seen in Israeli poet Dahlia Ravikovitch's reference to 'the sewage puddles of Sabra and Shatila' in her poem 'You Can't Kill a Baby Twice'.[76] These are the Beirut refugee camps that were the sites of infamous massacres of Palestinian and Lebanese civilians by Lebanese Christian Phalangist militias assisted by Israel during its 1982 invasion of Lebanon. This metonym suggests the extent to which unclean conditions in camps are produced by warfare and serve to 'legitimate' violence against their populations. At the same time, as Joseph Hall notes, this is a risky strategy with the potential to reaffirm stereotypes of an 'othered' population.[77] Elsewhere representations of sewage become symbols of the state of the nation, as in the pessimistic refrain 'sink into the mud, Palestine' of Sahar Khalifeh's 1976 novel *Wild Thorns*, written in the wake of the 1967 defeat, or, as Hall notes, in David Grossman's equation of uncontrolled Palestinian waste with radicalisation seeping across Israel's border in his non-fictional work *The Yellow Wind* (1988).[78] In this case, literature shows the socio-political origins and impacts of Palestine's environmental crisis, as well as the potential for representing this crisis to inadvertently reinforce notions of Israeli environmental superiority.

What Is Water?

I have discussed water so far as if it has a straightforward meaning. However, just as Israeli and Palestinian water is not 'merely' scarce and likely to cause wars, neither is water as simple as it seems. We typically imagine water as a substance that exists 'out there' in nature as the compound H_2O, ready to be turned by humans into a managed and measurable 'resource'. Yet to perceive water in this way would be a mistake. As geographers and environmental historians have long been aware, water is not simply acted upon by humans but influences human society, producing social relations. The most notorious version of this argument is Karl Wittfogel's 1957 notion of the 'hydraulic society'.[79] Focusing on ancient China, Egypt, India and Mesopotamia, Wittfogel argued that the need to find the huge workforce to build major irrigation and dam infrastructures resulted in centralised and socially controlling forms of government, producing what he called 'Oriental despotism'. Wittfogel was building on Marx's dialectical account of labour, in which, Marx wrote, '[t]hrough this movement he acts upon external nature and changes it, and in this way he simultaneously changes his own nature'.[80] Wittfogel's argument is, of course, deterministic and essentialising; scholarship since has found counterexamples, while his discussion of the ongoing 'despotism' of the Chinese state bears more than a trace of his American Cold War climate. Nevertheless, scholars including Donald Worster have built on Wittfogel's work to identify the ways in which hydraulic engineering projects are incorporated into narratives of national self-construction, intended not only to supply water but to centralise power, inspire national pride and solicit international admiration for a country's ability to control nature.[81]

More recent criticism has emphasised the co-constitutive relationship between water and society, in which neither water nor society is a pre-existing, independent thing; instead, they are created through their interaction. This is the notion described earlier in this introduction as 'hydrosocial relations' that informs the approach in this book. From this perspective water is not just something that we act on, or that acts on us; as Linton writes, 'water is what we make of it'.⁸² What we think of as plain 'water' is produced by a manifold series of social processes and discourses. While this may seem counterintuitive, Swyngedouw shows what this means:

> Nature's water is captured, pumped, purified, chemically adjusted, piped, bought and sold, regulated, used by households, agriculture and industry, transformed into electricity, biochemically metabolised by plants, animals and humans, integrated in public displays like fountains, often turned into sewage, eventually returned to 'nature'.⁸³

Water may appear to be unproblematically 'natural', but it is constituted by a combination of 'natural' and 'cultural' elements: what Bruno Latour describes as a 'hybrid'.⁸⁴ Understanding water as merely 'H_2O' erases this social component, producing an impression of a world in which '[e]ven though we construct Nature, Nature is as if we did not construct it'.⁸⁵ This is important because the making of water legible as a fact of 'Nature' is what allows us to conceive of it as a resource existing in quantities independent of human intervention which we might discover, access, exploit or improve.⁸⁶ What is more, water's literal transparency and biophysical necessity disguises the extent to which it is produced through social and cultural processes and the fact that estimates of water potential are tied to relations of power.

This point may be better understood through returning to concrete examples. In Israel/Palestine, estimates of water potential have been closely tied to the priorities of the Zionist movement, the British Mandate authorities and, later, the Israeli state. The belief that Israel/Palestine is a water-scarce land is so widespread today as to be unquestioned. However, the opposite view prevailed among Zionist leaders until the creation of Israel in 1948 and formed a key part of the Zionist case for the feasibility of a Jewish state in Palestine.⁸⁷ As I discuss in Chapters 1 and 2, the Zionist movement used high estimates of Palestine's water potential to contest the British government's claims that Palestine lacked the 'absorptive capacity' to receive more Jewish immigrants.⁸⁸ By claiming abundant supplies of water, Zionist leaders were able to cite greater areas of land available for cultivation and settlement.⁸⁹ As Alatout notes, the present narrative of scarcity emerged after 1948, with the new need for state management of water resources facilitating the centralisation of institutions and strengthening the Israeli state.⁹⁰

The rhetoric of climate change serves a similar role today, allowing Israel to depict scarcity as a permanent fact of life in the Middle East and continue to deny water to the Palestinians.[91] Literature can help us to understand estimates of water potential as socio-political in origin and use them to shape alternatives in the present.

Water Is the New Oil

In the preceding section I discussed water as a natural resource, challenging the received wisdom that resources are merely naturally 'discovered' and showing that they are also produced by and productive of social relations and social power.[92] Water is often discussed in political and environmental contexts in relation to another resource, oil. Corporations seeking to capitalise on water crisis claim that 'water is the new oil', while water and oil appear together in the immense harms caused to water by oil spills. Oil has been the focus of much recent literary critical discussion in petrofiction and petrocriticism. This book asks what it might mean for water to be 'the new oil' in a critical sense, considering how petrofiction methodologies might be adapted to understand water in literature.

The term 'petrofiction' was coined by Amitav Ghosh in a 1992 review of Abdulrahman Munif's *Cities of Salt* trilogy, which shows the impact of the discovery of oil on a remote oasis community in the Gulf.[93] Petrofiction is now a fast-growing discipline within the 'Energy Humanities', a field that posits dominant 'energy regimes' as a new way of approaching literary and cultural periodisation.[94] Michael Rubenstein offers a helpful summary of the task of the petrocritic:

> A petrocritic may be someone looking to say something about texts about oil; she may also be looking for oil in cultural places where it is otherwise unspoken or unspeakable, at once too close, too far, and too immense to be immediately perceptible; and she may be looking, in fictions, for the profoundly uneven distribution of oil's benefits and consequences to peoples and territories around the globe.[95]

It is a premise of this book that there are valuable critical resources to be extracted from research on oil that can enrich our thinking about literature and water and our understanding of the relationships between water and power. First it is worth sketching some of the correspondences and contrasts between the material and symbolic meanings of oil and water.

Oil is fundamental to the lives of those of us in the world's wealthiest countries, yet this is largely unacknowledged except during times of crisis. Our oil dependence, as Graeme Macdonald writes, 'remains mostly "offshore" in our social and cultural consciousness', in part because of the physical offshoring of zones of oil extraction and their environmental consequences in the world's peripheries.[96] Yet oil invisibly ties together the local and global. Sixty-five per cent of known reserves of oil are in the Middle East, yet '[a]s soon as oil is struck, its site is internationalized' because of the capital, technology and expertise necessary to bring it to the world market, often leading to destabilising foreign interference.[97] Oil is the foundation of every coffee we drink and meal we eat via industrial production, packaging and transportation; it fuels our cars, makes our roads and heats our homes; it funds social services through tax revenue and supports us in old age through pension fund investments. Oil's role is not just material but cultural, producing our conception of the neoliberal 'good life' including, as Imre Szeman notes, 'the fantasy of suburban living and the freedoms of highways'.[98] Oil is everywhere trivially in the literature of a modern world premised on 'hydrocarbon culture' yet in few places substantially.[99]

Water is at the same time everywhere and nowhere in our lives and in literature. Much like oil, it provides the invisible, unacknowledged basis for our life activity, not least because, unlike oil, it is a biophysical necessity. Yet many of us, most likely anyone reading this book, have lives in which we take water's availability for granted and think little about the processes bringing it to our tap unless it stops. Water is crucial for sanitation and hygiene, used in food production (particularly if we eat animals or animal products) and in the industrial manufacturing and transportation of consumer goods, including physical books (growing trees, producing and bleaching wood pulp), while also bearing many of the environmental costs of industrial production, particularly oil extraction in the peripheries.[100] Like oil, water requires significant capital, technology and expertise to make it usable, and this can entrench international and local relations of domination. At the same time, water itself is already internationalised by the water cycle and the transboundary locations of key water bodies, which allow contamination to spread. Water shapes cultural norms and aspirations; Szeman's oil-fuelled suburban fantasy might also include the water to keep the lawn green, to produce the beefburgers grilling on the barbecue and to clean the bodies of its inhabitants and their domestic spaces, marking their gendered, racialised and class distinctions. At the same time, few literary texts take water as their theme.

The main way in which oil and water are brought together in political and media discourse is in their supposed shared ability to generate conflict, as in Serageldin's prediction of water wars. This takes us to significant differences between oil and water. While this notion has proven imaginatively compelling for authors including Paolo Bacigalupi, Emmi Itäranta and Gavron, as well as in blockbuster films such as *Mad Max: Fury Road* (2015), there is scant historical evidence of water wars, in stark contrast to the frequent role of oil in generating conflict. As Selby has pointed out, this thesis misunderstands the contrasting political economy of oil and water, emphasising a neo-Malthusian picture that elides the role of human institutions in producing water scarcity.[101] These comparisons primarily serve to justify the privatisation and securitisation of water by politicians, militaries and corporations.[102] Another key contrast is in the materialities and symbolic resonances of each resource. While oil and water both circulate, flow, flood and dry up, water is life, as the mantra says, and oil is death. Fresh water is crucial to the survival of human and much nonhuman life, holding related religious connotations of rebirth and providence, while oil leaks spell disaster. Water and oil have different cultural, economic and political meanings that I do not wish to elide, yet engaging their comparisons allows us to unravel what it might mean to think about water as a motor of literature in the same way as oil.[103]

In this book I propose the category of hydrofiction as a way of bringing the meanings and effects of water in literature and our lives to light. I seek to explicate what we might call literature's 'hydrological unconscious', a parallel to Yaeger's 'energy unconscious', in which she builds in turn on Fredric Jameson.[104] From petrocritics I also take an interest in the formal and generic modes, tropes and themes of hydrofiction and their relation to dominant water management strategies, an interest also found in the work of the Warwick Research Collective (these groups often overlap).[105] Macdonald argues that petrofiction manifests recurrent concerns with topics including 'volatile labor relations and ethnic tensions, war and violence, ecological despoliation, and political corruption', often framed in 'a narrative of uneasy and uneven encounter', and driven by 'proleptic inevitability or by a sudden acceleration in events'.[106] In hydrofiction we find plots of travel and migration, of uncanny and uncontrollable returns, and a preoccupation with language and imagery of flux, circulation, floods and droughts, frequently transferring into representations of the body as thirsty, saturated or overflowing, as well as narrative forms that flow between styles or come to jarring stops.

As with oil, all fiction is potentially a hydrofiction. The selection of texts for a hydrocritical project is difficult to narrow down. I have chosen texts in which water is a major theme and which focus on the major Israeli and Palestinian bodies of water: the River Jordan, the swamps of the Jezreel and Hula Valleys, the Mediterranean Sea and – taking 'body of water' more loosely – the pipes of the West Bank, Gaza and Israeli Palestinian communities within Israel. Together the texts illustrate key moments in the history of Israeli and Palestinian attitudes towards water and illuminate the changing relationships between water and power in Israel/Palestine, from the emergence of political Zionism in the late nineteenth century to the present. This is by no means an exhaustive account of water in Israeli and Palestinian writing. I hope that the case studies offered here will encourage other critics to extend this approach within Israeli and Palestinian literature and to other world-literary contexts.

I have also restricted myself to texts in English translation. This is in part due to the limits of my linguistic skills as a student of Arabic and Hebrew, although I have at times consulted the untranslated texts. At the same time, I reject a hierarchy between 'originals' and an 'inferior' translation. As Anna Bernard rightly notes, translated texts have their own life and circulation and the writers of all of these texts write knowing that their work will reach an international audience.[107] Any project of decentring the United Kingdom and North America in literary studies and, in this case, the Blue Humanities, will necessarily involve reading in translation and this is to be encouraged. The Anglophone circulation of these texts bears an additional significance given the topic of water. Water is a crucial mediating factor between Israelis, Palestinians and the countries of the world's core, with Israel seeking to foreground its water management strategies and environmental sensibilities as part of a bid for Euro-American support, while water shortages are frequent features of Palestinian calls for international solidarity. By turning to literature that circulates in the Anglophone world, I aim to bring to light how literature reflects and intervenes in these projects of national self-construction on a world stage. Finally, my chief aims are to raise the profile of Palestinian and Israeli literatures as environmental writing to Anglophone readers who are unlikely to have encountered them in this context and to promote a way of reading literature as hydrofiction, of which I offer Palestinian and Israeli literatures as a crucial test case. The approach developed here offers many possibilities for a new environmental approach to literature by focusing on a substance which is crucial to life, but which in literary criticism has too often been overlooked.

This book comes at a time at which we are increasingly told that 'water wars' are on the horizon, with Israel/Palestine seeming to offer both a frightening vision of the future and an answer to the problems of the world's core. Our era may not produce 'water wars', but it is nonetheless a time of increasing privatisation, securitisation and enclosure of water by multinational corporations, militaries and world powers, trends which threaten to heighten the already vast and unjust differences in access to water that cause 4 billion people around the world to suffer water scarcity for at least one month a year.[108] This book reads Israeli and Palestinian literature in the light of world water crisis, showing that water is not merely an issue for technical, scientific and political calculation and that practices of narration and representation are crucial to how the politics of water are understood locally and internationally. In reading Israeli and Palestinian literature as hydrofiction I propose a new approach both to these literatures, so long defined by a relationship to land, and to literature more broadly, one that is crucial as we move into a climate-changed future. Taking the Blue Humanities into Israel/Palestine is a reminder that we must be alert not only to our changing world but to colonialism's ongoing environmental aftermaths, and to the need to combine climate politics with a commitment to justice.

Notes

1. Gavron, *Hydromania*.
2. The word 'cli-fi' is generally acknowledged as having been coined in 2007 by journalist Dan Bloom, who maintains a website tracking uses of the term. Bloom, *The Cli-Fi Report*.

3. Malka, 'To the Last Drop'.
4. Cited in Selby, *Water, Power and Politics in the Middle East*, p. 49.
5. On the revival of 'water wars' discourse, see Cascão et al., 'Why Are Water Wars Back on the Agenda?'.
6. See, for example, Senor and Singer, *Start-Up Nation*; Siegel, *Let There Be Water*.
7. Rinat, 'Collapsing Environmental State of Gaza Poses Threat to Israel's National Security, Report Warns'.
8. Bhattacharyya, 'Globalizing Racism and Myths of the Other in the "War on Terror"', p. 46.
9. Linton and Budds, 'The Hydrosocial Cycle', p. 170.
10. Swyngedouw, *Liquid Power*.
11. Big dams have once again emerged as a favoured – and deeply flawed – solution to water shortages and a driver of 'green growth'. Boelens et al., 'Contested Knowledges', p. 416.
12. Messerschmid, 'Hydro-Apartheid and Water Access', p. 61; 'UK Climate Averages'. See 'Not Enough Water in the West Bank', *Visualizing Palestine*.
13. Selby, *Water, Power and Politics*, p. 51; Selby and Hoffmann, 'Rethinking Climate Change, Conflict and Security', p. 748; Messerschmid, 'Nothing New in the Middle East', pp. 423–59.
14. Alatout, '"States" of Scarcity', pp. 959–82.
15. Ibid., p. 961.
16. Linton, *What Is Water?*
17. Tvedt and Oestigaard, 'Introduction', p. xv.
18. The classic study of Palestinian environmental imagery is Barbara McKean Parmenter's foundational, if now out of date, *Giving Voice to Stones*. There is a small body of criticism on space and place in Israeli literature, including useful studies of the kibbutz, the desert and Tel Aviv. See Brauch et al., *Jewish Topographies*; Grumberg, *Place and Ideology*; Mann, *A Place in History*; Mann, *Space and Place in Jewish Studies*; Omer-Sherman, *Israel in Exile*; Omer-Sherman, *Imagining the Kibbutz*; Zerubavel, *Desert in the Promised Land*.
19. Contemporary criticism on Israel/Palestine increasingly uses a settler colonialism paradigm. See Busbridge, 'Israel-Palestine and the Settler Colonial "Turn"'; Salamanca et al., 'Past Is Present'; Porter and Yiftachel, 'Urbanizing Settler-Colonial Studies'; Veracini, 'Israel-Palestine Through a Settler-Colonial Studies Lens'. As Busbridge notes, the revival of this framework has been influenced by the work of Patrick Wolfe. See Wolfe, *Traces of History*. Palestinians, however, have understood Zionism as a settler colonial project since long before the establishment of

the State of Israel. The Socialist Organization in Israel (Matzpen, founded 1962) also used this framework. For older uses of a settler colonial framework, see Hanegbi et al., 'The Class Nature of Israeli Society'; Rodinson, *Israel: A Colonial-Settler State?*; Sayegh, *Zionist Colonialism in Palestine*.

20. Swyngedouw, *Liquid Power*; Swyngedouw, *Social Power and the Urbanization of Water*.
21. Selby, *Water, Power and Politics in the Middle East*. I also count here the work of Samer Alatout, Strang's *The Meaning of Water* and Naguib, *Women, Water and Memory*.
22. Williams and Ball, 'Where Is Palestine?', p. 128. As this introduction was being revised in July 2019 a wave of protests was taking place in Israel against the killing of a nineteen-year-old Ethiopian-Israeli man by an off-duty police officer.
23. Ibid., p. 128.
24. Nixon, *Slow Violence*, p. 33.
25. Young, *Postcolonialism*, pp. 10, 20.
26. Notable moves in this direction are the forthcoming special issue of *Humanities* on 'World Literature and the Blue Humanities' edited by Alexandra Campbell and Michael Paye, and Deckard, 'Water Shocks'. Some of the most interesting recent works on the ocean are from Black Studies and are not typically categorised within the Blue Humanities. This may prompt us to consider the whiteness of the 'blue' and the politics of classifying a work as 'environmental'. See Sharpe, *In the Wake*; King, *The Black Shoals*.
27. Crutzen and Stoermer, 'The Anthropocene'.
28. Chakrabarty, 'The Climate of History', p. 213.
29. Gregory, *The Colonial Present*. In this project I draw on works including Davis and Todd, 'On the Importance of a Date'; Haraway, 'Anthropocene, Capitalocene, Plantationocene, Chthulucene'; Malm, *Fossil Capital*; Moore, 'The Capitalocene, Part I'.
30. Yusoff, *A Billion Black Anthropocenes or None*, p. 2.
31. The phrase is used by Simon Schama in the recollection of childhood tree-planting ceremonies with which he begins *Landscape and Memory*, p. 5.
32. Layla 'Allush, 'The Path of Affection', trans. by Salma Khadra Jayyusi and Naomi Shihab Nye, in Jayyusi (ed.), *Anthology of Modern Palestinian Literature*, pp. 106–7.
33. I adapt this term from Bear and Bull, 'Water Matters'.
34. Abufarha, 'Land of Symbols'; Bardenstein, 'Trees, Forests'.
35. Malkki, 'National Geographic'.
36. Darwish, *Unfortunately, It Was Paradise*, p. 7; Handal, *The Lives of Rain*, p. 43.

37. Zimmerman, *World Resources and Industries*, p. 3.
38. Shpigel, 'It's No Longer That Hard to Walk on Water at the Sea of Galilee'.
39. Lidman, 'Desalination Isn't the Magic Bullet, Water Authority Warns Israelis'.
40. Allan, *Virtual Water*. Allan argues that virtual water has in fact already solved the region's water shortages. Allan, 'Hydro-Peace in the Middle East'.
41. Avgar, *Israeli Water Sector—Key Issues*, p. 14.
42. Garb, 'Desalination in Israel', p. 240.
43. Marin et al., 'Water Management in Israel', p. 22.
44. 'Seawater Pollution Raises Concerns of Waterborne Diseases and Environmental Hazards in the Gaza Strip'.
45. Official accusations are contained in 'Palestinian Obligations as Per Note for the Record of the Hebron Protocol of 15 January 1997'. See Cohen, 'Eitam Prohibits Palestinians from Drilling for Water in West Bank'.
46. Cited in Farrier, 'Washing Words', p. 5.
47. Selby, 'Cooperation, Domination and Colonisation'.
48. See Alexandre Goetschmann and Guy Davidi's documentary *Interrupted Streams*.
49. State of Palestine Palestinian Water Authority, 'Water Sector Damage Assessment Report', p. 10.
50. Roy, *The Gaza Strip*, pp. 3–5; Roy, *Failing Peace*, pt 3.
51. This is Neil Smith's term, used in the context of desalination in Swyngedouw, 'Into the Sea', p. 262.
52. Cited in Alatout, 'Towards a Bio-Territorial Conception of Power', p. 613.
53. Swyngedouw, *Liquid Power*, p. 194.
54. Ben-Gurion, *Recollections*, pp. 145, 148, 137.
55. Ibid., p. 148.
56. In this point I build on Swyngedouw, who is himself borrowing from David Harvey. *Liquid Power*, p. 7.
57. Scott, *Seeing like a State*, ch. 3.
58. Ibid., pp. 89–90.
59. Allan, 'IWRM/IWRAM: A New Sanctioned Discourse?'. See Linton, *What Is Water?*, ch. 7; Swyngedouw, *Liquid Power*.
60. Worster, *Rivers of Empire*; Mikhail, *Water on Sand*.
61. Nixon, *Slow Violence*, p. 156.
62. Massad, *The Persistence of the Palestinian Question*, ch. 3.
63. The line is also sometimes translated as '[i]f you will, it is no fairy-tale'. Herzl, *Altneuland*, p. 1.

64. The socialist character of the Zionist movement and early Israeli state has been the subject of considerable scholarly debate. Ze'ev Sternhell frames socialism as a Zionist 'mobilizing myth' rather than a concrete commitment, while Gershon Shafir and Zachary Lockman highlight the ways in which early-twentieth-century Zionist Labour unions actively marginalised Mizrahi Jewish and Palestinian Arab workers. Capitalism is often understood as having 'arrived' in Israeli in the late 1980s. Adam Hanieh argues against this claim, noting that Labour Zionism encouraged the growth of an indigenous capitalist class. Lockman, *Comrades and Enemies*, p. 50; Shafir, *Land, Labor and the Origins of the Israeli-Palestinian Conflict*, pp. 81, 115; Sternhell, *The Founding Myths of Israel*, p. 20; Hanieh, 'From State-Led Growth to Globalization'.
65. Alatout, 'Towards a Bio-Territorial Conception of Power', p. 613.
66. Bakker, *An Uncooperative Commodity*.
67. Siegel, *Let There Be Water*, p. 170.
68. On conflict over land in the Negev, see Manski, 'Blueprint Negev'; McKee, *Dwelling in Conflict*; Weizman, *The Conflict Shoreline*.
69. Zerubavel, 'Desert and Settlement', p. 205. See also Shohat, *Israeli Cinema*, pp. 15–53.
70. Davis and Burke, 'Imperialism, Orientalism, and the Environment in the Middle East', p. 2; Nixon, *Slow Violence*, p. 152; Guha and Martinez-Alier, *Varieties of Environmentalism*, ch. 5.
71. B'Tselem, 'National Parks in East Jerusalem'; Kadman, *Erased from Space and Consciousness*, ch. 5.
72. See Schulman, 'Appendix: Brand Israel and Pinkwashing', in *Israel/Palestine and the Queer International*, pp. 179–85.
73. B'Tselem, *Made in Israel*.
74. Tuffaha, *Water and Salt*, pp. 41–2.
75. Ashly, 'Drowning in the Waste of Israeli Settlers'.
76. Ravikovitch, *The Window*, pp. 103–4.
77. Hall, 'Shared Sorrow, Shared Abundance', p. 260.
78. Khalifeh, *Wild Thorns*; Hall, 'Shared Sorrow, Shared Abundance', p. 260.
79. Wittfogel, *Oriental Despotism*.
80. Linton and Budds, 'The Hydrosocial Cycle', p. 173.
81. Worster, *Rivers of Empire*.
82. Linton, *What Is Water?*, p. 3.
83. Swyngedouw, *Social Power and the Urbanization of Water*, pp. 1–2.
84. Latour, *We Have Never Been Modern*, p. 1.

85. Ibid., p. 32.
86. Linton, *What Is Water?*, p. 182. On 'legibility', resources and power, see Scott, *Seeing Like a State*, p. 2. Richardson and Weszkalnys, 'Introduction: Resource Materialities', p. 14.
87. Alatout, 'Bringing Abundance into Environmental Politics'; Alatout, '"States" of Scarcity'; Alatout, 'Towards a Bio-Territorial Conception of Power'.
88. Alatout, 'From Water Abundance to Water Scarcity (1936–1959)', pp. 200, 208.
89. Wolf, *Hydropolitics along the Jordan River*, pp. 35–6. Lowdermilk, *Palestine: Land of Promise*, pp. 223–9.
90. Alatout, '"States" of Scarcity', p. 961.
91. Messerschmid, 'Hydro-Apartheid and Water Access', pp. 53–76.
92. Richardson and Weszkalnys, 'Introduction: Resource Materialities', p. 14.
93. Ghosh, 'Petrofiction'.
94. Yaeger et al., 'Editor's Column'.
95. Rubenstein, 'Petro-'.
96. Macdonald, 'Oil and World Literature', p. 7.
97. Ibid., p. 7.
98. Szeman, 'Conjectures on World Energy Literature', p. 280.
99. Macdonald, p. 31.
100. On the water impact of pulp bleaching, see Langston, *Sustaining Lake Superior*.
101. Selby, 'Oil and Water'.
102. Cascão et al., 'Why Are Water Wars Back On the Agenda?'.
103. Selby's 'Oil and Water' (2005) offers a valuable account of their comparative political economy.
104. Yaeger et al., 'Editor's Column', p. 306.
105. WReC, *Combined and Uneven Development*.
106. Macdonald, 'Oil and World Literature', p. 31.
107. Bernard, *Rhetorics of Belonging*, p. 5.
108. Mekonnen and Hoekstra, 'Four Billion People Facing Severe Water Scarcity'.

1

CROSSING THE RIVER: HOME AND EXILE AT THE RIVER JORDAN

'The Jordan River figures as the border where both Palestinian and Israeli identities are constructed, contested, and mythologised.' – Rachel Havrelock[1]

'I wouldn't want to be baptised there, I can tell you that' – Gidon Bromberg, Director, EcoPeace Middle East[2]

The River Jordan plays two intersecting roles for Israelis and Palestinians: it is a national border and a major reserve of surface water. As a border, the Jordan is currently a site at which Palestinians travelling between Jordan and the West Bank endure lengthy and often humiliating encounters with Israel's occupation. As a resource, the river is claimed by both sides, but is diverted at present almost in its entirety into Israel's National Water Carrier and used upstream to a lesser extent by Jordan, Syria and Lebanon. The 'mighty Jordan' of popular imagination is now a contaminated trickle of sewage, saline spring water and agricultural runoff from farmland and fishponds that sometimes disappears almost entirely.[3] The Jordan's parlous ecological state is one of the best-known and most widely reported aspects of hydropolitics in Israel/Palestine. This is partly because the river's contemporary despoliation provides a compelling contrast with the historic fertility and abundance described in biblical accounts of the Holy Land, serving as an appealing narrative hook for journalists.[4] Conflict over the Jordan's waters is also the most frequently cited example of past and future 'water wars'.[5] The River Jordan is overloaded with material and symbolic significance for Israelis, Palestinians and the international community, particularly the Christian world, and for this reason I take it as the starting point for this work.

In this chapter I examine three texts in which the River Jordan plays a major narrative role. The first is writer and president of the Jewish Farmers' Federation Moshe Smilansky's largely forgotten short story 'Hawaja Nazar', initially published in four instalments from 1910 to 1911 in the World Zionist Organisation journal *ha-Olam* and included in English translation in Smilansky's 1935 collection *Palestine Caravan*.[6] The second half of the chapter turns to works by the two most widely read contemporary Palestinian poets, Mahmoud Darwish and Mourid Barghouti. The first is Darwish's poem 'A River Dies of Thirst', published in Arabic in 2008 and translated into English by Caroline Cobham the following year in a collection of the same name.[7] The second is Barghouti's memoir *I Saw Ramallah*, published in Arabic in 1997 and translated into English by Egyptian novelist Adhaf Soueif in 2000.[8] While these texts span genres and periods and are by authors of varying reputations, all take the river as a site for the exploration of key national questions at different moments in time in a way that makes them productive to examine together. Of these texts, Barghouti's acclaimed memoir has received the most critical attention; criticism on Smilansky is sparse, while there is no work to draw on in the case of Darwish's poem. Where it exists, work on these texts has largely overlooked the significance of the river.[9] By focusing on the role of the Jordan, I show that it is as important in Israeli and Palestinian environmental imaginaries as the better-known symbols of the pine or olive tree, the sabra cactus or the orange. In all three texts the river is fundamental to understandings of home and exile, more traditionally associated with land-based imagery, with water's distinct material properties forming the basis of its national significance. Representations of the land's water border, meanwhile, prompt reconsiderations of how the land itself might be inhabited in the future.

'Hawaja Nazar' is one of the best known of the many short stories published by Smilansky in Hebrew and Yiddish periodicals in Palestine, Europe and North America from 1902 onwards for around thirty years. Smilansky was a member of the First Aliyah, the earliest wave of Jewish immigration to Palestine in the 1880s and 1890s. Today his writing is largely forgotten and out of print. He is remembered more commonly in histories of Hebrew literature as the great uncle of the Israeli novelist S. Yizhar (Yizhar Smilansky), author of the powerful 1948 war novel *Khirbet Khizeh* (1949). Smilansky's work was not well regarded in his lifetime and was notably condemned as 'genre fiction' by pioneering Hebrew novelist Yosef Haim Brenner.[10] Nevertheless, it was widely read, with his 1911 short story collection *Sons of Arabia* (*Bnei Arav*) going into multiple reprints. For readers outside Palestine, as Gershon Shaked notes, Smilansky's work provided 'exotic tales that depicted for their readers a heretofore unknown world', functioning as a form of 'virtual propaganda'.[11] Smilansky's stories are widely viewed as Zionist versions of the colonial adventure tale, offering naïve glorifications of Jewish life in Palestine and presenting Zionist values positively to audiences abroad.

Existing criticism has focused on Smilansky's representation of Palestinian Arabs and their implications for the Zionist project. Risa Domb and Gilead Morahg argue that Smilansky's writing manifests typical Zionist attitudes of the time, portraying Arab characters as thinly sketched stereotypes and depicting Jewish pioneers as quasi-colonial figures bringing civilisation to the 'backward' East.[12] Yaron Peleg views Smilansky's work more favourably, arguing that he presented a romanticised image of Palestinian life as a model for Jewish attempts to become 'native' to Palestine, while Gila Ramras-Rauch foregrounds Smilansky's concern for the exploitation and poor living conditions of Arab workers.[13] Discussion of 'Hawaja Nazar' has followed similar lines, focusing on Smilansky's apparently simplistic portrayal of a 'New Hebrew Man' who proves the legitimacy of Zionist settlement through his zeal for working the land and the admiration he receives from the Arab population.[14] There has been little close attention, however, to the protagonist's obsession with the River Jordan, or to the fact that his apparent right to Palestine is proven not just by his skills as a farmer, but as a sailor and swimmer. Crossing the river and being immersed in it are crucial to this story's negotiation of national politics. In this chapter I reappraise Smilansky's story through the lens of his binationalist politics and work in the citriculture industry, showing the importance of the Jordan's waters in providing material and metaphorical sustenance for the future of Jewish settlement in Palestine at this time and arguing that his story carries a rather more ambivalent message about Zionist ambitions than has been recognised so far.

In the second half of the chapter I focus on Darwish's poem 'A River Dies of Thirst' and Barghouti's memoir *I Saw Ramallah*. Darwish does not directly name his river, but, as I discuss, many aspects of the poem evoke the Jordan. Barghouti, meanwhile, reflects on the river at a pivotal moment in his text as he waits at the border on his return to the West Bank following a prolonged period of forced exile. Darwish is often described as Palestine's national poet while Barghouti, long a highly visible figure, has to some extent inherited this mantle since the death of Darwish in 2008.[15] The crossing of the Jordan figures frequently in Palestinian writing, particularly life-writing, because of its central role in the Palestinian national narrative of displacement and exile. As a result, many texts are of potential interest here. I focus on Darwish and Barghouti's works in part because of their authors' international profile – these works are particularly prominent representations of the river – and because of their shared concern with the river's ecological state, which in both cases forms part of an exploration of nationalist politics.

Darwish's poem has attracted little critical interest, while Barghouti's memoir has primarily been analysed as an example of the 'literature of the checkpoint', with critics focusing on his interactions with Israeli soldiers at the border.[16] In this chapter I highlight the environmental dimensions of these works and the significance of the River Jordan in Palestinian environmental imaginaries. I show that the Jordan plays a key role in imaginaries of a lost Palestine alongside more familiar 'terrestrocentric' symbols, with the crucial distinction being water's capacity to stand in for the movement or stoppage of national time. While in Darwish's poem the dried-up river represents Palestine's lost rural past and the 'unnatural' disruption of previously harmonious relations between people and place, in Barghouti's memoir the river signifies a lost future and the process of 'de-development' to which Palestinians have been subjected, in part, through Israel's restrictions on Palestinian water access.[17] Darwish and Barghouti's different representations of the Jordan show the manifold impacts of its loss on Palestinian life, indicating the need to consider the way that the river is imagined alongside political demands for just access to its waters.

A key framing term in this chapter is 'riverscape'. Just like landscapes, riverscapes play central roles in national myth, serving as a medium in which social and economic power structures are inscribed and reproduced in turn as 'natural', invisible and inevitable. The movement of rivers allows them to play a particular role in a national environmental imaginary, standing in, as Tricia Cusack writes, 'for the passage of time, for life, and for renewal'.[18] As a result, rivers often serve as metaphors for 'the uninterrupted "flow" or "course" of national history'.[19] 'Solid' landscapes move and change too, of course. As Barbara Bender notes, 'landscapes, like time, never stand still'.[20] The key difference is one of immediacy. Except in the cases of rapid events such as earthquakes or landslides, landscape change occurs over a longer period of time, often on a geological scale. By contrast, the change and movement of liquids is readily apparent, making them more immediately available as a metaphor. In this chapter I widen Cusack's approach by discussing the Jordan riverscape not only as a site at which 'elite' perspectives are constructed and naturalised but as a location at which nationalisms are negotiated and alternative perspectives emerge, even if sometimes only temporarily. In these cases, a move away from the land to its fluid and changing border allows for different ways of inhabiting the land and imagining its future to come to the fore.

Smilansky's 'Hawaja Nazar'

I begin with Smilansky's story of early-twentieth-century Jewish settlement in Palestine. Smilansky arrived in Palestine in 1891 as a young Jewish immigrant from Kiev, Ukraine.[21] He worked as a labourer in Baron de Rothschild's vineyards before helping to found the famous moshava Hadera and eventually settling in another moshava, Rehovot.[22] In Rehovot Smilansky switched his crop from grapes to citrus and became an early Jewish citriculture expert, producing the Zionist movement's emblematic export commodity.[23] He was a prominent public spokesperson for farmers as founder and president of the Jewish Farmers' Federation and wrote regularly for the newsletter of the Labour Zionist group Hapoel Hatzair until 1911, when there was a dispute over the issue of 'Hebrew labour'.[24] While Second Aliyah immigrants advocated the employment of an entirely Jewish agricultural workforce – a 'conquest of labour' which was, for them, inseparable from the 'conquest of land' – Smilansky, by contrast, employed Arab and Jewish labourers.[25]

This decision can, in one sense, be explained as a result of Smilansky's capitalist priorities: Arab labourers were both cheaper than Jewish workers and, not unrelatedly, unorganised.[26] While this is surely relevant, Smilansky's employment of Arabs and Jews also stemmed from political beliefs. He was a follower of the spiritual Zionist thinker Ahad Ha'am (Asher Hirsch Ginsberg), whose 1891 article 'Truth from Eretz Yisrael' famously and presciently described his concern with the condescending attitudes he encountered among the Zionist movement towards Palestine's existing Arab population and argued that these threatened the success of Jewish settlement.[27] Smilansky, similarly, wrote that '[o]ur country [Palestine] is not an unsettled wasteland' and that '[t]he inhabitants of our land are not savages who may be treated with disregard'.[28]

This apparently humanistic approach to Palestine's Arab population remains problematic, to say the least. While Smilansky demonstrated a more concessive approach than many of his contemporaries, advocating explicitly for binationalism, these views derived from efforts to model the Jewish settlement of Palestine on European settler colonialism and seem to legitimate the long history of European colonial violence towards any populations viewed as 'savages'. Such statements also sat alongside essentialising portrayals of Arab 'primitivism' and Eastern 'mystery' in Smilansky's stories and other writings, as well as an active strategy of purchasing land for Jewish ownership and wish to see a Jewish majority in Palestine. Some of these contradictions did not escape his critics at the time.[29] Nevertheless, Smilansky's background in the citrus industry and concern with the effects of Jewish settlement on Palestine's existing population indicate an intriguing alternative reading of 'Hawaja Nazar' in which a representation of the river tells us much more about what might be possible or permissible both on land than is apparent on the surface.

The story centres on a young Russian immigrant, Lazar, who arrives unannounced at an unnamed Jewish colony in Palestine and is taken under the guardianship of the similarly unnamed narrator. It quickly becomes apparent that Lazar is obsessed with the River Jordan. He longs to see it and is unable to countenance the thought that it may not be as full or as wide as he had imagined. When a visitor to the colony describes the Jordan at Galilee as 'only a thin ribbon', adding that '[a]t the end of the summer it grows dry' to the extent that 'there are places where you can cross on foot', Lazar is distressed.[30] When he and the narrator eventually visit the river Lazar is disappointed to see the visitor's description apparently confirmed, until they later discover a broad, fast-flowing section. At this point he is filled with a delight which turns increasingly manic. He strips off and dives in but, unable to fight the strong current and to negotiate the river's dangerous weeds, drowns. After Lazar's naked body washes up on the bank it becomes apparent that he is not circumcised. Earlier in the story we have learnt that he is the son of a Jewish father and non-Jewish mother, so is not Jewish on the crucial mother's side. Shocked, the Hevra Kadisha (Burial Society) refuses to inter Lazar's body. The body is drawn back into the Jordan and disappears downstream.

Lazar is presented in the story as a Zionist hero, suggesting a greater national significance to his obsession with the Jordan. This begins from the title itself. 'Hawaja Nazar' is spoken by the character Ibrahim, who appears briefly after attempting to rob Lazar before being unexpectedly overpowered by his strength.[31] Ibrahim prefaces Lazar's name with the honorific title 'Hawaja' to indicate his new-found respect for Lazar, while mispronouncing his name as 'Nazar'. This initiates a pattern of interactions in which Lazar demonstrates exemplary aptitude for (Smilansky's version of) Palestinian Arab culture and traditions that serves to naturalise his, and, by extension, Jewish, belonging in Palestine. Lazar 'rapidly' learns Arabic; begins to dress in *'abaya, keffiyeh* and *agal*'; 'outstripped' the Arabs in their farm work; honours his guests appropriately; and is invited to Arab villages to 'help them settle their disputes'.[32] One character declares: 'He is like one of us – a son of Arabia!'[33]

The term of respect 'Hawaja' and Lazar's skill at working the land emphasise his affinity with the 'native' Arabs of Palestine, suggesting his own 'natural' belonging to the land even as a new arrival and implying in turn the 'naturalness' of Zionist settlement. This naturalisation is amplified by Smilansky's use of Arabic terms in the list of clothing and the title, which mirrors a trend in literary representations of Jewish workers in Palestine at this time for using Arabic to emphasise the authenticity of life in the Yishuv.[34] This technique also tapped into the fin-de-siècle European appetite for the 'exotic' and 'Oriental', appealing to Smilansky's prospective readers.[35] Smilansky himself drew on this convention, publishing his first

Hebrew stories as 'Hawaja Mussa'. Smilansky's portrayal of Lazar's aptitude for Palestinian Arab life and culture suggests not just 'natural' belonging, however, but 'natural' rule. Lazar's agricultural skills are greater, while his interventions in Palestinian Arab life suggest the benefits of his presence and, by implication, Zionist settlement, to Palestine's local population.

While Zionist narratives of return and settlement are typically understood as focused on 'working the land', in Smilansky's story Lazar's 'natural' belonging is underscored by his aptitude for sailing. When travelling to the Jordan, Lazar and the narrator pause at Lake Kinneret before staying overnight at Tiberias. Lazar initially mistakes the lake for the Jordan but declares it 'lovely' once he learns the Jordan runs through it. This prompts a page-long rhapsodic description from the narrator that simultaneously provides an account of Palestine's beauty for readers abroad.[36] Lazar persuades the narrator to sail on the lake with three Arab sailors, going faster and faster until even 'the two sailors turned pale' and another tries to intervene.[37] Lazar, however, shows his skill and the skipper 'gazed at him with love and wonder', seeing what the narrator describes as 'a fellow spirit'.[38] This moment can be understood in the light of a less well-known history of efforts to encourage Jewish seafaring and revive an apparently ancient Jewish maritime history. The Palestine Maritime League was founded in 1937 with the aim of encouraging Jewish seafaring, while the Hakibbutz Hameuchad settlement movement promoted the idea that being a fisherman or dockworker was as worthwhile an occupation for pioneers as farming.[39] Lazar's skills on water further 'naturalise' his belonging to Palestine while anticipating the later emergence of the 'conquest of the sea' as a Zionist goal, a topic to which I return in Chapter 3.

Lazar's physical appearance is described repeatedly and is similarly significant to Smilansky's apparent portrayal of the glory and success of Zionist settlement, reinforcing the sense that his obsession with the Jordan possesses a greater national significance. His body draws admiration from both the Arab population and the narrator, with the narrator describing his physique at length:

> The Arab looked at [Lazar] admiringly, nor could I myself take my eyes off him. He was a youngster of about eighteen or twenty, with all the freshness of boyhood still clinging to him. The morning dew was not yet dry on him. His

face was smooth and clean as that of a woman, without a sign of hair or any mark of beard or moustache. His skin shone like polished metal, and he was full of exuberant vitality. The whole of his big, supple frame told of strength, bravery and the glory of youth.[40]

Descriptions such as this mirror the 'New Hebrew Man' of early-twentieth-century Zionist thought, intended to negate the supposedly 'degenerate' traits of Diaspora Judaism. This was specifically conceived of as a project of masculine regeneration, with Diaspora life seen to have produced weak, deformed and effeminate Jewish men (in this sense, of course, Zionist thinkers replicated antisemitic tropes).[41] Lazar's enormous size epitomises the new, forceful and athletic male Jewish body valorised in early-twentieth-century Zionism, resembling the 'deep-chested, sturdy, sharp-eyed men' of Zionist leader Max Nordau's 'muscular Judaism'.[42] Elsewhere in the story Lazar encounters offensively stereotyped portrayals of religious Jews whom he describes as 'repulsive', underscoring his seemingly virtuous distance from the Diaspora Judaism that Zionists sought to leave behind in Europe.[43]

Repeated references to Lazar's youth in the passage above emphasise his vigour and nobility to Smilansky's readers abroad, qualities which are transferred to the Zionist project. It is hard, however, not to read the narrator's attraction to Lazar as homoerotic, while the narrator's comparisons between Lazar and a woman also seem to pose problems for Lazar's status as a Zionist ideal. Both elements potentially mirror antisemitic fin-de-siècle associations between Jewish men and homosexuality that formed part of a wider antisemitic equation of Judaism with gender ambiguity.[44] These traits are not, however, incompatible with a new Zionist masculinity. Lazar's gender ambiguity indicates a valorised emotional sensitivity, underscored later by his passionate declarations of love for the Jordan.[45] The narrator's reference to Lazar's lack of a beard, meanwhile, positions him as the epitome of Ancient Greek male desirability, placing their relationship in the context of the homoerotic socialisation valorised within nationalist movements of the time, with Lazar as youthful novitiate to the narrator's wise elder.[46] In this way Smilansky's descriptions of Lazar's body suggest the success of the regeneration both of Jewish masculinity and of the land of Palestine, indicating that his obsessive attachment to the river possesses greater national meaning.

The Jordan as Resource and Riverscape

Lazar's fixation with the Jordan's size and flow indicates its material and metaphorical centrality to the success of Jewish settlement in Palestine. Palestine's water potential – and therefore its capacity to support greater Jewish settlement – was a major topic of discussion in the Zionist movement in the early years of the twentieth century, when Smilansky's story was written. In contrast to today's assumption that Israel/Palestine is a region of 'natural' water scarcity, estimates of abundant water supply were a crucial means by which Zionist leaders countered British estimates of Palestine's 'absorptive capacity', spelled out in Churchill's 1922 White Paper, which were at this time being used to restrict Jewish immigration.[47] The River Jordan was seen as playing a vital future role in agriculture as part of the envisioned future state's breadbaskets of the Jezreel Valley, discussed in the next chapter, and the Jordan Valley.[48] It was also identified as a potential source of hydroelectric power, with American soil scientist Walter Clay Lowdermilk developing detailed plans for a 'Jordan Valley Authority' in the 1940s based on the Tennessee Valley Authority that were subsequently extended by American engineer James B. Hays.[49] If the Jordan were only a small river, this would seem to undermine the long-term stability of Jewish settlement in Palestine in multiple material ways. Lazar, with his unwavering commitment to the Zionist project, would be right to be concerned.

As a citrus farmer, Smilansky would have been well aware of debates over the importance of water and waterpower to the future of Jewish settlement. The industry was known as the driver of new, 'rational' irrigation methods and technologies in Palestine. These included the introduction of a technique of digging grids of irrigation furrows known as the 'California method' that promised cost savings and efficiency through the use of animals and machines, as well as increased mechanisation more generally in cultivation and the pumping of water, both of which depended on a reliable electricity supply.[50] Smilansky himself wrote of the value of technology in accessing 'hidden water wealth' to expand the area of potentially cultivable land and praised the Jewish introduction of new intensive irrigation practices that replaced earlier Arab methods he perceived as 'primitive'.[51] These advances helped to shore up the production rate of the orange in Palestine's Jewish agricultural sector. Lazar's investment in the size of the Jordan, then, seems to suggest a concern with the capacity of Palestine to support increased Jewish immigration through water for drinking and for sustaining high levels of agricultural productivity. Water supply was crucial to both the state's economic survival and to sustaining notions of the capacity of the Jewish people to successfully 'rebuild' both the land of Palestine and themselves through agricultural labour. This was a principle to which Smilansky subscribed, as a Hovev Tsiyon, or believer in a Jewish return to the land.[52]

Lazar's references to the biblical Jordan and Russia's national river, the Volga, are similarly significant in terms of the story's commentary on the success and legitimacy of Zionist settlement. Lazar's citations of the Bible suggest that this provided the main source for his images of Palestine and the Jordan, as it did for many visitors and immigrants to Palestine at this time and historically. After hearing the Jordan described as narrow by the visitor to the colony, Lazar invokes the Bible as evidence for what he believes to be the river's true size, protesting to the narrator:

> Friend, it is impossible! 'When the Jordan overflowed its banks all the harvest season!' 'And the waters stood still, rose in a single pile.' 'And all the people passed through on the dry land . . .'[53]

All of these references are abruptly cut short, like Lazar's imagined full-flowing river, indicating his distressed emotional state. As Lazar's quotations suggest, the Jordan and its surrounding valley are portrayed in the Bible as abundant, fertile and even heavenly. Genesis 13: 10, for instance, states that the Jordan Valley was 'well-watered everywhere, like the garden of the Lord'.[54] Lazar's expectations of a biblical Jordan suggest a desire for continuity between ancient times of plenty and, crucially, of Jewish ownership of Palestine and the present-day Zionist 'rebuilding' of the Jewish people and the land.[55] The Jordan's reported narrowness and small volume causes Lazar distress by undermining claims of divine support for the Zionist mission, at the same time as actively inhibiting the potential for Jewish settlement. Low levels of water may even suggest divine disapproval, given the longstanding associations in Jewish and Christian theology between providence and a 'well-watered earth'.[56] A narrow Jordan, then, is a bad sign about the future success of Jewish settlement not just in a material sense, but in a metaphorical and spiritual one.

Lazar's biblical references are all taken from Joshua 3: 1–17, a source which points towards an additional meaning to his comments. In these passages, the overflowing waters of the river miraculously part, allowing Joshua to lead the twelve tribes of Israel out of the wilderness and onto the western bank. The Joshua narrative is a story of a return from exile, providing an obvious precursor and source of legitimation for the Jewish 'return' to Palestine in the twentieth century. It is also, however, a narrative of conquest.[57] As Havrelock points out, the men of the twelve tribes are transformed in the crossing into an army, while the 'pile' or 'heap' of waters provides evidence of God's domination of nature and points towards the future submission of Israel's enemies.[58] Lazar's attachment to this representation of the Jordan in particular tells us that his interest in the river is also about an instance of historical Jewish control over the river in which it provides the source of Jewish military might. These allusions foreshadow his subsequent attempts, discussed later in the chapter, to cross the river to the land beyond and claim both as Jewish-owned.

Lazar's distress at the Jordan's lack of resemblance to the biblical river is compounded by its failure to mirror the Volga. Earlier in the story, we learn that Lazar is deeply attached to the Volga. On his arrival in the colony, he is reserved until asked about the river, which passes through his home town of Samara in south-east Russia. The narrator describes Lazar's immense enthusiasm for the river:

> In flowing and picturesque words he began telling me of the beauty of the Volga – how broad it was, how bright and clear were its waters. An ocean of a river! Often your eyes could not see across to the other bank.[59]

It emerges that with his recent Jewish awakening Lazar's passion for the Volga was translated onto the Jordan. He declares: 'And I began to love the Jordan more than the Volga. How lovely that word is: J-o-r-d-a-n! How fine it sounds.'[60] Lazar's new-found love for the Jordan is associated here with an enjoyment of the new sound of the Hebrew language that, as the narrator notes, 'flows' from his mouth, suggesting that love for the river is as much a part of becoming 'native' to the land of Palestine for Lazar as learning

Hebrew. After the visitor's talk, Lazar's assumption of a resemblance between the Jordan and the Volga is undermined, as it was for the biblical Jordan. He repeats a version of his earlier comments: 'The Volga . . . Sometimes the eye cannot see the farther bank. A sea . . .'.[61] The fragmentation of these remarks illustrates, again, Lazar's distress and disbelief at the Jordan's seeming failure to match the river of his homeland and of biblical history.

One way to understand Lazar's desire for a likeness between the Jordan and the Volga may be in terms of security. His references to the Volga as an 'ocean' and a 'sea' recall the way in which seas are often thought of as a particularly effective 'natural border'.[62] If the Jordan were to resemble a sea in its great expanse, it might serve as a buffer between Jewish settlements and potentially hostile Arab countries, providing a greater degree of safety. Indeed, the Jordan became a border between Arab and Jewish forces in 1948, while Likud leader and later Prime Minister of Israel Yitzhak Shamir advocated the Jordan as a border on defensive grounds, declaring in 1978 that 'there is no other natural border'.[63] This defensive purpose is hinted at by Lazar in a reference to the military history of the Jordan, in which he states that '[d]uring warfare, [armies] used to capture the fords of the Jordan' so that enemy forces were unable to cross the river.[64] Lazar's attachment to the Volga is also significant in this respect. Riverscapes, as noted above, are frequently incorporated into nationalist imagery and become symbols of the persistence of the nation through time. Lazar's wish for the Jordan to resemble the Volga suggests his desire for a new Jewish state in Palestine to become as powerful as his home country of Russia, with these countries' strength and projected ancient roots symbolised by the image of a wide, perpetually flowing river.

Lazar's desired similarity between the Volga and the Jordan is also noteworthy in terms of his attempt to become 'native' to the land of Palestine and to feel 'at home' in a new and unfamiliar environment. Jewish immigrants to Palestine, anticipating a biblical land of milk and honey, were instead met by the uncompromising realities of the often harsh Palestinian landscape which differed immensely from the environments of their home countries in Central and Eastern Europe and often led to feelings of discomfort and alienation rather than of homecoming.[65] Reports of the Jordan's narrowness are disappointing for Lazar, then, in an additional sense. They seem to affirm Palestine's distance and difference from Europe through its seemingly 'abnormal', 'strange' and' defective' waterscapes, which are in fact a result of misplaced expectations about Middle Eastern environments and the 'normal' hydrological cycle.[66] A narrow Jordan undermines Lazar's ability to be at home on his 'return' to Palestine, challenging his faith in the Zionist project.

The Jordan as National Border

As indicated above in relation to the Joshua narrative, Lazar's fixation with the size of the Jordan has implications for Zionist territorial ambitions. When the narrator agrees to take Lazar on a journey along the entire length of the Jordan, Lazar insistently seeks assurances that the river's true size will eventually become apparent: 'And the further we go, the broader it will become, broader and broader?'[67] Moving from questions to a declarative tone, Lazar states his ultimate hope: 'And we will reach the place where it is broadest, overflowing its banks and its water rising in waves and waves. The place where its waters cover the whole of the countryside.'[68]

In this image the Jordan is not a border of the state, as it is today, but rather seems to make the entire idea of a border impossible through its spreading, liquid form. The overflowing Jordan suggests an apparently unlimited supply of water resources for use by Jewish immigrants to Palestine at the same time as indicating similarly limitless possibilities for Zionist territorial expansion. Lazar's status as an embodiment of ideal Zionist masculinity appears to underscore the legitimacy of his territorial claims.

Lazar's implicitly territorial ambitions recall a debate within the Zionist movement at the start of the twentieth century over the appropriate borders of a potential future Jewish state in Palestine. Palestine under the Ottoman Empire spanned both sides of the Jordan until British Mandatory authorities divided it along the course of the river in 1921. When approved by the League of Nations in 1922 this modification created two countries: Transjordan in the East and Mandate Palestine in the West. Britain restricted the area in which it intended to implement the Balfour commitment to a Jewish national home to the land west of the river, but the Revisionist Zionist movement, founded in 1925, held the idea of a 'whole land of Israel' including Transjordan as a core aim. Revisionist founder Ze'ev (Vladimir) Jabotinsky maintained that the Jordan was not a border of Israel, but in fact, as he wrote in his 1930 poem 'The Left Bank of the Jordan', its 'backbone' and 'spine'.[69]

The poem's line '[t]here are two banks to the Jordan – This one is ours, and that one as well' became a Revisionist rallying cry.[70] This view of 'the whole land of Israel' has since largely become the preserve of the religious right, such as the now-defunct settler movement Gush Emunim.[71] The geographical referent of the phrase 'the whole land of Israel' has changed so that when used today, even by Likud politicians, it stretches to the River Jordan but not beyond.[72] Nevertheless, when Smilansky was writing this was a mainstream debate, with the World Zionist Organisation petitioning the British authorities in the early twentieth century for a much larger territory, including land on the river's eastern side.[73] Lazar's hoped-for resemblance between the Jordan and Volga takes on another meaning in the light of the militant Zionist group Lehi's (also known as the Stern Gang) later claim that the Jordan was 'as little a frontier of border demarcation between states as the Thames in England or the Vistula in Poland', suggesting that the Jordan is no more a border than other national rivers of Europe.[74] Lazar's obsession with the Jordan can hence be read as the staking of a territorial claim on both sides of the river.

This reading is underscored by the story's penultimate scene in which the narrator and Lazar eventually reach a broad and fast-flowing section of the Jordan. At this point, the usually sceptical narrator takes on Lazar's tone of religious awe in describing the river:

> Its waves no longer rippled but beat with force, and were grey in colour. It seemed as though the small stream had become a river, and that from here onward it would grow broader and stronger until the whole earth would be filled with its glory. We could not imagine that from this spot onward the Jordan would again be quiet and dwindle down to a stream as before.[75]

In these comments, the spatial reach and 'force' of the river's flow seem to suggest a similar lack of spatial and temporal restrictions for a potential future Jewish state. Lazar strips naked to swim in the river, in an image which holds several connotations. The immediate connotation is of sexual fulfilment. Swimming in the Jordan is the culmination of Lazar's fixation with the river, which throughout the story is called the object of his 'longing', 'love' or 'yearning' for which he 'can wait no longer'.[76] This response is not as unusual or implausible as it may seem, given the romantic and even erotic language used by some Jewish 'pioneers' to express their feelings on their 'return' to Palestine. Ofer Nordheimer Nur, for instance, quotes a new arrival who wrote: 'I celebrated my wedding with the land. I clung to it, ate it, and was drunk with it'.[77] It might also be read in the light of Lazar's parental background: Lazar describes his father as an 'assimilationist', while his mother was not Jewish.[78] His immersion in the river might be seen as an affirmation of his Jewishness through literally entering into the motherland, Eretz Israel. This is compounded by common associations between the weightless sensation of floating in water to experiences of being in the womb or in infancy, as in Gaston Bachelard's comments: 'Water carries us. Water rocks us. Water puts us to sleep. Water gives us back our mother.'[79] For Lazar, entering the Jordan suggests the ultimate fulfilment of his dream of 'return' and the inextricable connection between the 'renewal' of the Jewish people and of the land.

Immersion in the river also evokes associations of ritual bathing as a cleansing and purifying experience. The Jordan, of course, provides the stage for the most famous example of water's ritual significance in the Christian tradition as the site for John's baptism of Jesus. Lazar's removal of his clothes to appear 'naked as on the day he was born' similarly suggests a moment of rebirth and renewal, while offering a further opportunity for the reader to be reminded of Lazar's admirable physique and its national connotations.[80] The impression of renewal is emphasised by descriptions of Lazar's transformed facial expression, which previously 'bespoke deep suffering' but in the river is 'bright with a laugh of happiness and satisfaction'.[81] The description of Lazar's new-found joy gains a further religious hue from the line 'drops of water scattered all round him and gleamed in the sun like sapphires'.[82] This image recalls the biblical trope of 'bejewelled Jerusalem', suggesting the blending of the earthly and heavenly worlds and an apparent divine blessing for the Zionist project of 'renewing' the people and the land. The suggestion in this image of an immigrant being nourished by and 'reborn' in the environment of his new home is again familiar from Zionist writing and seems unsurprising in a story by Smilansky, given his romantic views of Jewish settlement and the cultivation of Palestine's soil.[83] While we typically associate this narrative of renewal with the land, Smilansky's story shows that the rivers of the homeland can hold similar connotations that are intensified through the ability to literally enter into water. Lazar's immersion in the river appears to be a depiction not just of his personal rebirth and renewal in the land of Palestine, but of the Jewish people.

Lazar's embodiment of ideals of Zionist physicality indicates that his entry into the water can be read as the enactment of ownership claims both on the water of the Jordan and on the territory beyond. It represents a translation onto water of the Zionist practice of 'knowing the land' through direct environmental experience, which in itself represented an assertion of ownership. The equation of presence and ownership in relation to water similarly occurs when Lazar swims to the opposite side of the bank and declares: 'Greetings from beyond Jordan'.[84] He then moves further into the territory: Smilansky writes that Lazar twice 'climbed the bank, stood upon it, gazed over the whole district, and dived down into the water'.[85] In surveying the district from a high vantage point, Lazar performs something like the 'prospect view' of the European landscape tradition, demonstrating his authority and possession of the land.[86] Lazar's incorporation of the 'whole district' – both the western and eastern banks of the river – into a single visual frame from a 'commanding' viewpoint suggests an assertion of ownership claims on the entire territory. At the same time, with Smilansky's references to 'yearning' and 'love' in mind, this scene recalls the colonial trope of depicting exploration and possession of land in the language of sexual conquest, with a 'New Hebrew Man' looking over his territory and claiming it for exclusive Jewish possession.[87]

Lazar's death in the staking of a claim over territory and natural resources seems, as Peleg notes, to make him as much of a 'national hero' as did his life.[88] His death in the service of attempting to unite the two banks manifests the Zionist and Israeli virtue of sacrifice for the nation in which, as Yael Zerubavel writes, 'the loss of individual life contributes to the survival of the collectivity'.[89] Lazar battles to bring the natural environment of Palestine under Jewish control, including the river's deep water, 'strong current' and 'stiff grass', even while aware of the risks.[90] While Palestine's environment defeats him, what we know of Lazar's noble character casts his actions in a positive light and seems to have laid a path for other pioneers to follow – perhaps Smilansky's readers. The drawing of Lazar's body into the river at the end of the story suggests that this is a 'beautiful death' in which his body will serve the important purpose of sanctifying the water as Jewish, just as the blood of halutzim served to regenerate the land.[91]

The negative portrayal of the Hevra Kadisha underscores the story's alliance of Lazar and the narrator with a 'new' and 'progressive' form of Judaism. They travel in a disorderly manner on 'mules' rather than the noble horses preferred by Lazar, the narrator and the Arab characters, and are associated negatively with the group behaviour of animals: 'a crowd of black ravens', 'a screech', 'like wild beasts'.[92] Their emblems of traditional Orthodox Jewish dress are described unflatteringly, even comically: 'The tails of their long coats swung in the air, while their "zizith" swung between their legs'. Their refusal to bury Lazar because he is uncircumcised – even after his apparent death in the service of the nation – suggests a 'backward' attachment to traditions that should, the story implies, have been left behind in Central and Eastern Europe. Lazar and the narrator, by contrast, are offered as appropriate and noble models of Jewish masculinity in the new land of Palestine.

At the same time, elements of the story suggest it may not be a simple narrative of national triumph, even if the prominence of the Zionist myth of sacrifice means that Lazar's death does not immediately register as tragedy or folly. Lazar's strange glee at the river's dangerous currents and weeds in fact seems to indicate something improper, even pathological, in his relation to the Jordan. When in the river, he declares to the worried narrator: 'The water is deep here, friend. And there's a very strong current indeed underneath. You can easily drown . . . .'.[93] The narrator reflects: 'How happy he sounded as he spoke! . . . I began to grow frightened'.[94] In what turn out to be prophetic last words, Lazar exclaims: 'The river bottom is covered with stiff grass. Once get your legs caught in them [sic] and you won't get out again easily!'[95] What the narrator describes as Lazar's 'victorious cry, "You can drown!"' mirrors his earlier glee at risking his life and the lives of his passengers on the Kinneret. We might in one sense read Lazar's enjoyment of the risk of drowning in relation to Freud's notion of the 'oceanic feeling', a wish to restore an earlier sense of completeness in the watery womb which is also linked to an idealisation of death.[96] In this sense, Lazar's urge to return to the motherland through entering its waters takes him to a dangerous and ultimately self-destructive place which suggests that he may represent less of a nationalist ideal than it may initially seem.

Lazar's death highlights the value of the narrator's bookish caution, offered by Smilansky as part of a necessary 'balance' in the Zionist project. In particular, the death shows the narrator's suspicion of Palestine's landscapes and waterscapes to be well founded. Lazar refuses to encounter the Jordan on its own terms, repeatedly comparing it to the full-flowing Volga or the biblical river and being disappointed when it fails to match them. It is, however, the specifics of the local environment that prove his undoing. The narrator, meanwhile, has a careful, even fearful, attitude to Palestine's environment. In sharp contrast to Lazar, he feels 'a strange sense of orphanage and loneliness' in the countryside's expanse, imagining '[t]he whole environment seems to be at enmity with you and to hate you in secret for having pitched your tent or built your house in its midst'.[97] The narrator's personification of hostile nonhuman nature evokes the threat of an unfamiliar environment and of Palestinian resistance to Jewish settlement, suggesting the dangers of Lazar's passionate attachment to an imagined landscape detached from Palestine's reality, which includes inhabitants likely to be displeased or harmed by his exploits.

The point of the river at which Lazar drowns is similarly significant. We are told that 'before he was halfway across the water reached his neck', with this symbolic point suggesting that Lazar ought to have turned back instead of attempting to reach and symbolically claim the eastern bank and river's water.[98] Lazar's death after crossing the mid-point of the river suggests the risks to Jewish settlement that would be likely to increase if his expansionist fervour were to be pursued. In this sense the story might be read in relation to Smilansky's concern – even if, as noted above, this was problematic and complicated – for Palestine's existing population, suggesting the dangers of disregarding local landscapes and people in the pursuit of solely Jewish ownership of land and resources. While Smilansky's stories were popular for what Peleg describes as their 'regenerative promise', 'Hawaja Nazar' is ultimately an ambivalent tale, casting doubt on aims and methods of the Zionist movement of the time through its representation of the River Jordan.[99]

The Palestinian River Jordan

Smilansky's project was, of course, impossible. While he may have argued that '[w]e are coming to redeem our land, not to grab it', the project of acquiring

Palestine for Jewish ownership and a Jewish majority could hardly not be a violent one, as both Smilansky's settler-colonial inspirations and Palestine's subsequent history showed.[100] In the following section I turn to Palestinian experiences of the Jordan in the wake of the inestimable changes in Palestinian relationships to the river after 1948. The Jordan was first designated as a border by the British Mandate authorities in 1922, a decision that initially made little difference to day-to-day Palestinian life in the border zone. Movement of people and goods across the river remained relatively fluid, as it had been under Ottoman rule. This fundamentally changed after the 1948 War, known by Israelis as the War of Independence and by Palestinians as the Nakba, or 'Catastrophe'. Around 100,000 of the estimated 700,000 Palestinians forced to leave their homeland after the creation of Israel in 1948 fled across the Jordan.[101] More refugees took the same route in 1967, fleeing across the ruins of the Allenby Bridge, which Israel had destroyed at the start of the war. At this point Israel occupied the West Bank and extended the area of historic Palestine under its control to the Jordan. The river came to represent, as Edward Said writes, '*the* border: the closest one spiritually, the one travelled across most painfully, the one that most fully characterises the displacement and the proximity of its cause'.[102] In the following section I examine two portrayals of the River Jordan in Palestinian literature, showing that the loss of the Jordan has been mourned by Palestinian writers alongside the land and its symbolic features, with the capacity of rivers to stand in for the passing of time crucial to the Jordan's national meanings.

Darwish's poem 'A River Dies of Thirst' is a lament for an unnamed river personified as an infant that dies after being separated from its nursing mother. Written in his characteristic free verse, the poem provides botanical, geographical and social details that indicate its subject as the River Jordan. The river in Darwish's poem bears marked resemblances to the Jordan, with the most immediate parallel being the exhausted state of both rivers. Darwish's river has dried up, 'died of thirst', mirroring the shrinking of the Jordan and foreshadowing the demise that may not be too far in its future. The 'small river' of Darwish's poem similarly mirrors the Jordan's historically narrow width, while its route also bears comparison with that of the Jordan. Darwish describes the river as 'descending from the mountain peaks/visiting villages and tents like a charming lively guest'. Its mountain source suggests the Jordan's headwaters in Mount Hermon and the Golan Heights, while its visits to many villages evoke the Jordan's meandering course, which render its length over twice the direct distance from source to end.[103] Darwish's description of the river as 'descending' also provides an etymological link to the Jordan, recalling its Hebrew name: Ha-Yarden, or 'Descender'. Darwish's use of the verb '*nazilan*' in the original poem, which derives from the root 'n-z-l', meaning 'to descend', indicates that this connection was not introduced in translation. What is more, 'descend' (نازل) shares its root with 'guest' (نزيل), echoing the description of the river as a 'lively guest' of different villages in a time before Israel's militarised borders as well, perhaps, as the temporariness of its designation as a border.

Darwish contrasts two distinct periods of time in the life of the river and of the community on its banks through depicting the diminishing flow of water. These periods are unspecified, but other lines of the poem, discussed below, indicate that they refer to pre- and post-1948. Darwish depicts nonhuman nature prior to the drying-up of the river as abundant, with it 'bringing oleander trees and date palms to the valley'. The proliferating oleander trees around Palestine's rivers, including the Jordan, were mentioned frequently in narratives by nineteenth-century European visitors to the Holy Land. James Silk Buckingham wrote that the Jordan's banks were 'so thickly wooded with oleander and plane trees', among other plants, 'that we could not perceive the water through them from above'.[104] The scented pink-white flowers of oleander trees make them a decorative plant, while date palms have historically provided a major food source and income in the Middle East. Darwish's reference to the oleander and palm, with their very different connotations, illustrates both aesthetic and practical contributions made by the river to village life.

The river in Darwish's poem is an important locus of village activities. It hosts 'nocturnal revellers on its banks' and provides 'the milk of the clouds' for villagers and their horses to drink. The villagers' revelry is mirrored in the personification of the river as 'laughing' and having 'sang', a correspondence which draws on a longer poetic history of imagining the sound of water and rivers as a human voice and points towards a harmonious and intersubjective relationship between the villagers and river.[105] The reference to 'nocturnal revellers' by the river perhaps hints at a role for the Jordan in the villagers' own fertility as well as that of their crops, reproducing the village's human population into the future. Palestinian culture, like many cultures, has found places for rivers and water in fertility rituals and celebrations of marriage.[106]

This link between the river and Palestinian reproduction is heightened by Darwish's reference to milk and nursing, with the river's water described as the 'milk of the clouds' and the river itself as 'nursed' by 'a heavenly mother'. This equation of Palestine's water with milk builds on a common metaphor identified by Bachelard in his catalogue of the poetics of water, *Water and Dreams* (1942), and in doing so emphasises the role of Palestine itself in nourishing and sustaining the Palestinian people.[107] It also echoes a common trope in Palestinian nationalist art and literature of imagining Palestine as a woman – usually, in Anna Ball's words, as 'mother, nurturer and object of desire'.[108] While this trope is typically discussed in relation to representations of land and its beauty or fecundity, it derives in this case from the necessity of water in sustaining human bodies, showing that the material properties of water can be incorporated into Palestinian national imagery even if water's changeability and movement might seem to make this less likely. In this context, the associations of nursing with innocence, intimacy and maternal care heighten the violence of what is to come in the poem, emphasising the tragedy of the loss of the river and the need for it to be protected as part of a (masculine, heteronormative) nationalist commitment.

A final point worth noting in the context of the river's links to village life is the correspondence between the flow of the river and human mobility. The personified river urges, '"water the horses / and fly to Jerusalem and Damascus"'. There is no sense in the poem of the Jordan as the militarised border it is today. Instead, the possibility of this journey being undertaken with speed ('fly') hints at a time prior to the region's present-day national borders, or the roadblocks, closures and other restrictions on movement endured daily by Palestinians in the West Bank. In providing water for horses the river directly facilitates this mobility and crossing of borders, while its own journey from Syria to Palestine provides a metaphor for the international 'flows' of villagers and their visitors around the region. Darwish's account of the history of the river recalls the ease with which it could be crossed during the Ottoman and Mandate periods, as discussed above. It is worth noting that the Jordan is not, in fact, a very suitable border. It runs through a chalky landscape that can erode rapidly in times of heavy rainfall, allowing the course of the river to alter and causing land on one side of the river to end up on the other.[109] British officials tasked with drawing the border between East and West Palestine in the 1920s were forced to take this capriciousness into account, deciding to draw it along the Jordan's thalweg (deepest point of flow). As a result, sovereignty shifts with the changing riverbed.[110] Darwish's poem emphasises the 'unnaturalness' of the British and later Israeli designation of the Jordan as a border, highlighting the capacity of rivers to function instead as points of transnational connection.

The level of geographical and botanical detail in Darwish's poem suggests it might play another role. In these aspects the poem bears similarities to the vast numbers of Palestinian 'memorial books' produced in the wake of the displacement of 1948.[111] These collections of narratives about destroyed or unwillingly abandoned villages form part of a process of 'active remembrance' which unites Palestinians in the diaspora through reconstructing a shared history at the same time as countering the erasures of official Israeli narratives.[112] In its elegy for the dried-up river, Darwish's poem provides an account of a lost human and nonhuman world that functions as both a document of Palestinian loss and what Catriona Mortimer-Sandilands calls an 'archive of ecological trauma'.[113] In this way, the 'thirst' of the title performs a dual role, invoking not just the drying-up of the river, but the painful longing for a homeland of exiled Palestinians. While land and its features may dominate Palestinian environmental imagery, Darwish's poem indicates the cultural and ecological loss represented by the separation of Palestinians from the River Jordan.

Darwish's disruption of the poem's cyclical structure underscores the apparent tragedy and 'unnaturalness' of the river's death. The poem begins with the lines:

> A river was here
> and it had two banks
> and a heavenly mother who nursed it on drops from the clouds.

These recur towards the end of the poem with a small variation: the first two lines are compressed into the more declamatory '[i]t was a river with two banks'. What initially seems like a return is abruptly cut short by three curt lines that announce the river's death:

> But they kidnapped its mother
> so it ran short of water
> and died, slowly, of thirst.

Darwish's account of the river's 'kidnap' and death dramatises the diversion of the Jordan's waters by Israel, with 'kidnap' recalling both the high numbers of Palestinians held by Israel in the legal limbo of administrative detention and Israel's appropriation of Palestinian water resources. While a full-flowing river typically signifies national strength and persistence over time, the death of Darwish's river mirrors the parallel dispersal of the Palestinians and the end of a continuous period of national history in the land of Palestine. The interruption in the flow of the poem mirrors the interruption of the movement of the water cycle by Israel's act of 'kidnapping', reinforcing the sense of a forced ending of an ancient, natural, potentially even 'sacred' order and balance by an 'alien' interferer not attuned to local patterns of nonhuman nature.[114] The 'unnaturalness' of the kidnapping and pathos of the poem is heightened by Darwish's personification of the river and its source as a mother and her nursing child. This is a powerful image, even with its reliance on normative ideas of maternal womanhood common to both nationalist and environmentalist rhetoric.[115]

The contrast between Darwish's vision of earlier social and ecological harmony along the river and this violent event represents what Laurence Buell describes as a '[t]rauma of pastoral disruption'.[116] This trope features frequently in environmental writing, particularly in postcolonial indictments of imperial environmental degradation.[117] As Shaul Cohen notes, an inflection of this trope is common to Palestinian environmental narratives:

> For Palestinians, the environment is a vessel for the idyll of Palestinian independence and a place that has been despoiled by Israeli (de)construction. It is also an hourglass that shows the erosion of opportunity for (re)creating a garden of Eden that Palestinian nationalism has promised will materialise upon the termination of the occupation.[118]

The juxtaposition of 'A River Dies of Thirst' with the poem 'The Wall' on the opposite page underscores Cohen's point.[119] 'The Wall' addresses

Israel's separation barrier, describing it as '[a] huge metal snake' consisting of 'a nightmare of cement segments reinforced with pliant metal'. Darwish transforms the snake of the Garden of Eden into a monstrous manifestation of Israel's apparent alienation from nonhuman nature, suggesting the environmental 'Fall' described by Cohen. The reference to the Wall, a hard, modern border, contrasts with the depiction of free-flowing mobility across the Jordan in 'A River Dies of Thirst'. In this sense, the two poems suggest the 'unnatural' character of both borders and in turn, Israel's own lack of environmental sensitivity.

By depicting a flourishing environment in Palestine's past, Darwish's poems challenge Zionist narratives of having 'drained the swamps and made the desert bloom'. Drastic environmental alterations were frequently presented by the Zionist movement and later the State of Israel as part of a process of undoing Palestinian 'neglect', with these claims serving to naturalise exclusive Jewish or Israeli ownership of land and resources. These assertions of superior environmental aptitude were seen earlier in this chapter in Lazar's exceptional ability to work the land and sail its waters and are discussed in the following chapter in greater depth when I turn to the Zionist and Israeli history of swamp drainage. Darwish's 'A River Dies of Thirst' and 'The Wall' imply instead that Israeli alterations of the landscape have caused a parallel 'environmental Nakba', in which the displacement of Palestinians for the creation of Israel was accompanied by devastation of Palestine's environment.[120] 'A River Dies of Thirst' evokes a history of seemingly superior Palestinian environmental stewardship, providing an implicit counter-claim of rightful Palestinian sovereignty over land and water in Israel/Palestine and suggesting Israel's separation from nature. Darwish's depiction of ecological harmony along the river shows the importance of representations of the Jordan riverscape in articulating Palestinian ideas of loss and belonging to the homeland, beyond the more familiar symbolism of the land, with the capacity of flowing water to stand in for the passing of time indicating a historic relationship that has been lost just as the Palestinian nation has been forcibly dispersed.

A River without Water

Barghouti's memoir *I Saw Ramallah* was published at the turn of the millennium to widespread regional and international acclaim, including winning the Naguib Mahfouz Medal for Literature. It has often been hailed, not unproblematically, as an archetypal representation of Palestinian experience, including by Said in its foreword.[121] The book recounts Barghouti's return to Israel/Palestine after an enforced thirty-year exile in the wake of the Six-Day War, covering his visits to Ramallah and his home village of Deir Ghassaneh. It begins with Barghouti's entry into Palestine from Jordan via the Allenby Bridge, also known as al-Karama Crossing and the King Hussein Bridge. Forced to endure a typically lengthy wait, Barghouti looks out of the door at the river and reflects:

> I was not surprised by its narrowness: the Jordan was always a very thin river. This is how we knew it in childhood. The surprise was that after these long years it had become a river without water. Almost without water. Nature had colluded with Israel in stealing its water. It used to have a voice, now it was a silent river, a river like a parked car.[122]

Barghouti and Darwish use similar strategies to critique Israel's impact on the River Jordan. The arid riverscape features again, conveying a comparable impression of national loss, disunity and tragedy to that found in 'A River Dies of Thirst' and becoming, as Bernard notes, 'a symbol of loss and defeat'.[123] Barghouti's spare tone and short, largely descriptive phrases communicate a sense of restrained outrage, much as in Darwish's poem, particularly its concluding lines. In Barghouti's account, the river's 'death', if not described with the overt personification which makes such strong affective demands in Darwish's poem, is still conveyed through the metaphor of a silenced 'voice', another trope identified by Bachelard as common to representations of water.[124] As in 'A River Dies of Thirst', this passage juxtaposes two distinct periods in its timeline of the river's environmental degradation: before and after Israel's occupation of the West Bank. Darwish's language of Israel's 'kidnap' of Palestinian resources recurs here, too, in Barghouti's description of 'nature' and Israel 'stealing' the river's water. Like Darwish's poem, Barghouti's lines echo Cohen's account of Palestinian environmental imagery and rhetoric that portrays Palestine as a 'place that has been despoiled by Israeli (de)construction', with the loss of the river a result of Israeli occupation and what is portrayed as Israel's ultimately self-defeating desire to bend nonhuman nature to its will.

Barghouti's incongruous simile 'a river like a parked car' contrasts sharply with the nostalgic, pastoral tone of Darwish's poem and is key to the political distinctions between their representation of the Jordan. Bernard reads this image in relation to Barghouti's wider use of 'absurd' metaphors, which she describes as a strategy with 'Brechtian affinities'.[125] The river and car 'share immobility, but nothing else', producing a clash that compels the reader to reflect on the material impact of the loss of the river on the Palestinian inhabitants of the West Bank.[126] Yet, as Farrier notes, Barghouti's references to water highlight the operation of Israeli regimes of power in the West Bank.[127] Farrier points out that Israelis have access to what Zygmunt Bauman describes as 'liquid modernity', allowing them to travel freely, while Palestinians are subject to 'heavy modernity', with their movement curtailed by Israel's roadblocks and checkpoints, and, most visibly, the separation wall. In this case, considering the Jordan's contemporary riverscape reveals that the image of river-as-car is more than merely incongruous, evoking the actual parked cars queuing on both sides of the river as Palestinians wait to cross the Jordan.

The queues of cars at the Allenby Bridge appear frequently in literary representations of the Jordan, including Raja Shehadeh's memoir *A Rift in Time* (2010) and Joe Sacco's graphic novel *Palestine* (2003).[128] While these queues are out of view in *I Saw Ramallah*, they are a prominent feature in an account of crossing the Jordan that appears in the book's sequel, *I Was Born There, I Was Born Here* (*Wulidtu Hunak, Wulidtu Huna*), published in Arabic in 2009 and translated into English in 2011 by Humphrey Davis.[129] Barghouti describes '[h]undreds of human beings standing outside their cars waiting their turn', adding that '[t]he rows of cars have no end'.[130] As noted above, the power of rivers as national symbols derives from the potential of water to suggest the movement, hence the continuity, of the nation through time. Movement, too, is an inherent part of the function and symbolic connotations of the car, 'invented', as André Gorz notes, 'to allow its owner to go where he or she wishes, at the time and speed he or she wishes'.[131] Barghouti's 'absurd' simile, then, points to the obstruction of two parallel flows under Israeli occupation: of the River Jordan and of the movement of Palestinians into, around and out of the West Bank. These flows, of course, intersect: idling cars at checkpoints and the circuitous routes Palestinians are forced to take as a result of Israel's checkpoints serve, ultimately, to further diminish the flow of the Jordan through their contribution to carbon emissions and to regional desertification, underscoring the environmental impact of the occupation.

These obstructed flows are bound up with another stalled flow, that of capital. The loss of the Jordan drastically constrains the potential of the Palestinian agricultural sector, while Israel's stranglehold on Palestinian movement inhibits the development of the Palestinian economy, instead producing 'de-development'. The loss of the Jordan and limited access to the Mountain Aquifer means that West Bank residents are forced to purchase water from Israel at inflated prices, harming Palestinian health, wellbeing and quality of life.[132] Lack of access to reliable and affordable supplies of clean water has a significant impact on the Palestinian economy through inhibiting agriculture. Only 21 per cent of Palestine's agricultural land is currently irrigated, depriving the Palestinian economy of what even conservative estimates put at over a billion dollars in annual income.[133] Israel's diversion of the Jordan's waters materially limits the Palestinian Authority's capacity to support its population and to build an independent economy, even if changes to Israel's border regime would be needed to export the products of Palestinian agriculture.[134] Darwish's representation of the Jordan evokes a lost national past, whereas Barghouti's concern is with the future from which Palestinians have effectively been cut off by Israel's appropriation of Palestine's natural resources. The capacity of the river to suggest the movement of time is crucial to its national meanings in both texts.

Barghouti's emphasis on the economic impacts of occupation marks a sharp difference between his approach and that of Darwish. It is true that at some points in his memoirs Barghouti advances a romantic, pastoral perspective on Palestinian relationships with nonhuman nature which bears comparison with Darwish's imagery in 'A River Dies of Thirst'. Farrier, for instance, cites Barghouti's account of traditional irrigation methods in the village of Ein al-Deir as an example of 'sustained agro-ecological harmony'.[135] This scene mirrors the harmonious relations between humans, water and place depicted in Darwish's poem. Similarly, an account of the separation wall in *I Was Born There, I Was Born Here*, which Barghouti describes as 'a cruel and disfiguring intervention' to which nature has been 'subjected', resembles Darwish's description of the wall discussed above.[136] At the same time, the reference in the above passage to 'nature' is salient here again. Barghouti writes that 'nature had colluded with Israel in stealing [the Jordan's] water'.[137] Collusion, or collaboration, is a practice with high stakes in Palestine, and Barghouti's use of personification links 'nature' to the most serious possible betrayal of the Palestinian national cause. Darwish, by contrast, presents the causes of 'nature' and the Palestinians as inherently aligned, treating environmental harm solely as the result of the expulsion of the Palestinians in an association familiar from Palestinian literature.[138] While Darwish's text illustrates the affective impact of the loss of water and its disruption of a way of life, Barghouti's approach provides a reminder of the potential for the pastoral to give a misleading impression of history and to reinforce a perception of the lost Palestine as a land of rural peasant life that can be counterproductive.[139]

Elsewhere in *I Saw Ramallah*, Barghouti describes the flourishing urban life in Ottoman Palestine and emphasises the significance of the loss of Palestine's urban culture of the early twentieth century over the more traditionally mourned village life. He writes:

> The occupation has kept the Palestinian village static and turned our cities back into villages. We do not weep for the mill of the village but for the bookshop and library. We do not want to regain the past but to regain the future and push tomorrow into the day after. Palestine's progress in the natural paths of its future was deliberately impeded, as though Israel wished to make of the whole Palestinian community a countryside for the city of Israel. More than that, it plans to turn every Arab city into a rural hinterland for the Hebrew State.[140]

While villages form the mainstay of Palestinian nationalist myth, a surprisingly high proportion of Palestinians – a third – lived in urban areas prior to 1948, and the harmonious idyll depicted by Darwish would probably not have survived the increasing urbanisation of Palestinian life which was already taking place prior to the creation of Israel.[141] If Darwish's romantic depiction of village life derives to an extent from the ways in which history tends to figure in poetry, Barghouti highlights the potential for a Palestinian nationalist emphasis on lost rural life to elide Israel's destruction and distortion of the development of Ottoman Palestinian urban life, perhaps of greater national consequence for Palestine's future. What is more, Barghouti's comments underscore a risk of suggestions of a Palestinian alliance with 'nature', which is that these carry the potential to reproduce Zionist imaginative erasures that served to justify claims that Palestine was a 'land without a people'.[142] Barghouti's representation of water, rather than land, allows him to challenge potentially reactionary norms of land-based nationalist imagery and to imagine the ways that Palestine has been cut off not just from its past, but from its future.

Barghouti's emphasis on the material impact of occupation continues in his depiction of the Allenby Bridge. In this image, Barghouti contests Israel's claiming of the river as a national border through what Bernard calls his 'existential materialist aesthetic'.[143] Barghouti describes his crossing of the bridge in terms which, as Bernard notes, are 'almost purely sensory' and stripped of the symbolic connotations which might be expected in an account of an event loaded with nationalist significance.[144] He writes: 'It is very hot on the bridge. A drop of sweat slides from my forehead down to the frame of my spectacles.'[145] The bridge itself is portrayed in similarly bare terms: 'a bridge no longer than a few meters of wood and thirty years of exile', or merely 'a piece of dark wood' with the implausible ability 'to distance a whole nation from its dreams'.[146] In these images, Barghouti juxtaposes his own bodily perceptions and the bridge's banal materiality with the immeasurable consequences for Palestinians of the Jordan's designation as a border. As Bernard points out, in setting up this contrast Barghouti highlights the roots of the bridge's metaphorical significance in human decisions and practices rather than as an apparently inevitable natural fact.[147]

Barghouti directly engages with the issue of 'natural' borders, suggesting, like Darwish, that rivers are not 'natural' divisions between peoples. Barghouti writes: 'I do not thank you, you short, unimportant bridge. You are not a sea or an ocean that we might find our excuses in your terrors. You are not a mountain range inhabited by wild beasts and fantastical monsters.'[148]

The extensive, dangerous and difficult to navigate spaces of oceans or mountain ranges, Barghouti suggests, might present more obvious borders. The River Jordan, by contrast, seems an unlikely candidate for a dividing line between peoples, particularly when, as Barghouti writes, '[t]here is very little water under the bridge'.[149] Here, Barghouti invokes a well-known idiom which explains everything that should make the Jordan easy to cross at the same time as demonstrating why this is not the case. The remark is a literal description of the state of the Jordan – always narrow, shrunken more than ever in the present – but also a summary of the state of the conflict and a reference to one of its exacerbating factors, the effective 'water war' against Palestinians that is enacted by Israel through the diversion of the Jordan.[150]

Conclusion

In this chapter I have examined representations of the River Jordan in a short story, poem and memoir by a Hebrew author and two Palestinian authors writing at different times and with sharply contrasting reputations. While Smilansky's story 'Hawaja Nazar' was written at the very start of the twentieth century and is barely read today, Darwish's poem 'A River Dies of Thirst' and Barghouti's memoir *I Saw Ramallah* are contemporary texts with wide readerships that may well be two of the highest-profile Palestinian literary engagements with hydropolitics. Nevertheless, like Smilansky's story, Darwish's poem has received no attention for its hydropolitical themes, while Barghouti's memoir has received little. This is surprising, given the high visibility of the River Jordan in international debate over 'water wars' and the global scale of concern over the disastrously degraded condition of a sacred river, but reflects the general critical tendencies set out in this book's introduction, in which the water of Israel/Palestine is seen as a matter for technical and political calculation rather than literary reflection.

The three texts, as I have shown, use depictions of the riverscape to engage with key issues in Israeli and Palestinian national politics at their times of writing. Smilansky demonstrates the importance of the Jordan's water resources in realising Zionist plans for settlement, at the same time as warning of the dangers of territorial overambition and of falsely expecting the Palestinian environment to mirror the landscapes of Europe. Darwish and Barghouti's texts, meanwhile, provide a crucial reminder of the manifold impacts of the loss of the Jordan on Palestinians and nonhuman nature in the region. They emphasise the ways in which Israeli overuse of the Jordan's water has harmed the river's ecology and disrupted Palestinian social relations, with Darwish offering a vision of disrupted pastoral harmony and Barghouti emphasising the loss of Palestinian urban life. Like Smilansky's character Lazar, Darwish and Barghouti both suggest that the Jordan is not a 'natural' border. While Lazar does so for reasons of territorial expansionism, Darwish and Barghouti instead argue for the social and environmental harms of Israel's designation of the Jordan as a border. In all three texts, the capacity of water to stand in for time is crucial to its national significance and its distinction from familiar land-based environmental imagery.

Water in Israel/Palestine is often understood as 'naturally scarce', an apparently incontrovertible scientific fact which provides the basis for many claims of past, present or future 'water wars' over the Jordan. In this chapter I began with a period of time in which Zionist leaders sought to prove that water resources were abundant and existed in sufficient quantity to support high numbers of Jewish arrivals from Europe, a belief that formed the basis of Lazar's hopes for a wide Jordan. The following chapter extends this theme, examining attempts during the Second Aliyah to deal with spaces which were judged to contain too much water: Palestine's swamps. In Chapter 2 I turn to the Zionist movement's swamp drainage projects of the early twentieth century, tracking their legacy through their revival in the early years of the Israeli state and their rejection during the formative years of the Israeli environmentalist movement in the 1980s and 1990s. While drainage provided the foundation for ongoing claims of Zionist and Israeli technological superiority, it also served – for both Palestinian and Israeli critics – as the basis for criticism of Zionism's elevation of national priorities over the long-term survival of nonhuman nature.

Notes

1. Havrelock, 'My Home Is over Jordan', p. 105.
2. Quoted in Udasin, 'Sewage Clogs Jordan River South of Baptism Site'.
3. De Châtel, 'Baptism in the Jordan River', p. 224.
4. For example, Schwartzstein, 'Biblical Waters'.
5. Selby, *Water, Power and Politics*, p. 49.
6. Smilansky, 'Hawaja Nazar'.
7. Darwish, *A River Dies of Thirst*, p. 54.
8. References to this text are to the 2004 UK edition. Barghouti, *I Saw Ramallah*.
9. A notable exception which I draw on in this chapter is Farrier's 'Washing Words'.
10. Cited in Ramras-Rauch, *The Arab in Israeli Literature*, p. 20.
11. Shaked, *Modern Hebrew Fiction*, p. 68.
12. Domb, 'The Arab in Fact and Fiction'; Morahg, 'New Images of Arabs in Israeli Fiction', p. 149.

13. Peleg, *Orientalism and the Hebrew Imagination*, pp. 75–6; Ramras-Rauch, *The Arab in Israeli Literature*, p. 15.
14. Peleg, 'Heroic Conduct'; Shaked, *Modern Hebrew Fiction*, p. 69.
15. Bernard, '"Who Would Dare to Make It into an Abstraction"', p. 665; Bernard and Elmarsafy, 'Intimacies', p. 1.
16. Mattar, 'Mourid Barghouti's "Multiple Displacements"'. See also Bernard, '"Who Would Dare to Make It into an Abstraction"'; Havrelock, *River Jordan*, pp. 272–3.
17. Roy, *The Gaza Strip*.
18. Cusack, *Riverscapes and National Identities*, p. 2.
19. Ibid., p. 2.
20. Bender, 'Time and Landscape', p. 103.
21. Karlinsky, *California Dreaming*, pp. 23–4. While there is no biography of Smilansky or dedicated account of his literature or politics, Karlinsky's detailed footnote on p. 227 provides an extensive list of available works, and his book itself is a key source for this chapter. Major points of reference for Smilansky's biography are his six volumes of autobiographical novels, published in Hebrew from 1944 to 1954.
22. Ibid., p. 24. The moshava differs from the better-known forms of early Zionist collective agricultural settlements, the kibbutz and moshav, in that all land and property are privately owned.
23. Karlinsky, *California Dreaming*, p. 24.
24. Ibid., p. 24.
25. Ibid., p. 27.
26. Shafir, 'Capitalist Binationalism in Mandatory Palestine', p. 614. On the history of relations between Jewish and Arab workers in Palestine and the role of the Jewish labour union Histadrut in promoting Hebrew Labour, see Lockman, *Comrades and Enemies*; Shafir, *Land, Labor and the Origins of the Israeli-Palestinian Conflict*.
27. For an English translation, see Dowty, 'Much Ado about Little'.
28. Cited in Karlinsky, *California Dreaming*, p. 27.
29. Ginsburg, *Rhetoric and Nation*, pp. 80–1.
30. Smilansky, 'Hawaja Nazar', p. 163.
31. Ibid., p. 149.
32. Ibid., pp. 159, 151, 160.
33. Ibid., p. 160.
34. Saposnik, *Becoming Hebrew*, p. 162.
35. Peleg, *Orientalism and the Hebrew Imagination*, p. 79.

36. Smilansky, 'Hawaja Nazar', p. 173.
37. Ibid., p. 174.
38. Ibid., p. 174.
39. Azaryahu, 'The Formation of the "Hebrew Sea" in Pre-State Israel', p. 262.
40. Smilansky, 'Hawaja Nazar', p. 148.
41. On Zionism and the (male) Jewish body, see Boyarin, *Unheroic Conduct*; Nur, *Eros and Tragedy*; Presner, *Muscular Judaism*; Weiss, *The Chosen Body*.
42. Cited in Reizbaum, 'Max Nordau and the Generation of Jewish Muscle', p. 133.
43. Smilansky, 'Hawaja Nazar', p. 172.
44. These are associated most notoriously with the work of (Jewish) sexologist Otto Weininger. Boyarin, *Unheroic Conduct*, pp. 208–16.
45. Nur points out that such a sensibility was part of some visions of the new Jewish man. *Eros and Tragedy*, ch. 8.
46. Peleg, 'Heroic Conduct', p. 40. Also relevant here in a way that may not be immediately apparent is the work of the antisemitic German ideologue Hans Blüher, writing roughly contemporaneously to Smilansky. Blüher positioned the homosexual as the manliest of all and emphasised the centrality of homosocial, potentially even homosexual, bonding to the emergence of the state, providing the theoretical basis for the German same-sex sports and hiking associations which fed into Zionist youth movements (for Blüher, as Todd Presner points out, Jewish men were not homosexual enough). Reading the apparent attraction between the narrator and Lazar in this light underscores its significance as a necessary precursor to statebuilding. See Nur, *Eros and Tragedy*, ch. 7; Presner, *Muscular Judaism*, pp. 137–8.
47. Sufian, *Healing the Land and the Nation*, p. 123. On the historical transition from Zionist perceptions of abundance to today's dominant narrative of scarcity, see Alatout, 'Bringing Abundance into Environmental Politics'.
48. Havrelock, *River Jordan*, pp. 227, 248.
49. Ibid., pp. 227, 248; Lowdermilk, *Palestine: Land of Promise*; Hays and Barrekette, *T.V.A. on the Jordan*.
50. Karlinsky, *California Dreaming*, pp. 18–19, 121–2.
51. Smilansky, *Jewish Colonisation and the Fellah*, pp. 5, 39.
52. Karlinsky, *California Dreaming*, p. 24.
53. Smilansky, 'Hawaja Nazar', p. 164.
54. Cited in Peppard, 'Troubling Waters', p. 113.
55. Lazar's reliance on the Bible mirrors a wider Zionist deployment of biblical precedent in support of claims of exclusive Jewish sovereignty over the land and resources of Israel/Palestine, on which there is a rich body of scholarship. See

Abu El-Haj, *Facts on the Ground*; Masalha, *The Bible and Zionism*; Whitelam, *The Invention of Ancient Israel.*
56. Benstein, *The Way Into Judaism and the Environment*, pp. 85–7; Tuan, *The Hydrologic Cycle and the Wisdom of God*, p. 144. See also Linton, *What Is Water?*, ch. 5.
57. Havrelock, *River Jordan*, p. 88.
58. Ibid., pp. 88, 92.
59. Ibid., p. 152.
60. Ibid., p. 154.
61. Ibid., p. 154.
62. See, famously, Johann Gottfried von Herder, who saw 'natural' borders as a crucial part of the 'organic' emergence of nations, writing that: 'Seas, mountain-ranges, and rivers are the most natural boundaries not only of lands but of peoples, customs, languages, and empires, and they have been, even in the greatest revolutions in human affairs, the directing lines or limits of world history. If otherwise mountains had arisen, rivers flowed or coasts trended, then how very different would mankind have scattered over this tilting place of nations.' Cited in Penrose, 'Nations, States and Homelands', p. 286.
63. Shelef, 'From "Both Banks of the Jordan"', p. 147, note 63.
64. Ibid., p. 164.
65. Ramras-Rauch, *The Arab in Israeli Literature*, p. 45; Zerubavel, 'The Conquest of the Desert and the Settlement Ethos', pp. 34–5.
66. Davis and Burke, 'Imperialism, Orientalism, and the Environment in the Middle East', pp. 3–4.
67. Smilansky, 'Hawaja Nazar', p. 165.
68. Ibid., p. 165.
69. Cited in Shelef, *Evolving Nationalism*, pp. 82–3.
70. Ibid., pp. 82–3.
71. Masalha, *Imperial Israel and the Palestinians*, pp. 107–9.
72. Kaplan, *The Jewish Radical Right*, p. 159.
73. Biger, *The Boundaries of Modern Palestine*, p. 161.
74. Shelef, 'From "Both Banks of the Jordan"', p. 135.
75. Smilansky, 'Hawaja Nazar', p. 177.
76. Ibid., pp. 166, 163, 175, 162.
77. Nur, *Eros and Tragedy*, p. 147. See also Neumann, *Land and Desire*, p. 52.
78. Smilansky, 'Hawaja Nazar', p. 153.
79. Bachelard, *Water and Dreams*, p. 131. See also Strang, *The Meaning of Water*, pp. 54–5.
80. Smilansky, 'Hawaja Nazar', p. 178.

81. Ibid., pp. 177, 178.
82. Ibid., p. 178.
83. Ramras-Rauch, *The Arab in Israeli Literature*, p. 13.
84. Smilansky, 'Hawaja Nazar', p. 178.
85. Ibid., p. 178.
86. Barrell, 'The Public Prospect and the Private View', p. 27; Cosgrove, 'Prospect, Perspective and the Evolution of the Landscape Idea', p. 55.
87. McClintock, *Imperial Leather*, p. 3.
88. Peleg, 'Heroic Conduct', p. 39.
89. Zerubavel, *Recovered Roots*, p. 227.
90. Smilansky, 'Hawaja Nazar', p. 178.
91. In this point I draw on Neumann, *Land and Desire*, p. 95.
92. Smilansky, 'Hawaja Nazar', p. 180.
93. Ibid., p. 178.
94. Ibid., p. 178.
95. Ibid., pp. 178–9.
96. On psychoanalytic readings of literary representations of water and drowning, see Baker, 'Fears and Fantasies of Swimming and Being in Water'.
97. Smilansky, 'Hawaja Nazar', p. 146.
98. Ibid., p. 178.
99. Peleg, *Orientalism and the Hebrew Imagination*, p. 78.
100. Cited in Karlinsky, *California Dreaming*, p. 27.
101. Havrelock, *River Jordan*, p. 256.
102. Cited in Havrelock, *River Jordan*, p. 253.
103. Kliot, *Water Resources and Conflict in the Middle East*, p. 143.
104. Buckingham, *Travels in Palestine*, pp. 108–9.
105. Bachelard, *Water and Dreams*, p. 189.
106. Strang, *The Meaning of Water*, p. 85; Naguib, *Women, Water and Memory*, pp. 110, 113–14; Salim Tamari, *Mountain Against the Sea*, p. 32.
107. Bachelard, *Water and Dreams*, p. 189.
108. Ball, *Palestinian Literature and Film*, p. 21.
109. Biger, *The Boundaries of Modern Palestine*, p. 187. Raja Shehadeh writes that this has been known to happen over the course of a single day. *A Rift in Time*, p. 57.
110. Biger, *The Boundaries of Modern Palestine*, p. 188.
111. Davis, *Palestinian Village Histories*; Slyomovics, *The Object of Memory*.
112. Slyomovics, *The Object of Memory*, pp. xiv, xii.

113. Mortimer-Sandilands, 'Melancholy Natures, Queer Ecologies', p. 342.
114. Tuan, *The Hydrologic Cycle and the Wisdom of God*, p. 122.
115. On nationalist discourse and imagery more generally, see Yuval-Davis, 'Gender and Nation'. On the Palestinian context see Ball, *Palestinian Literature and Film*, ch. 2. On environmental politics, see Seymour, *Strange Natures*.
116. Buell, *Writing for an Endangered World*, p. 37.
117. DeLoughrey and Handley, 'Introduction: Towards an Aesthetics of the Earth', p. 23.
118. Cohen, 'Environmentalism Deferred', pp. 248–9.
119. Darwish, *A River Dies of Thirst*, p. 55. All subsequent references to this poem are to the same page.
120. Al Butmah et al., 'Environmental Nakba'.
121. Bernard, '"Who Would Dare"', p. 666; Edward Said, 'Foreword', in Barghouti, *I Saw Ramallah*, pp. vii–xi.
122. Barghouti, *I Saw Ramallah*, p. 5.
123. Bernard, '"Who Would Dare"', p. 671.
124. Bachelard, *Water and Dreams*, pp. 187–96.
125. Ibid., p. 671.
126. Ibid., p. 671.
127. Farrier, 'Washing Words', p. 189.
128. Shehadeh, *A Rift in Time*, p. 54; Sacco, *Palestine*.
129. Barghouti, *I Was Born There, I Was Born Here*.
130. Ibid., pp. 133, 134.
131. Gorz, 'The Social Ideology of the Motorcar', p. 75.
132. Isaac et al., 'The Economic Costs of the Israeli Occupation of the Occupied Palestinian Territories', p. 9.
133. Ibid., pp. 10–12.
134. Ibid., p. 16.
135. Farrier, p. 196.
136. Barghouti, *I Was Born There, I Was Born Here*, p. 128.
137. Barghouti, *I Saw Ramallah*, p. 5.
138. Bardenstein, 'Trees, Forests', p. 152; Parmenter, *Giving Voice to Stones*, p. 81.
139. On Palestinian imagery of the peasant, see Swedenburg, 'The Palestinian Peasant as National Signifier'.
140. Barghouti, *I Saw Ramallah*, p. 147.
141. Benvenisti, *Sacred Landscape*, pp. 6–7.
142. Zerubavel, 'Desert and Settlement', p. 205.

143. Bernard, '"Who Would Dare"', p. 666.
144. Ibid., p. 670.
145. Barghouti, *I Saw Ramallah*, p. 1.
146. Ibid., p. 9.
147. Bernard, '"Who Would Dare"', p. 671.
148. Barghouti, *I Saw Ramallah*, pp. 9–10.
149. Barghouti, *I Saw Ramallah*, p. 11.
150. Zeitoun, *Power and Water in the Middle East*, pp. 1–7; Dajani, 'Drying Palestine'.

2

'THE DENSE, MURKY WATER OF THE PAST': SWAMPS, NOSTALGIA AND SETTLEMENT MYTH IN MEIR SHALEV'S *THE BLUE MOUNTAIN*

the true creators of our Old-New-Land ... were the hydraulic engineers –
Theodor Herzl, *Altneuland* (1902)[1]

When I was young I believed with all my heart the
Huleh swamp had to be drained.
Then all the bright-coloured birds fled for their lives.
Now half a century later they are filling it with water again
Because it was all a mistake. Perhaps my entire life I've been living a mistake. –
Yehuda Amichai, 'Once I Wrote *Now and in Other Days*' (2000)[2]

The neatly ordered arable farmland of the Jezreel Valley in northern Israel is commonly viewed as the central example of Israel's success in 'redeeming' the land of Palestine. The Jezreel Valley is popularly known in Israel as the 'Emek' ('Valley') and in Arabic as Marj Ibn 'Amer. Until the early twentieth century the Jezreel Valley was a swamp. In 1921 it was purchased by the Jewish National Fund (JNF) and from 1922 to 1924, like most of Palestine's swamps, it was drained by the halutzim, or 'pioneers', of the Second (1904–14) and Third (1919–24) Aliyot. The JNF included more images of the Valley in pre-state publicity and fundraising materials than any other part of the country and continues to celebrate the project on its website today.[3] In the pre- and early state periods drainage was valorised in left-wing literature, song and curricula, with schoolchildren sent to tour and work in the new settlements.[4] The history of swamp drainage tells us something intriguing about perceptions of the 'natural' state of water in Israel/Palestine. While water in Israel/Palestine is consistently framed today in terms of scarcity, the Zionist movement's extensive drainage projects indicate that an opposing view of the land's water potential was once prevalent. Water was considered abundant, to the extent that its 'excess' was a nuisance which had to be managed.

In this chapter I examine the history and mythology of swamp drainage in Israel/Palestine through a discussion of Israeli novelist Meir Shalev's bestselling first novel *The Blue Mountain* (*Roman Russi*, 1988), translated into English in 1991 by Hillel Halkin. Shalev is one of Israel's most popular novelists and his work has been translated into more than twenty languages. Still, his work is not well-known outside Israel. In the Anglophone world this may be due to a low appetite for translated literature in general, even if this has increased in recent years.[5] Anglophone readers' expectations of Israeli literature may also be a factor. Readers of literature from a 'conflict zone' may not expect Shalev's comic, magical realist style, while his lightness of touch differs sharply from the seemingly weightier works of Israel's best-known literary exports, David Grossman, Amos Oz and A. B. Yehoshua. This may explain why Shalev's work has also received little critical attention.

The style of Shalev's work has often caused it to be read as escapist. A recent online profile is typical, describing Shalev as an author who 'never mixes fiction with politics' and who writes 'whimsical and satirical novels [that] are grounded in the history and legends of pre-state Israel'.[6] Shalev's interest in the natural world may reinforce an impression of his books as gentle middlebrow entertainment, since nature writing is not usually known for its political commitment. This interest is well-documented in interviews, while Shalev's novels often contain detailed descriptions of nonhuman nature and have won awards for environmental accuracy.[7] A handful of critics have noted that despite his playful tone, Shalev offers sharp critiques of the early years of Zionist settlement in the same tradition as the authors above.[8] In this sense his work emerges out of the challenges to orthodox narratives of Israeli history levelled in the 1980s by Israel's 'New Historians' within the phenomenon of 'post-Zionism', as Israeli scholars sought to restore the Palestinian side of the story discussed in the latter half of the previous chapter. These critiques have not, however, been read in the light of Shalev's environmental interests. In this chapter I reframe *The Blue Mountain* as an environmental text, showing that its questioning of Israel's national myths is also, crucially, an environmental critique. In doing so, this chapter foregrounds the novel's links with another developing social trend in Israel during this period: the environmental movement.

At the same time as Benny Morris, Ilan Pappé, Avi Shlaim and others were questioning Israel's national mythology, Israeli environmentalists were articulating their own critiques of the activities of Israel's founders that centred on the draining of the swamps, particularly the Hula Valley.[9] Draining the swamps was gradually being redefined from a triumph of Zionist ingenuity to an emblem of its environmental hubris. Shalev's depictions of resurgent swamps and water become part of a reckoning with Israel's political and environmental history which asserts that dominant stories are no longer, in all senses of the word, sustainable. His use of magical realism, while easily readable as a quirky aesthetic choice, is central to his critique of dominant Zionist histories and Zionism's environmental politics.

Magical realism is a genre that is concerned with how history gets written, whose histories are canonised and whose are erased. As Brenda Cooper writes, magical realism 'opposes fundamentalism and purity' and undermines the 'quest to tap roots, origins and homogeneity', qualities that allow Shalev to use it to question orthodox national narratives and recover marginalised histories.[10] Magical realism not only reflects history, but, as Wendy B. Faris writes, 'it may also seek to change it, by addressing historical issues critically and thereby attempting to heal historical wounds'.[11] It does so through blending 'different realms' of the ordinary and extraordinary in a way that cannot be explained through rationalist logic, including the realms of the human and nonhuman.[12] It is these qualities that also make magical realism vital to Shalev's critique of what we might read as Zionism's similarly 'magical' thinking about the environment.

Magical realism is a tricky category to use in an Israeli context given its long association with postcolonial writing. It is often seen as a characteristically postcolonial mode.[13] Israel's relationship to the postcolonial, meanwhile, is fraught. As a country founded in part to escape European antisemitism, yet whose creation was inspired and aided by European colonial powers and led to the expulsion of the Palestinians, Israel is best understood, as noted in the introduction to this book, as what Joseph Massad calls a 'post-colonial colony'.[14] Nevertheless, magical realism has proliferated since the 1970s in a country with a similar status, Canada, where authors have used it to navigate Canada's relationship with Britain and the United States, the regional politics of 'heartland' and 'hinterland', and its destruction and subjugation of its Indigenous peoples.[15] Shalev's text sits within this wider context of the use of magical realism to engage with settler-colonial legacies while offering a specific critique of the Zionist attitude which saw Jewish labour and modern science as having the capacity to entirely transform Palestine's landscape. I conclude by raising some concerns about Shalev's emphasis on the emergence of a more ecocentric Israeli environmental sensibility in the present, discussing the capacity for 'green' projects in Israel today – including the 'restoration' of part of the Hula Valley – to contribute to similar acts of settler-colonial erasure.

Decline of the Pioneer Dream

The Blue Mountain is set in the village of Nahalal in the Jezreel Valley, one of the earliest Zionist settlements and Shalev's birthplace. Nahalal was established in 1921 and was the first moshav, a collective agricultural settlement that, in contrast to the better-known kibbutz, permitted private ownership of farms and property by individual families. The novel moves between different periods in the history of the village, from its founding era to the present day, when the myths of the 'pioneers' have long lost their lustre. Since its heyday in the early to mid-twentieth century the agricultural economy of the village has gone into terminal decline, as in Israel more widely, where it has come to play an ever-diminishing role in the country's identity and national income.[16] This decline is illustrated through the occupation of Baruch, grandson of one of the village's founding fathers, Mirkin. Baruch has considerable knowledge of agriculture: he was raised by renowned farmer Mirkin after the death of his parents in an Arab bombing and educated by teacher-naturalist Pinness.[17] However, in a macabre storyline, Baruch plants not bulbs but bodies. He founds a cemetery, Pioneer Home, after uprooting the fruit trees in his grandfather's famous orchard.[18] Here – for a significant fee – Baruch buries any Jew with a tangential connection to the Second Aliyah. The majority of his clients are wealthy Americans who made minimal contributions to the 'redemption' of Palestine, such as having 'worked in Baron de Rothschild's winery for three weeks'.[19] Shalev's description of the arrival of the bodies is a darkly parodic version of pioneer migration to Palestine, which sends up the Zionist message of self-realisation through return to the land by taking this metaphor literally.[20]

Baruch is portrayed as a quiet, unimaginative man and a mildly tragic figure. He appears incapable of freeing himself from the grip of the pioneers and beginning his own life, a trait implied particularly through his lack of interest in women. He starts the graveyard not out of greed, but to fulfil Mirkin's last request for revenge on his fellow villagers.[21] The reasons for Mirkin's desire for vengeance lie in the early days of the village. Mirkin was coerced into marrying against his will, supposedly in the name of the collective good.[22] He is finally reunited with his true love in an old people's home not long before his death.[23] Mirkin is also resentful of the villagers' treatment of his son Efrayim, who returned home with severe facial disfigurements after fighting with the British in the Second World War only to be ostracised.[24] Cemeteries are frequently charged with national symbolic meaning, so Baruch's project must be read in this light. They provide a connection to the nation's historical roots, a reminder of the 'sacrifice' of previous generations and a site for the performance of commemorative rituals.[25] In Israel, military and kibbutz cemeteries play a similar role, with their national significance amplified because, as noted in the previous chapter, of the prominence of heroism and sacrifice in Israel's national mythology.[26] Baruch disrupts these conventional nationalist meanings by founding a cemetery which illustrates the harmful effects of Israel's collectivist pioneering mythology and hastens its demise.[27]

To fully grasp the significance of Baruch's construction of a cemetery over agricultural land it is necessary to understand the history of swamp drainage in Israel/Palestine. Drainage was the greatest alteration of Palestine's hydrological map conducted by the Zionist movement prior to the creation of the State of Israel in 1948, after which it was superseded by the construction of the National Water Carrier in 1964. Both of these projects emerged out of the Zionist adherence to an ideology described in the Introduction as 'high modernism', a faith in the ability of progressive technological advancements to 'conquer' nonhuman nature in order to improve human life.[28] The pursuit of these projects for their national meaning over their practical feasibility has historically led to severe unintended environmental consequences around the world. An additional factor applies in the case of Zionism's mega-hydraulic projects. These were motivated not just by a faith in modern science and technology, but by a belief in the capacity of specifically Jewish labour to 'redeem' the desolate land. As Chaim Weizmann, later to become Israel's first president, wrote: 'It seems as if God has covered the soil of Palestine with rocks and marshes and sand, so that its beauty can only be brought out by those who love it and will devote their lives to healing its wounds.'[29] In the face of such a divinely ordained reconciliation between land and people, what in other contexts might appear to be 'natural limits' seemed not to apply. In a 1998 chapter for a commemorative volume on Israeli history, Shalev recounts a 1950s JNF meeting in a similar vein, in which a Dutch hydrologist warning against the draining of the Hula swamp was sharply told by a JNF hydrologist: 'Our turf is good turf, it is Zionist turf!'[30] As I discuss later in this chapter, the turf, or peat, under the swamp was in fact the project's undoing. The hydrologist's refusal to listen, in Shalev's telling of the story, indicates Zionism's mistake in believing that nonhuman nature was on its side.

Draining Israel/Palestine's swamps was a major project of the Zionist movement and later, Israel, for much of the first half of the twentieth century. Swamps were drained using a range of techniques. These included digging channels and planting eucalyptus trees, known for needing large amounts of water and thought of as having the capacity to purify malarial air.[31] Water-intensive crops such as cotton were also planted.[32] In the case of the draining of the Hula Valley in the 1950s, drainage involved altering the width and gradient of the River Jordan at the points at which it entered and left Lake Hula.[33] The draining of Palestine's swamps played a central role in Zionist settlement plans and ideology, yet it is important to note that draining Palestine's swamps did not begin with Zionism. The British Mandatory authorities undertook some drainage activities, as did the Ottoman Empire.[34] The diaries of Sami ʾAmr show enthusiasm for modernisation schemes among the Palestinian urban middle classes, reminding us not to reproduce a stereotype of Palestinians as always aligned with what is 'best' for nonhuman nature.[35] However, efforts to drain Palestine's swamps remained piecemeal until the JNF began drainage in earnest in the 1920s.

One of the major reasons cited by British and Jewish scientists for draining swamps was public health. Standing water, whether in swamps, cisterns or even a cattle hoofprint can provide a habitat for the *Anopheles* mosquito, the vector for the *Plasmodium* parasite which causes malaria.[36] British health surveys and anecdotal evidence indicate that malaria was a widespread problem in Palestine prior to and during the Mandate period, with frequent epidemics.[37] Nahalal, the Jezreel Valley village in which *The Blue Mountain* is set, was entirely encircled by swamps prior to drainage, so its prospects did not look good.[38]

Zionist interests in reducing the prevalence of malaria were not purely a matter of benevolence towards the local population, as they were often presented, but were closely connected to the perceived potential for success of settlement in Palestine.[39] In this way Zionist anti-malarial initiatives mirrored earlier European colonial public health projects, also historically motivated by anxiety about the potential for disease to disrupt settlement.[40] Malaria, of course, was 'the quintessential colonial disease', so its history can hardly be separated from colonial history.[41] Hebrew writer and farming spokesperson Moshe Smilansky, whose short story 'Hawaja Nazar' (1910) I discussed in the previous chapter, lamented the swollen spleens of many Jewish children in Palestine – a sign of a history of malaria – because of the disease's potential to affect the success of Jewish settlement. He declared: 'Almost every child in Palestine has a swollen abdomen like a pregnant woman. What a generation of labourers and colonisers will grow up from them!!!'[42] These swollen malarial bellies are a grotesque mirror of the enlarged pregnant stomachs Smilansky presumably wanted to see in order to effectively populate the country with more 'labourers and colonisers' and ensure the success of the Zionist project.

Eradicating malaria was seen by Zionist health experts as having the potential to fulfil several valuable ends. First, it would maintain the health of settlers who had already arrived and reduce expenditure of limited resources on treatment.[43] At the same time it was seen as crucial, along with drainage, to releasing 'new' agricultural land which could be used to feed large numbers of anticipated future immigrants, provide employment and perhaps eventually produce crops for export.[44] Making more land and water available through drainage and malaria reduction was closely linked to Zionist ambitions for Jewish immigration. Both were an essential part of demonstrating the land's capacity to absorb future waves of Jewish settlers to the sceptical British authorities. Drainage was seen by the British authorities as part of a wider water redistribution programme which was fundamental to any plans for expanding Jewish settlement, as a Mandatory document cited by Sandra M. Sufian demonstrates: 'The extent of this immigration depends almost entirely on schemes of irrigation, water-power development and public works, opening up for settlement land in Palestine which is now uninhabited and uncultivated.'[45]

Draining wetlands was expected to appease the British authorities and help the Zionist cause in a further sense. The willingness of Zionist agencies to undertake this task demonstrated their commitment to 'developing' Palestine, underscoring their rightful ownership of the land.[46] In doing so, drainage provided further support to the argument for permitting increased Jewish immigration and increased Jewish land purchase in Palestine.[47]

Anxiety about the impact of malaria on the possibilities for settlement suffuses earlier scenes in *The Blue Mountain*. Many of the older characters have suffered from the disease, including the central character Mirkin and his wife Feyge.[48] Pinness' wife Leah is described as having died of malaria while pregnant with twins, with her death symbolically emphasising the effect of malaria on the settlers' capacity to reproduce themselves.[49] The cause of Leah's death is later disputed by another pioneer, suggesting the ease with which memory may be distorted by dominant narratives of national history.[50] In this case, there is a hint that the prominence of malaria in Israel's settlement mythology, to which Pinness is passionately attached, perhaps causes him to retrospectively rewrite his wife's death as a heroic fall in the service of the nation. The potential of malaria to destroy settlements casts a shadow over the early years of settlement in the novel. There are repeated references to an earlier group of German Templars in the Valley, 'every one of whom died of malaria'.[51] German ghosts around a village spring remind the settlers of the possibility that their own efforts could be wiped out: 'the reedy death shrieks of their blond children could still be heard there, haunting the rushes and elecampane'.[52] Malaria is depicted as a risk to Jewish settlement in Palestine in its potential to cause settlers to abandon harsh conditions and leave: 'malaria and depression' are described as the two major factors against which settlers hoping to remain must develop 'resistance' in their 'sweet blood'.[53] The threat of the diseased swamp in these early years is so great as to shape even the architecture of the village, with pioneer cabins raised above the ground in order to avoid damp and insects.[54]

Repeated comparisons between malaria and Palestinian resistance emphasise the threat it poses to Zionist settlement. These are listed together as causes of equivalent numbers of deaths in accounts of 'the victims of malaria and of Arab bandits, the suicides and the fallers by the wayside' and claims that '[t]here wasn't a house without its dead, whether from malaria or from a bullet'.[55] The universal impact of these causes of death is suggested by Baruch's own family history: his parents are killed by an Arab bomb, while his guardians after their death, Pinness and Mirkin, are both affected by malaria.[56] Further connections between disease and Palestinian resistance are found in the oppositional and often militaristic language used to describe the pre-drainage landscape and its nonhuman inhabitants. In one of many examples, Baruch recounts a childhood memory of eating in 'the woods behind the meeting house where the wild garlic grew', an area he recalls as the 'last remnant of the days when anopheles mosquitoes warred on us and the water buffalo stuck its long tongue out at us'.[57] Wild garlic prefers moist soil, so its presence is a 'last remnant' of the area's former life as a swamp. The Palestinian environment is depicted in these lines as hostile and uncooperative through anthropomorphic, militaristic language ('warred') and the comically rude gesture of the buffalo sticking its tongue out at the pioneers. This language literalises the historical role of militaries in antimalarial campaigns while deploying ironic exaggeration that mimics and undermines the hyperbole of accounts of pioneer heroism.[58]

From a Swamp to a Wetland

Draining the swamps was not just about eliminating malaria or opening up 'new' land, but about notions of hygiene and aesthetics. In the draining of Palestine's swamps, as in programmes of swamp drainage around the world in the early to mid-twentieth century, modern germ theory and bacteriological sciences circulated alongside older ideas about miasma as a cause of disease. The term 'malaria' originates in the Italian for 'bad air' and in the nineteenth century was attributed to 'noxious vapours' from stagnant water.[59] The eradication of all types of wetland was long thought of as part of producing a 'sanitary' landscape.⁶⁰ In recent decades, the rise of the term 'wetland' over the term 'swamp' has accompanied changing perceptions of their ecological, aesthetic and economic value.⁶¹ The stigmatisation of wetlands on supposed health grounds can be seen as part of a hierarchy of water purity with religious origins. In this schema water's flow is seen as a sign of sacredness and divine providence (hence the prominence of 'living water' in a range of religious rituals), while its purity is measured on a vertical axis, from the 'clean' water of rain or the mountain spring down to the 'low' and symbolically 'corrupted' water of the swamp.⁶² Scientifically, too, as Jamie Linton discusses, the constant flow of the hydrological cycle is often seen as the 'proper' state of water, regardless of the actual applicability of this model outside the well-watered environments of the Northern European countries from which it originated.⁶³ Swamp water falls down on this count, too. Water does of course flow through swamps, if slowly, providing the basis of their vital ability to filter and purify water and act as 'the kidneys of the landscape'.⁶⁴ The Hula swamp filtered the waters of the River Jordan before they reached Lake Kinneret, Israel's largest water reservoir; indeed, as I discuss later in this chapter, the redirection of the river eventually put Israel's water supplies into a perilous condition.⁶⁵ Since the flow of water through swamps is not as immediately visible as in the case of rainwater, springs or rivers, the swamp then appears as a 'deviant' landscape in both sacred and scientific terms.

Wetlands fail to conform to dominant European categories of landscape aesthetics. They blend water and land in a 'viscous' and unstable landscape which refuses to fit into the favoured aesthetic categories of the European landscape tradition, offering neither the awe and sublimity of mountain scenery, nor a 'prospect view' over a picturesque patchwork of fields.⁶⁶ The draining of Palestine's wetlands mirrored wider colonial environmental alterations intended to make 'dysfunctional' environments productive and 'correct', according to Eurocentric standards of a 'properly' functioning ecosystem.⁶⁷ Equally, in their apparently unproductive mix of land and water, wetlands have often fallen victim to what Philip Garone calls the 'agricultural mystique'.⁶⁸ Until recently, intensive agriculture has been promoted around the world as the optimal use of rural land, with swamps seen as idle capital waited to be extracted and their existence as the outcome of local neglect.⁶⁹ The often negative ecological effects of drainage were either missed or glossed over in an urge to develop and 'modernise' the landscape and extend a country's territory through incorporating its 'frontier'.[70]

The unifying factor in these various iterations of 'swamp stigma' is the material and symbolic in-betweenness of the swamp. Writing on swamps in the American South, Anthony Wilson frames the distaste for swamps' ambiguous state through Mary Douglas' work on purity and classification and Julia Kristeva's writing on the 'abject', which builds on Douglas.[71] Swamps, Wilson writes, unnerve because they cannot be classified as either a liquid or a solid. They are a 'treacherous mix of land and water that can give way at any moment beneath the unwary foot', with this uncertainty rendering the swamp 'abject'.[72] Similarly negative characteristics have often been projected onto human inhabitants of swamps, portrayed historically and today as unclean, unproductive, morally corrupt and potentially corrupting. These assumptions derive in part from the persistence of theories of 'miasma', but also have a material component: swampland is generally cheaper to buy or rent because of the risks of flooding and disease, meaning that its populations are frequently racially or economically marginalised communities. The attribution of negative traits to swamp inhabitants is, then, a racialised and classed discourse, as I discuss below in relation to Zionist perceptions of inhabitants of the Jezreel and Hula Valleys.

Shalev's depiction of the early years of settlement similarly suggests that the swamps were viewed by Zionist pioneers as unhygienic landscapes in need of 'correction'. Shalev uses magical realist techniques to echo their distorted perception of their environment and amplify it for comic effect. The use of the pioneers' views as a source of comedy flatters Shalev's contemporary readers by implicitly suggesting that we, particularly readers in Israel, possess a superior attitude towards the environment, an implication I examine further later in the chapter. The early village is described as 'barely visible through a miasmic veil of swamp gas and mosquito wings'.[73] Exaggeration such as this is common in magical realist writing and serves to mirror and underscore the apparent 'excess' of the Palestinian landscape, particularly its water. Shalev uses magical realist hyperbole to illustrate the pioneers' attitude towards their own activities and their subsequent valorisation in Zionist myth. Baruch describes the 'execrable waters' in the region '[b]efore they were dried and ploughed', while the villagers are described as flying across the valley '[m]ounted on hoes... over poisonous swamps' and through 'a rank cover of rushes and crabgrass'.[74] By portraying the pioneers as literally flying above the ground with their hoes like farmer-gods, Shalev parodies both the pioneers' own messianic beliefs in their ability to 'transcend' the limits of nature and dominant Labour Zionist mythologies of this period, which were being called into question in the 1980s.

The result of drainage is an ordered and seemingly rationalised landscape, observed by Pinness from the top of the blue mountain of the title, probably Mount Tabor or Mount Carmel. This scene can be read as an example of the 'prospect view', a way of observing and visually organising the external world which establishes a separation and relationship of dominance between viewer and viewed that makes the object of vision potentially subject to the observer's power and control. Pinness is described as 'looking down on the broad, obeisant, fertile Valley at his feet', in which the 'geometric fields of the pioneers' can be distinguished in a 'patchwork' shape.[75] This symbolically elevated position suggests Pinness' ownership of the landscape. Meanwhile, the emphasis on visual perception – Pinness is 'looking down' – underscores his separation from and control over the landscape through the historical association in European rationalist thought between vision, knowledge and reason.[76] This valorisation of sight as the highest sense has been criticised by feminists, among others, for ignoring non-visual forms of knowledge acquisition and facilitating an attitude of environmental and social domination.[77] Shalev's description of the transformed valley as 'broad, obeisant, fertile' has clearly gendered connotations, suggesting a feminised landscape which has been subdued by both masculine Zionist labour and Pinness' discerning eye.

The 'prospect' over a landscape has an imperial history.[78] As W. J. T. Mitchell notes, it allows 'a projected future of "development" and exploitation' to be mapped out, a vision which resonates with the Zionist project of 'improvement' depicted by Shalev.[79] In this projection the observer's vision for the land's future is mapped *over* existing uses of the land by earlier or current inhabitants, imagined as incapable of achieving a similar separation from nature. Such a perspective is evident in Israeli geographer Yehuda Karmon's description of the Hula not long after drainage, which has much in common with Pinness' account of the Jezreel Valley. Karmon writes:

Gone are the many narrow and twisted irrigation channels. In their place are the straight channels of the Banias and Hatsbani [sources of the River Jordan], and between them broad fields where one can see tractors and agricultural machines all year round.[80]

Karmon's and Shalev's descriptions are similar in their valorisation of the order and symmetry produced by Zionist agriculture, and indeed the well-ordered kibbutz landscape was a common feature of JNF educational posters of the early to mid-twentieth century. David Zak's 'From a Wasteland to a Settlement', for instance, produced around 1955, depicts a page being turned from left to right, peeling away an image of empty brown scrubland filled with zigzagging cacti to reveal the straight lines of the green fields, houses, water tower and tall, European-like trees of an Israeli kibbutz.[81] In this poster Israeli farming is depicted as an improvement and modernisation of the unruly Palestinian landscape, showing the technological skill of Israeli agriculturalists and demonstrating the Jewish right to the land by transforming a seemingly 'unproductive' Middle Eastern landscape into a Europeanised one. Zak's image is literally the turning over of a page of a book, indicating both the role of Hebrew literature such as Smilansky's in building the nation and, significantly for this chapter, suggesting that the main constraint on this process is imagination. As noted in this book's introduction, Herzl's famous epigraph to *Altneuland* was '[i]f you will it, it is no longer a dream'.[82]

Karmon's and Shalev's accounts are also comparable in their implications about Palestinian environmental management. Karmon positions the transformed landscape as a dramatic improvement on Palestinian uses of the Hula. He celebrates the removal of 'the Arab villages', lauding the 'sharp contrast to the picture of poverty and degeneration' presented by the newly drained Valley.[83] In this account the presumed degradation of the environment and its inhabitants are deterministically linked, with Karmon claiming that: '[p]oor conditions and diseases have created a uniform type out of the ... Ghawarna, weak in body and spirit, helpless against the forces of nature'.[84] Karmon transfers the stigma of the swamp onto its already socially marginalised inhabitants of the Ghawarna tribe, whose supposed inability to separate themselves from nature sets them apart from Zionist and Israeli technological ingenuity. The same association is mirrored in Shalev's ironic metaphorical associations between nonhuman nature and Arab resistance, discussed above. This imagery assimilates Palestine's existing population to its environment, evoking pioneer perceptions of the challenges of settlement in which the views of existing residents were rarely considered. An issue here, however, is whether Shalev's evocation of these views in fact reproduces them. I return to some complications with Shalev's politics later in the chapter.

Redeeming the Land, Redeeming the Nation

European and American visitors to Palestine in the nineteenth and early twentieth centuries often described the apparent degradation of the Palestinian landscape. Mark Twain and even Herzl recounted their disappointment on visiting the Holy Land, with Twain famously declaring that 'Palestine sits in sackcloth and ashes'.[85] Shalev's characters echo this narrative of desolation, with Baruch reflecting: 'It's hard to imagine that it was all a wilderness once' and adding that photographs of the early-twentieth-century Palestinian environment 'looked like they were taken elsewhere'.[86] Others are typical of early settlers in becoming depressed by the 'desolation of the countryside', which the pioneer Levin, like Smilansky's Lazar in the previous chapter, views as 'dead and pitiful' compared to the 'vast green expanses' of Eastern Europe.[87] As noted above, this seeming desolation was widely attributed to neglect by its Palestinian inhabitants and cited as a reason why Palestine was appropriate for Zionist colonisation. One of the most famous iterations of this argument comes from British author Israel Zangwill, who claimed in 1920, not long after the Balfour Declaration, that:

> If Lord Shaftesbury was literally incorrect in describing Palestine as a country without a people, he was essentially correct, for there is no Arab people living in intimate fusion with the country, utilising its resources and stamping it with characteristic impress; there is at best an Arab encampment.[88]

Here, Palestine is presented as *terra nullius*, lacking in civilisation and available for – indeed, requiring – occupancy and development. 'Improving' the land becomes a performance of an ownership claim, in a familiar colonial trope which has its origins in Locke's theory of ownership as 'mixing' one's labour with land discovered in a 'state of nature'.[89]

'Improvement' performed an important role in aligning the Zionist movement and later the State of Israel with its European and American allies, with management of water viewed as crucial. Its significance can be seen in Herzl's utopian novel *Altneuland* (1902), in which Herzl lays out a vision of a future Jewish state in Palestine. Out of all that they view on their tour of the state, Herzl's protagonists Friedrich and Kingscourt are 'most impressed by the technical marvels achieved by the water engineers', who are described by their guide David Litwak in the epigraph to this chapter as 'the true creators of our Old-New-Land'.[90] These 'marvels' include regulating the Jordan for agriculture, draining the swamps and producing hydroelectricity by constructing a canal from the Mediterranean Sea to the Dead Sea.[91] Herzl stresses the European and American origins of the new society's technological innovations, which are 'not built in Palestine, but . . . in England and America, in Germany and in France'.[92] These innovations ensure that 'every single drop that fell was put to good use' and Herzl's fiction was ultimately mirrored in the employment of American water experts Walter Clay Lowdermilk and James B. Hays to produce the Zionist movement's water management plans for Palestine.[93] By drawing explicitly on European and American water innovation and expertise, Zionist leaders made an implicit case for European and American support of their project based on shared technological aptitude and a shared hydromodernist principle of mastering nonhuman nature for the improvement of human life.

The project of drainage was seen not just as a means of 'improving' the land but as part of the Zionist project of national 'regeneration' discussed in the previous chapter. These processes were seen as intimately connected, with the 'desolation' of the land imagined as the inevitable result of Jewish exile and agricultural labour perceived as having the capacity to 'renew' both the people and the land, ridding Jewish settlers of the negative and 'degenerate' traits presumed to have been acquired in the Diaspora.[94] The supposed Jewish distance from nonhuman nature and preference for 'intellectual' work over physical labour were the targets of particular disdain.[95] Herzl's protagonist Friedrich repeats this narrative of a parallel decline of land and people in *Altneuland*, describing on his first visit to Palestine, prior to its reformation, a landscape of 'almost nothing but sand and marsh'.[96] This environment leads him to conclude that '[i]f this is our homeland . . . then it has been brought just as low as we are'.[97] 'Redeeming' the land instantiated discourses of health and disease in multiple ways, with drainage appearing to not just 'cure' the neglect supposedly caused to the land by Palestinians, but serving to purge qualities of the 'sick' Diaspora Jew from new settlers and allowing them to become 'native' to the land of Palestine.

In *The Blue Mountain*, the process of 'curing' immigrants of Diaspora traits is made literal in an encounter between the pioneers and a character named Zeitouni, master of a travelling circus. Zeitouni is a lapsed Hasidic Jew who makes his living through magic, numerology and superstition.[98] He is explicitly linked to old Jewish culture in Eastern Europe through his esoteric activities, described as learnt in his 'Hasidic life'.[99] He adopts a nomadic lifestyle with a group of 'wandering players', suggesting the stereotype of the 'wandering Jew' instead of the appropriate activity for a new 'Hebrew' man of working the land.[100] Zeitouni's troupe is not welcomed in the village, with one of the founders declaring with scorn, '[w]e saw enough of that nonsense in the Hasidic courts of the Ukraine'.[101] One of the villagers, Tsirkin, attempts to force Zeitouni to leave in a unique way:

> The deeper he dug, the louder the earth growled, until finally, when the hoe struck the crust of the pent-up swamp, sharp blades of rushes popped up in a loathsome cloud of mosquitoes and lanced Zeitouni's skin. Muscular leeches shinnied up his pale calves and hung on there, while pale worms sought to drag him down into the depths.[102]

Tsirkin's attempt to 'swamp' Zeitouni represents a literalisation of the capacity of the worked-on land to 'consume' the supposed negative traits of Diaspora Judaism.[103] These are encapsulated in Zeitouni, who narrowly escapes being 'drag[ged] down into the depths'. Zeitouni's 'pale calves' are the opposite of the tanned, healthy pioneer ideal, who later morphs into Israel's iconic 'Sabra'.[104] They are so weak, in fact, that Shalev even contrasts them comically with the '[m]uscular leeches' of Palestine.[105] The act of 'swamping' itself, meanwhile, exaggerates the myth of the pioneers 'taming' the land of Palestine through portraying them as possessing the ability to make the swamp disappear and appear at will. At the same time this image is ambivalent about the pioneers' success: it indicates that the swamp remains beneath the surface, with a power that, as I discuss below, might not always stay under human control.

Post-Zionist Environmentalism

The influence of Israel's founding national myths, including the stories of swamp drainage by heroic Zionist pioneers, has faded dramatically in recent decades. This process was hastened by scholarly trends of the late twentieth century. In the late 1980s, just prior to the publication of *The Blue Mountain*, a group of predominantly Israeli academics known as the 'New Historians' or 'Revisionists' (not to be confused with Ze'ev Jabotinsky's right-wing Revisionists, discussed in Chapter 1) began to challenge dominant Israeli historiographical interpretations of the 1948 war, often relying on newly released archival material. Scholars such as Simha Flapan, Benny Morris, Ilan Pappé, Tom Segev and Avi Shlaim questioned accepted truths including the assumption of Israel as an innocent victim of Arab aggression and intransigence, the claim of Israel as a home for all Jews (undermined by the negative experiences of Arab Jews) and the myth of Palestinian refugees as having willingly left their homes.[106] Their work often prompted significant public controversy.

The 1970s and 1980s also saw social, political and economic changes that further diminished the appeal of earlier Zionist-collectivist narratives of Israeli identity. Developments included the decline of Israel's previously dominant Labour movement and the rise of the right-wing Likud party, consolidated in Likud's election victory of 1977; the growth of Israel's settler movement and religious right; greater demands from Israel's Mizrahi Jewish population for national recognition and inclusion; and a hastening of economic liberalisation, shrinking of the state and promotion of free-market individualism.[107] This period also saw a strengthening of Palestinian nationalism, paralleled by a growing unease among some Israelis with the country's historic and contemporary treatment of Palestinians. Traditional narratives of Israeli identity based on Labour Zionist mythologies of agricultural settlement seemed inadequate as a way of accounting for Israel's increasingly disparate national collective. The term 'post-Zionism' emerged around this time, first used in a theoretical sense in 1993 by Israeli sociologist Uri Ram.[108] The rise of a post-Zionist sensibility saw academics and the Israeli public becoming newly sceptical about the accuracy and ongoing relevance of Israel's earlier Zionist national narratives. At the same time, as Eran Kaplan notes, this critique was only able to emerge once Zionism had accomplished its task and the modern State of Israel was a 'fait accompli'.[109]

As noted above, Shalev's novel has frequently been linked to post-Zionism, with Baruch's transformation of productive agricultural land into a profit-making cemetery indicating the decline of older collectivist myths of Israeli identity. However, despite its environmental themes and close attention to Israel/Palestine's landscapes and waterscapes, it has not been read in relation to environmentalist developments of the same period, which intersect in important ways with the post-Zionist critique of dominant narratives of Israeli national history. *The Blue Mountain* was published in 1988, at the end of a decade in which Israel's environmental movement became particularly active. This period is described by Israeli environmental historian Alon Tal as the dawning of a 'new era of environmentalism'.[110] Like post-Zionist historians and sociologists, environmentalists often sought to reassess the activities of Israel's founders, attracting widespread public attention – and intense criticism – for doing so. A major focus of these debates was the history of drainage in the Jezreel and Hula Valleys. The Hula was by this point the site of an unfolding ecological crisis which presented a serious threat to Israel's population by endangering its supplies of clean drinking water. The project of draining the swamps, a celebrated part of Israel's national narrative of rebuilding the Jewish people and the land, now seemed to have put the nation at risk.

The Hula basin was once the largest wetland in Palestine.[111] Situated in the northern Jordan Valley, it sustained a diverse ecology of plants and animals. These included, twice a year, a world-renowned temporary population of migratory birds that travelled the major migratory corridor of the Great Rift Valley from Syria to East Africa.[112] The valley was home to around 5,000 human inhabitants, mainly Palestinian Arabs but also Jewish residents living in newer settlements.[113] The valley's Arab inhabitants were largely of the Ghawarna tribe, whose economy consisted of producing papyrus products, grazing water buffalo, fishing and cultivating a range of crops, including rice and cotton.[114] The Hula had been targeted for drainage by Zionist leaders for much of the early twentieth century and, before this, the Ottoman government. Drainage was delayed for a combination of reasons including difficulty and expense; complex land ownership arrangements; local resistance and the wider Arab revolt; continuing uncertainty over partition plans; and World War Two.[115] It was only undertaken in the 1950s after the creation of

Israel and finally completed in 1958. The expulsion of the valley's Palestinian inhabitants during the 1948 war had removed the obstacles of local opposition and ownership disputes.[116]

The need for drainage, however, was no longer obvious. Concerns about malaria, which had provided at least the explicit motivation for earlier drainage projects, were no longer relevant as widespread use of pesticides such as DDT had largely eradicated the disease in Israel (this would later cause its own problems).[117] Speculation continues on the reasons. Draining the Hula may well have brought Israel benefits including securing its northern border, helping it to gain control over the Jordan's headwaters or providing peat for use in agriculture and industry.[118] One indisputable advantage brought to Israel by undertaking a massive drainage project in the early years of the state was its nation-building symbolism. After its success in the 1948 war, re-enacting the activities of the original pioneers provided a reminder for new Israeli citizens and to the world of Zionism's founding national triumphs, harnessing the powerful myths of drainage and settlement to the nation-building efforts of the new state.[119] The success of the project in this respect could be seen in the popularity of photographer Peter Merom's 1960 book *The Death of the Lake*, which documented the draining of the Hula in a series of iconic photographs and could be found in many Israeli homes in the 1960s.

The draining of the Hula was lauded as a technical triumph. However, this was not to last. Underground fires burnt beneath the former swamp as its dried-out peat spontaneously combusted, while dust storms blew away the region's once-fertile topsoil. The ground level dropped alarmingly in places by several metres as a result and the area's promised agricultural potential seemed lost.[120] The drastic changes produced by drainage had already caused a dramatic loss of the area's previously rich biodiversity and ended the possibility of a revival of a unique Palestinian way of life.[121] Now the loss of the Hula posed an immediate threat to Israel's human population. While wetlands have historically been viewed as 'unhealthy' environments and sources of disease, the Hula had played a vital role in filtering water passing into Israel's main reservoir, Lake Kinneret. Without the swamp, nitrates and sulphates from decomposing peat, along with further nitrates and phosphorus by-products of Israel's historically fertiliser-heavy farming techniques, flowed into the lake and caused dangerous levels of eutrophication.[122] Drainage the Hula had put the safety of the Kinneret's water at risk. A series of droughts from 1984 to 1986 and 1989 to 1990 which have continued periodically to the present day had already prompted concern over the state of Israel's water supplies. The problems with Israel's pursuit of national priorities without concern for their environmental consequences were beginning to become apparent.

The story of the Hula is closely associated with the emergence of the Israeli environment movement as well as being linked to global environmental trends. Opposition to the initial drainage project helped to precipitate the founding of the Israeli environmental organisation Society for the Protection of Nature in Israel (SPNI), which managed to persuade a reluctant JNF to reflood 3,100 dunams of the Hula swamp five years after drainage.[123] By 1994 the JNF had been forced to reflood more of the swamp and create a small new lake, Lake Agmon, in an attempt to restore some of the Hula's historic biodiversity and protect Israel's drinking water.[124] Since the success of this project there have been moves to 'restore' further wetlands in Israel.[125] This reappraisal of the value of Israel's wetlands has taken place in the context of a wider international shift in perception of these waterscapes. Wetlands are no longer seen as unproductive, harmful or morally dangerous environments. Instead, their varied ecological functions have been widely recognised and their aesthetic status has shifted such that they have become popular sites on 'ecotourism' itineraries. Wetlands also offer valuable 'ecosystem services' through their capacity to act as carbon sinks, leading to the emergence of the dubious practice of 'wetlands mitigation banking'.[126] As this suggests, the re-evaluation of wetlands is motivated not purely by new-found environmental awareness but by the rise of neoliberal environmentalism.

The drainage of the Jezreel swamps involved a similarly drastic environmental transformation to the Hula and led to Palestinian displacement and dispossession. This time thousands of Palestinian tenant farmers and their families found their land sold to the Zionist Organisation by absentee landlords.[127] However, the drainage of the Jezreel Valley did not become an environmental catastrophe in the same way as the Hula. Post-Zionist scholars instead put the triumphalist narrative of drainage under scrutiny in a heated debate which spilled into the popular sphere in the years prior to the publication of *The Blue Mountain*. Initial controversy was prompted by the publication of a 1983 article titled 'The Swamps of the Jezreel Valley – Legend and Reality', by Israeli geographers Yoram Bar-Gal and Shmuel Shamai.[128] Bar-Gal and Shamai's article disputed the extent of the swamps in the Jezreel Valley prior to drainage, arguing that this had been greatly exaggerated in order to fortify the national narrative of pioneer triumph over a hostile landscape. The article caused widespread argument, becoming, as Tamar Katriel notes, 'a symbol in its own turn' of the presumed disloyalty of academics who sought to put national myths under closer scrutiny.[129] Bar-Gal and Shamai were attacked as anti-Zionists and 'PLO supporters', much as Israel's New Historians were criticised at this time for questioning national orthodoxies.[130] What is interesting here is not so much the possibility that Bar-Gal and Shamai might have discovered an environmental 'truth' behind the myth. Environmental historians regularly produce vastly differing interpretations even when they agree on the evidence.[131] Instead, what is significant is the strength of the reaction to this querying of Israel's swamp mythology. The vociferous condemnations of Bar-Gal and Shamai suggest that the narrative of draining the swamps had an almost sacred status until this time in Israel's 'civil religion'.[132]

Revenge of the Dying Lake

In the 1998 chapter on Israeli history cited above, Shalev writes at length about the draining of the Hula Valley and the resulting environmental catastrophe. His commentary on the lake is a forceful indictment of earlier Zionist attitudes to nonhuman nature which functions simultaneously as a critique of Israel's erasure from national history of its expulsion of the Palestinians. He states:

> The Hula Lake has been dried out, killed. It is gone but, like many other great victims, it refuses to be forgotten. . . . For us laymen, the Hula will forever be an allegory about brutality, blindness, arrogance, and the abuse of ideals. If this sounds familiar, let us not forget that we have acted the same way in other areas – hence the power of the allegory.
>
> It seems that the dying lake is fighting back with a vengeance. The water we had expected to collect is contaminated and contaminates Lake Kinneret. Wild animals and plants are disappearing, mice are multiplying, and the land – that virgin land that awaited us so – is not good Zionist turf, but simply barren wasteland. We could almost say that the Hula waters cry to

us from the ground. . . . brute force is a double-edged saber – it swings right back and wounds those who rattled it. The Hula is dead, and this is its last will and testament.[133]

In *The Blue Mountain* Shalev anticipates these comments by depicting a similar process of environmental 'vengeance' that functions as a political allegory. He includes a series of instances in which the swamp and its former human and nonhuman inhabitants appear to return, offering a conjoined critique of Zionism's environmental and political erasures.

Shalev's depiction of the returning swamp and its inhabitants merges Israel/Palestine's past and present, drawing attention to moments of founding violence in the history of Israel. It does so through the techniques of magical realism, a feature that is crucial to the text's critique of Zionism's environmental politics. Shalev interrupts the everyday with surreal reminders of the past that are treated by characters as if there is no distinction, a characteristic feature of magical realism. Magical realism, Faris writes, 'goes beyond the uncanny'.[134] The two modes are, however, closely connected, a link that is apparent in *The Blue Mountain*. Shalev's 'returns' evoke Freud's notion of the 'return of the repressed', which Freud identified as 'perhaps the most potent' example of the uncanny.[135] This notion is worth briefly unpacking further for its implications for Shalev's text. As Freud explained in his 1919 essay, the closest English translation of the German *unheimlich* is not 'uncanny' but 'unhomely'.[136] He argued that the uncanny derives not from something strange, but 'goes back to what was once well known and had long been familiar', endorsing the German philosopher F. W. J. Schelling's view that the uncanny represents 'everything that was intended to remain secret, hidden away, and has come into the open'.[137] The uncanny is hence something integral to the *heimlich* which has been repressed. This is a notion that has resonated in postcolonial literature, particularly in settler-colonial contexts, in which the legacies of colonial violence and oppression often figure as ghosts that return to 'haunt' the homeland.[138] The uncanny also recurs in environmental writing, particularly the genre known as 'ecogothic', in which the environmental violence of modernity 'returns' to threaten catastrophe.[139] Shalev's novel brings these two uses of the uncanny together in the context of Israel's national history.

Freud's notion of the uncanny is also pertinent in this context because one of his examples relates to water's materiality. He cites a lengthy 1860 dictionary entry by German lexicographer Daniel Sanders that features many examples, one of which involves a dialogue between two speakers attributed to German dramatist Karl Gutzkow. The first speaker recalls a feeling experienced near any 'buried spring or a dried-up pond', in which he has the impression that '[y]ou can't walk over them without constantly feeling that water might reappear'.[140] The other describes this feeling as 'uncanny'.[141] In spite of water's familiarity – it is, after all, essential to our lives – it is also mobile and unpredictable, making it, in some sense, always potentially uncanny. It is perhaps for this reason that swamps feature so widely in literary 'returns': Rod Giblett describes the swamp as 'the uncanny place par excellence', while William Tynes Cowan calls it 'the landscape equivalent of the gothic's haunted house'.[142] Swamps, then, are often sites at which unwanted histories rise to the surface.

One striking depiction of the reappearing swamp occurs as Baruch attempts to remove the weeds, which have grown with supernatural speed, from his grandfather Mirkin's cabin after Mirkin's death. Baruch removes a huge root from the ground, repeating the same arduous labours performed by the pioneers and lauded in national myth. This repetition, however, has the opposite effect, bringing the swamp back to life:

> A great hole remained in the ground, and from it rose a milky, pestilential vapour thick with swarms of mosquitoes. Peering down into it, I saw the dense, murky water of the past swirling slowly, little grubs clinging to its surface and breathing patiently through their short air tubes . . . I could have identified the larvae of the anopheles mosquito with my eyes closed.
>
> A deep gurgle sounded from the hole. Shut up by the founders in the bowels of the earth, imprisoned in the trunks of the eucalyptus trees they planted, the soughing swamp began to surge toward me . . .[143]

In this scene, the swamp's water is no longer allied to the success of Zionist agriculture through its use in irrigation or contained within the eucalyptus trees planted for drainage. Water in the early village is carefully regulated, channelled through taps, sprinklers, pipes, stored in the water tower, and travelling in smooth flows that are checked, adjusted, opened and closed.[144] In extreme contrast, the swamp Baruch encounters acts of its own accord. Its 'gurgle' and 'surge' suggest an unpredictable and seemingly autonomous movement that threatens to overwhelm him.

The 'dense, murky' appearance of the swamp water, meanwhile, suggests contamination and disease, echoed in the return of the mosquitoes and the miasmatic 'vapour'. Together these point towards the failure of the Zionist attempt to make the land 'hygienic' through rationalising its water resources and draining swamps. At the same time, the 'murky' colour of the water, which continues to 'swirl' rather than drain away, suggests the unresolved and messy questions surrounding Israel's founding that refuse to disappear. The depth of the hole, which goes down to 'the bowels of the earth', alludes to a deep and fundamental repression of political and ecological violence while simultaneously suggesting a fear of being 'engulfed' by a newly monstrous environment gendered as feminine.[145] This is the 'broad, obeisant, fertile' plain gone very wrong. In this scene water's 'liveliness' and capacity to act independently of human agency become malevolent, with water's movement promising the violent return of life-endangering reminders of a suppressed past.

Shalev's swamps remind us in an uncanny way of the lost human history of the Jezreel Valley by suggesting the agricultural economy of the various Bedouin groups that lived in the swamps of Israel/Palestine prior to their eviction. In one of the many swamp scenes Shalev describes 'reeds and rushes as tall as a man' that 'sprang up' in place of the 'pear trees', which are 'dragged . . . down into the pestilent muck' by 'thick, pale worms that coiled around' their trunks.[146] This scene hints at the way of life of the inhabitants of the Valley who would have cultivated 'reeds and rushes' from which they constructed buildings, baskets and other products. These plants return in a monstrously exaggerated size, consuming the neat, rationalised plantations of Zionist agriculture which replaced them. They demonstrate through their imposing height – 'as tall as a man' – the failure of the high modernist and Zionist project of 'man' subduing 'nature'. The appearance of 'ponderous water buffalo', animals previously farmed by the Valley's Palestinian inhabitants, compounds the impression of a ghostly return of the region's human population. The returned nonhuman contents of the swamp suggest the precariousness of Israel's territorial sovereignty by implying that its national myths are literally founded on unstable ground.

Baruch's failure to be disturbed by these events, while a tendency characteristic of magical realism, also suggests the capacity of Israelis to live with and ignore violent histories whose traces are right in front of them.

Shalev's depiction of the Israeli swamp as a site of political-ecological returns was paralleled over twenty years later in a 2009 text by Oz that indicates the ongoing power of the swamp as the 'haunted house' of Israel's landscape. Oz is the most visible representative of Shalev's generation of dissenting writers, even if, as I discuss in the following chapter, his dissent is less progressive than it initially seems. In the final short story of Oz's collection *Scenes From Village Life*, titled 'In a Faraway Place at Another Time', Oz depicts the battle of a lone civil servant deployed by the 'Office for Underdeveloped Regions' to a remote, unnamed village against a swamp which has definitively returned.[147] He writes:

> All night long vapours blow in from the poisonous swamp. A sweetish smell of decay spreads among our huts. Iron tools rust here overnight, fences rot with a damp mould, mildew eats at the walls, straw and hay turn black with moisture, as though burnt in fire, mosquitoes swarm everywhere, our homes are full of flying and crawling insects. The very soil bubbles.[148]

In Oz's text, which in plot and tone strongly recalls J. M. Coetzee's *Waiting for the Barbarians* (1980), the village is depicted as a frontier settlement, a last bastion of civilisation at the edge of the swamp. Its gradual permeation by water suggests the impossibility of repressing the violence which underlies the myth of agricultural settlement, whose symbols of 'straw and hay', and 'iron tools' are destroyed by the encroaching dampness. Borders, meanwhile, are threatened by the water, which fails to respect human impositions on the landscape and rots both 'fences' and 'walls', symbols of Israeli territorial control.

In both Shalev's and Oz's texts, the threat is portrayed as coming from beneath the earth. This vertical axis is crucial. The subterranean nature of the threat is particularly apparent when reading Oz's short story within its collection, alongside other stories that refer repeatedly to unidentified sounds and movements underground including flowing water, drains and what characters think might be digging.[149] In *The Blue Mountain* villagers are also described as 'always hearing things in the earth'.[150] With the region's more recent political history in mind, these subterranean anxieties might be read in relation to Israeli fears of Palestinians in Gaza using tunnels for munitions storage, cross-border attacks and abductions, a national panic which reached feverish levels during 'Operation Protective Edge' in July and August 2014. They might also be read, albeit more anachronistically, alongside calls for the release of Palestinians who have, like Shalev's swamp, been 'imprisoned', whether in Israel's jails or in Gaza, frequently characterised in activist discourse as the 'world's largest prison'.[151] Still, even as Oz and Shalev's texts critique dominant Zionist environmental and historical narratives, it is worth noting that their texts perform a similar erasure in relegating Palestinians to part of the landscape and associating their political demands with elements of nonhuman nature. As Barbara McKean Parmenter notes, this is an older trope that presents Palestinians as 'irrational [and] uncivilized'.[152] I return to this issue with Shalev's text later in the chapter.

Swamp Nostalgia

Shalev's target is not just Israel's pioneer mythologies of drainage and settlement, but a contemporary wave of nostalgia for this period which sought fervently to preserve these myths.[153] As noted above, Zionist historiography was increasingly challenged during the 1980s, yet it was simultaneously reasserted in a widespread popular enthusiasm for the settlement period manifested in the proliferation of museums.[154] This dimension of Shalev's critique can be seen in the activities of the character Meshulam, Baruch's cousin, an amateur historian obsessed with preserving the relics of the founding years. Meshulam starts a museum, 'Founder's Cabin', which includes objects of dubious historical value such as a stuffed cow displayed with a 'gold medal from the British High Commissioner' awarded for her famed milk production.[155] The museum is a stop-off point on the tours taken by '[b]usloads of tourists and schoolchildren' around the moribund village, described ironically by Shalev as 'the flourishing creation of the founding fathers'.[156] Meshulam, driven increasingly mad by what he perceives as modern Israel's sacrilegious forgetting of its roots, starts 'reswamping the village'.[157] He begins in the museum by constructing a 'diorama of the swamp and its draining' before attempting to produce real swamps by smashing water pipes.[158] Meshulam's obsessive 'reswamping' project, purportedly a mission to remind Israelis of their history, can also be seen as an attempt to repress the history of Palestinian expulsions and environmental harm by reasserting Zionism's mythology of heroic settlement.

Meshulam's 'reswamping' of the village at first seems to be a reversal of the pioneer generation's efforts to regulate and control Palestine's unruly hydrological landscape. He smashes water taps on irrigation pipes and blasts stolen fireman's hoses around the village to cause floods, declaring, in a parody of pioneer rhetoric, 'I'm founding a swamp' and '[a] swamp is born!'[159] Meshulam stands in the 'swamp' he has created 'waiting to be carried off by malaria' and urges others from the village to join him so that their deaths can be reported by 'comrades from the press'.[160] The potential news story of pioneer sacrifice is presumably intended to galvanise wider national sentiment, as it would have in the past, while Meshulam's use of collectivist language, 'comrades', indicates his comically outdated ideological fervour for the founding stories of Labour Zionism. Eventually Meshulam persuades some 'unemployed men' to put on a costume of 'old peasant's blouses and Russian worker's caps', take 'sickles and hoes' and participate in his drainage project while singing nationalist songs.[161] On another occasion, he employs an 'old Arab' to plough the land.[162] The inclusion of a silent Arab farmer in this scene recreates the Orientalist pastoral of early Hebrew literature, as found in the work of authors such as Smilansky.[163] Meshulam's efforts, however, are a pathetic pastiche produced by himself and fringe members of society, the desperate unemployed, rather than, as in the past, Israel's heroes.

Meshulam's project can be read as a manifestation of what Svetlana Boym calls 'restorative nostalgia'.[164] Boym identifies restorative nostalgia as particularly associated with nationalist movements and revivals, characterised by 'a return to national symbols and myths' which can sometimes involve 'total reconstructions of monuments of the past'.[165] Restorative nostalgics like Meshulam believe that their project is about recovering truth, although their motivation is often found in anxiety about attempts to call national traditions into question.[166] The swamp-draining pioneers were, of course, already participating in a form of restorative nostalgia in their attempt to redeem the land of Eretz Israel and restore the biblical 'land of milk and honey', meaning that Meshulam's activities can be seen, more absurdly, as nostalgia for nostalgia. Shalev indicates that by Meshulam's time the activities of the pioneers themselves had become an origin myth of similar significance and one which was under threat. In 'reswamping' the village, Meshulam seeks to restore the place of drainage and the valorisation of pioneer activities in Israel's national mythology, suppressing emerging challenges to this story by recreating the 'monument' of a swamp. The repetitive nature of Meshulam's project, meanwhile, recalls Paul Ricœur's transfer of Freud's work on compulsive repetition to a national context.[167] Ricœur highlights the extent to which the absences in official national histories – namely, moments of founding violence – are reaffirmed through commemorative public performances.[168] Shalev's depiction of the last defender of Israel's national history as a paranoid 'swamp revivalist', desperately performing swamp creation and drainage in front of bemused village onlookers, offers a parallel view of contemporary nostalgia for the founding period as hopelessly misguided.[169]

Meshulam's swamp obsession is prompted by outrage at the publication of an academic article on the Jezreel Valley with the same title as Bar-Gal and Shamai's controversial 1983 paper.[170] He sees the article as a possible catalyst for a wider 'epidemic of cynicism' threatening to afflict Israel and castigates the unnamed academics for their 'pathetic hunger for publicity and sensationalism'.[171] Meshulam's indignation over the article mirrors the furore over Bar-Gal and Shamai's work, in which their questioning of the founding national myth of draining the swamps was construed as the ultimate expression of anti-Zionist treason. Both Meshulam and Pinness see criticisms of pioneer narratives as part of increasing decadence in Israeli society, with Meshulam viewing a revival of the rite of passage of drainage as a way to reverse this process. 'The Jews of this country have forgotten what a swamp is', Meshulam laments, adding: '[t]he time has come to remind them.'[172] This decadence is primarily manifested in the novel through lack of respect for another primary feature of Zionist water history and settlement iconography: the water tower.[173] The novel begins with Pinness overhearing a comically obscene shout from the top of the tower, 'I'm screwing Liberson's granddaughter!', which recurs with various daughters and wives of the village until the shouter is discovered as Baruch's cousin Uri and given his comeuppance.[174] The 'debauchery' of this act enrages the uptight Pinness not just because it involves the celebration of adultery and promiscuity but because it defiles a once-powerful site of Israeli national myth.

Meshulam's 'reswamping' project fails, of course. It is met only with irritation or indifference by the villagers, who drain the swamps efficiently and without celebration each time they appear.[175] The pioneer myths of drainage and settlement are clearly no longer as compelling for the villagers as they are for Meshulam. A major reason for this, along with the economic, social and political changes in Israeli society described earlier in this chapter, is changing attitudes to the environment, notably the dramatic shift in estimations of Israel's water potential since the pre-state period from 'abundance' to 'scarcity'.[176] This is suggested by a remark by one of the village's former pioneers, Liberson, now in a nursing home. As one of the original drainers of the swamps, we might expect Liberson to be enthusiastic about Meshulam's project. Instead he is sharply dismissive, declaring, 'How silly can you get . . . Who cares about all that anymore? It's just a big waste of water.'[177] Liberson's scathing assessment of Meshulam's 'revivalism' indicates that the prevailing Israeli attitude to the environment has changed significantly, with even a former pioneer now disillusioned by the pioneering mythology in which he played a central role. Liberson's description of Meshulam's 'reswamping' as a 'waste of water' indicates a shift towards concern for an issue of global significance, in contrast to Meshulam's narrowly nationalist and ideological uses of nonhuman nature.

The Blue Mountain seems to suggest the emergence of a new Israeli environmental sensibility in which there has been a realisation that it is no longer ecologically or politically sustainable to manipulate nonhuman nature in the service of nationalist goals. This impression is reinforced by the novel's form and elements of Shalev's writing style. The novel is a family saga. Its original Hebrew title, *Roman Russi* ('Russian Novel' or 'Russian Affair') drew self-conscious attention to this form, suggesting an epic chronicle of family life against a historical background in a style familiar from classical Russian literature. This recalls the Tolstoyan aspirations of early pioneers such as A. D. Gordon, while hinting ironically at the Eastern European origins that Shalev's protagonists struggle to shed in the process of becoming 'native'. *The Blue Mountain* achieves a traditional form of narrative closure with the death of Pinness, the last founder, and the marriage of Uri, who has changed his ways and is now a contented father to four children.[178] This closure is mirrored in nonhuman nature. While Baruch's cemetery is described frequently earlier in the novel as having 'poisoned the orchard', by the end it has ceased to be a site through which the founders play out their resentments even in death, resolving the text's central conflict and suggesting a new ecological harmony in the Valley.[179] Farm crops and fruit trees grow wild over the graves, producing a 'thick cover' which resembles the mixed planting of a permaculture farm and which causes Uri to have to install flagpoles as grave markers.[180] Shalev's text itself, too, could be read as encouraging greater environmental awareness among its readers. It carefully details the native flora and fauna of Israel/Palestine and meticulously describes the pioneers' agricultural practices. In this way the novel accords with the priorities of 'first wave' ecocritics, who prized literature that enabled what Lawrence Buell called 'environmental reorientation'.[181] *The Blue Mountain* seems to both depict and facilitate a changing attitude to the environment in Israel.

Zionist Conservation

Shalev's novel offers a political and environmental critique of traditional Zionist narratives of draining the swamps that highlights the malign tendencies of nostalgia for this period at the time of writing. Still, his depiction of a newfound Israeli environmental sensibility, in which it is no longer acceptable to instrumentalise nonhuman nature for nationalist ends, sits uneasily with the many ways in which this process continues in present-day Israel. The IDF, for instance, professes a commitment to being an 'environmentally friendly military' and promotes its use of renewable energy sources.[182] The occupation, however, is hardly environmentally friendly and prevents Palestinians from enjoying nonhuman nature. In *Palestinian Walks* (2007) human rights lawyer and nature writer Raja Shehadeh chronicles the environmental damage and restrictions to Palestinian movement imposed by Israel's breaking up of the West Bank with walls, checkpoints and separate road networks, while the unexploded ordnance and land mines littering Palestinian urban and agricultural areas, particularly Gaza, put human and nonhuman populations at risk. In the northern Negev, meanwhile, the practice of tree planting by the JNF ostensibly operates as a means of combating climate change-induced desertification, yet also restricts access by local Bedouin communities to their ancestral lands and homes and is more likely to have caused environmental harm than benefit.[183] In these and other instances, a well-publicised commitment to 'green' principles serves to enhance Israel's territorial claims, mitigating the reputational harm caused by Israeli aggression and veiling its environmental impacts.

What is more, Shalev's emphasis on an emerging Israeli environmental ethic has led *The Blue Mountain* to be read as implicit justification for Israeli territorial claims. Alan Mintz argues that the novel's representation of non-human nature demonstrates 'an autochthonous attachment, a mythic pre-Judaic connection that derives from the earth and is rooted in the soil of a particular place'.[184] This Israeli sense of belonging is, he states, 'no less fierce and no less embroiled an attachment to the land' than that often found in Palestinian nationalist writing.[185] Shalev's text depicts settler colonialism and the dubious environmental practices pursued in the service of this end as elements of Israel's past that it needs to reckon with, yet these themes are very much of the present. This containment of political and ecological conflicts in Israel's past allows the novel to be read as a celebration of 'the good old days' and a relief from the present-day conflict. Shalev's own gently ironic nostalgia skewers the novel's potential political impact, even if it perhaps accounts for its commercial success in Israel. *The Blue Mountain* offers a critique of the harmful effects of nostalgia which itself never manages to escape the nostalgia trap.

This correspondence between contemporary 'green' narratives and earlier, ecologically harmful Zionist environmental projects can be seen clearly in promotional materials for the Hula Valley. Today the Hula Valley has become a popular 'ecotourism' destination, well known for birdwatching, although the effects of so many visitors on the birds themselves have not escaped note. The JNF website promotes the creation of a new area of swamp as a contemporary act of pioneering, stating that this was 'no less of a feat than the draining of the swamps sixty years ago'.[186] Meanwhile, the Israel Ministry of Tourism website declares that: 'The Hula valley is a place of miracles and wonders. Heroic people working together with Mother Nature have made the Hula valley into a place filled with abundant green beauty.'[187]

These accounts erase any history of anthropogenically induced environmental harm in the Hula Valley, at the same time as saying nothing about the populations who were displaced in order to drain the area who remain prevented from returning. Contemporary conservationists are portrayed as modern pioneers, in a narrative which indicates the ease with which present-day ecological concern can be assimilated into existing Zionist mythology.

Conclusion

Shalev's *The Blue Mountain* has much to tell us about Israeli and Palestinian hydropolitics, even if its environmental dimensions have been neglected in existing criticism. The novel illustrates the role played by hydraulic engineering projects in reshaping Israel/Palestine's waterscapes and producing Israeli national identity, underscoring the centrality of the narrative of draining the swamps to Israel's Labour Zionist national mythology. Shalev's seemingly whimsical magical realist style is key to his portrayal of the capacity of the swamp to bring forth troubling environmental and political 'returns' that Israel's national narratives have suppressed. Through descriptions of water's uncontrollability and mobility, Shalev suggests the possibility of a resurgence of claims for environmental and political justice in the present. *The Blue Mountain* appears to offer hope in the emergence of an Israeli environmental sensibility in which it is no longer acceptable to subordinate nonhuman nature to nationalist ends. However, 'green' priorities further Israel's ongoing appropriation of Palestinian land and resources, with the 'restored' Hula becoming just as invested with national sentiment as the drained swamp.

In this chapter I have emphasised the role of magical realism in Shalev's critique of Zionism's environmental politics. Shalev uses magical realist techniques including irony, exaggeration and the blending of worlds to reckon with the past in the present, highlighting the persistence of historical wrongs and of claims for justice. At the same time, Shalev's magical realism might be read as registering broader upheavals in 1980s Israel, in which dominant Labour Zionist narratives of Israel's national history were undermined not only by academics but by wider processes of economic, social and political liberalisation. As a result, by 1996 Jonathan Nitzan and Shimshon Bichler were able to write that '[t]he Zionist-collectivist ethos seems to have finally given way to the universal creed of business enterprise'.[188] Emerging at this time of transition, Shalev's magical realism fits Fredric Jameson's notion of the genre as 'constitutively dependent on a type of historical raw material in which disjunction is structurally present', in which there is a 'coexistence of precapitalist with nascent capitalist' tendencies.[189] In *The Blue Mountain*, we saw the disintegration of Israel's socialist national narratives through the story of an undead swamp. The following chapter turns to what promised to replace them in the 1990s amid optimistic hopes of both peace and a 'peace dividend': a turn to the sea.

Notes

1. Herzl, *Altneuland*, p. 175.
2. Amichai, 'Once I Wrote Now and in Other Days', p. 31.
3. Bar-Gal, *Propaganda and Zionist Education*, pp. 159–60; 'Third Decade: 1921–1930'.
4. Kellerman, 'Settlement Myth and Settlement Activity', p. 371.
5. Nielsen Bookscan reported in 2018 that sales of literature in translation were up 5.5 per cent from the previous year, with sales at the highest level since they began recording in 2001. Flood, 'Translated Fiction Enjoys Sales Boom'.
6. Cooper, 'Meir Shalev: Israel's Dictator-in-Writing'.
7. Sela, 'Meir Shalev Publishes New Novel'; Institute for the Translation of Hebrew Literature, 'Meir Shalev'.
8. Kaplan, *Beyond Post-Zionism*, p. 71; Peleg, *Israeli Culture between the Two Intifadas*, pp. 7, 11–14; Zerubavel, 'Revisiting the Pioneer Past'.
9. The most celebrated of this group is Benny Morris, who has since expressed rather different views. In a 2004 *Haaretz* interview following the publication of the expanded edition of his *The Birth of the Palestinian Refugee Problem*, Morris offered a justification for ethnic cleansing, stating: 'There is no justification for acts of rape. There is no justification for acts of massacre. Those are war crimes. But in certain conditions, expulsion is not a war crime. I don't think that the expulsions of 1948 were war crimes. You can't make an omelet without breaking eggs. You have to dirty your hands.' He argued that these actions were justified on the basis of the necessity of the creation of Israel: 'A Jewish state would not have come into being without the uprooting of 700,000 Palestinians. Therefore it was necessary to uproot them. There was no choice but to expel that population.' Shavit, 'Survival of the Fittest'. For discussion, see Joel Benin, 'No More Tears', pp. 38–47.
10. Cooper, cited in Bowers, *Magic(al) Realism*, p. 4.
11. Faris, *Ordinary Enchantments*, p. 138.
12. Ibid., p. 7.
13. Bhabha, 'Introduction: Narrating the Nation', p. 7; Bowers, *Magic(al) Realism*, p. 90; Slemon, 'Magic Realism as Postcolonial Discourse'.
14. Massad, 'The "Post-Colonial" Colony', pp. 13–40.
15. One of the founding essays on postcolonialism and magical realism is from a Canadian context: Slemon's 'Magic Realism as Postcolonial Discourse'. For a survey of these debates, see Andrews, 'Rethinking the Relevance of Magic Realism for English-Canadian Literature'.
16. Shalev, *The Blue Mountain*, p. 149; Tal, *Pollution in a Promised Land*, p. 238.

17. Shalev, *The Blue Mountain*, p. 161.
18. Ibid., pp. 19–21.
19. Ibid., p. 178.
20. Ibid., pp. 201, 30; Mintz, 'Tellers of the Soil', p. 40.
21. Shalev, *The Blue Mountain*, p. 27.
22. Ibid., p. 40.
23. Ibid., p. 232.
24. Ibid., pp. 67, 119.
25. Mosse, *Fallen Soldiers*.
26. Weiss, 'Bereavement, Commemoration, and Collective Identity in Contemporary Israeli Society'.
27. Grumberg and Mann briefly make related arguments. Grumberg, *Place and Ideology*, p. 104; Mann, 'Modernism and the Zionist Uncanny', p. 75.
28. Scott, *Seeing Like a State*.
29. Cited in Said, *The Question of Palestine*, p. 85.
30. Cited in Sufian, *Healing the Land and the Nation*, p. 5.
31. Penslar, *Zionism and Technocracy*, p. 25.
32. Sufian, *Healing the Land and the Nation*, p. 148.
33. Karmon, 'The Drainage of the Huleh Swamps', pp. 178–9; Sufian, *Healing the Land and the Nation*, p. 179.
34. Biger, 'Ideology and the Landscape of British Palestine', p. 189; Sufian, *Healing the Land and the Nation*, p. 17.
35. See the undated entry 'If I Were an Arab Leader' in 'Amr, *A Young Palestinian's Diary*, pp. 128–9.
36. McNeill, *Mosquito Empires*, p. 102.
37. Sufian, *Healing the Land and the Nation*, pp. 63, 81.
38. Ibid., p. 148.
39. Davidovitch and Zalashik, 'Pasteur in Palestine', p. 402.
40. Arnold, 'Introduction: Disease, Medicine and Empire', pp. 14–15. Bewell, *Romanticism and Colonial Disease*, pp. 10–11.
41. Sufian, *Healing the Land and the Nation*, p. 66. Colonial epidemiological exchange went both ways, with European settlers unwittingly introducing new diseases that decimated Indigenous populations. Crosby, *Ecological Imperialism*.
42. Cited in Sufian, *Healing the Land and the Nation*, p. 80.
43. Hirsch, '"We Are Here to Bring the West, Not Only to Ourselves"', p. 581.
44. Penslar, *Zionism and Technocracy*, p. 3.
45. Ibid., p. 121.

46. LeVine, 'The Discourses of Development in Mandate Palestine'.
47. Sufian, *Healing the Land and the Nation*, pp. 130–2.
48. Shalev, *The Blue Mountain*, pp. 29, 51.
49. Ibid., p. 3.
50. Ibid., p. 280.
51. Ibid., pp. 32, 78.
52. Ibid., p. 78.
53. Ibid., p. 39.
54. Ibid., pp. 5, 171.
55. Ibid., p. 114.
56. Ibid., pp. 161, 3, 29.
57. Ibid., p. 188. For similar examples, see pp. 26, 45, 111, 291, 16.
58. Mitchell, *Rule of Experts*, p. 26.
59. Sufian, *Healing the Land and the Nation*, pp. 43, 65.
60. Nash, *Inescapable Ecologies*, p. 82.
61. Buell, 'Wetlands Aesthetics', p. 670.
62. Strang, *The Meaning of Water*, pp. 91, 100; Tuan, *The Hydrologic Cycle and the Wisdom of God*, pp. 58–9.
63. Linton, *What Is Water?*, chs 5 and 6.
64. Wetlands ecologist William Niering, cited in Howarth, 'Imagined Territory', p. 520.
65. Karmon, 'The Drainage of the Huleh Swamps', p. 178; Sufian, *Healing the Land and the Nation*, p. 1.
66. Dorrian, 'Fluid and Viscous Landscapes', p. 22.
67. Davis and Burke, 'Imperialism, Orientalism, and the Environment in the Middle East', p. 3.
68. Garone, *The Fall and Rise of the Wetlands of California's Great Central Valley*, p. 14.
69. Howarth, 'Imagined Territory', p. 523.
70. Sufian, *Healing the Land and the Nation*, p. 112.
71. Wilson, *Shadow and Shelter*, p. 9.
72. Ibid., p. 9.
73. Shalev, *The Blue Mountain*, p. 43.
74. Ibid., pp. 85, 39.
75. Ibid., p. 268.
76. Cosgrove, 'Landscape and the European Sense of Sight', pp. 249–68.
77. For instance, Plumwood, *Feminism and the Mastery of Nature*, p. 94.
78. Mitchell, 'Imperial Landscape', p. 17.
79. Ibid., p. 17.

80. Cited in Gorney, '"Desolate" vs. "Wondrous" and "Wild" vs. "Rational"', p. 344.
81. Zak, 'From a Wasteland to a Settlement'.
82. Herzl, *Altneuland*, p. 1.
83. Cited in Gorney, '"Desolate" vs. "Wondrous" and "Wild" vs. "Rational"', p. 344.
84. Ibid., p. 344.
85. Herzl, cited in Eisenzweig, 'An Imaginary Territory', p. 282; Herzl, *The Complete Diaries of Theodor Herzl*, p. 745; Mark Twain, *The Innocents Abroad*, p. 607.
86. Shalev, *The Blue Mountain*, p. 258.
87. Ibid., pp. 43–4.
88. Cited in Masalha, *The Bible and Zionism*, p. 45.
89. Locke, *Two Treatises of Government*, pp. 328–9.
90. Herzl, *Altneuland*, pp. 177, 175.
91. Ibid., pp. 177, 175.
92. Ibid., p. 113.
93. Ibid., p. 177.
94. Zakim, *To Build and Be Built*, p. 60.
95. Hirsch, '"We Are Here to Bring the West, Not Only to Ourselves"', p. 582; Presner, *Muscular Judaism*, p. 12.
96. Herzl, *Altneuland*, p. 32.
97. Ibid., p. 32.
98. Shalev, *The Blue Mountain*, p. 173.
99. Ibid., p. 173.
100. Ibid., p. 174.
101. Ibid., p. 173.
102. Ibid., p. 173.
103. Ibid., p. 176.
104. Ibid., p. 173. On the 'Sabra', see Almog, *The Sabra*.
105. Shalev, *The Blue Mountain*, p. 173.
106. Flapan, *The Birth of Israel*; Morris, *The Birth of the Palestinian Refugee Problem*; Pappé, *Britain and the Arab-Israeli Conflict*; Segev, *1949*; Shlaim, *Collusion Across the Jordan*.
107. See Ram, 'From Nation-State to Nation-State'.
108. Ram, *The Changing Agenda of Israeli Sociology*. See Silberstein, *The Postzionism Debates*.
109. Kaplan, *Beyond Post-Zionism*, p. 4.
110. Tal, 'An Imperiled Promised Land', p. 118.

111. Kark and Levin, 'The Environment in Palestine in the Late Ottoman Period', p. 12.
112. Turner et al., 'Crossing the Jordan', p. 16.
113. Sufian, *Healing the Land and the Nation*, pp. 153, 159.
114. Khawalde and Rabinowitz, 'Race from the Bottom of the Tribe That Never Was'; Payne, 'A Longer-Term Perspective on Human Exploitation and Management of Peat Wetlands', pp. 3–5; Sufian, *Healing the Land and the Nation*, p. 159.
115. Sufian, *Healing the Land and the Nation*, pp. 163, 178.
116. Tyler, 'The Huleh Concession and Jewish Settlement of the Huleh Valley', pp. 853–4.
117. Anton, 'Blind Modernism and Zionist Waterscape', p. 79; Tal, *Pollution in a Promised Land*, p. 116.
118. Sufian, *Healing the Land and the Nation*, p. 3; Hambright and Zohary, 'Lakes Hula and Agmon', p. 85.
119. Sufian, *Healing the Land and the Nation*, p. 3; Tyler, 'The Huleh Concession and Jewish Settlement of the Huleh Valley', p. 840.
120. In a 1960 essay written in praise of the project, Karmon unknowingly predicted the problems which would result in the Hula's ruin. Karmon, 'The Drainage of the Huleh Swamps'.
121. Hambright and Zohary, 'Lakes Hula and Agmon', p. 87.
122. Tal, *Pollution in a Promised Land*, p. 234; Hambright and Zohary, 'Lakes Hula and Agmon', p. 87. Eutrophication is a process of rapid algal and plant growth that diminishes water quality. Lakes are left slime-covered and foul-smelling; decomposition of high volumes of plant matter rapidly exhausts the water's oxygen, causing fish to be starved of oxygen and die; and drinking water can become contaminated by toxic blooms of cynaobacteria, more commonly known as blue-green algae.
123. Tal, *Pollution in a Promised Land*, pp. 116–17.
124. 'Reflooding Hula Valley Begins, Reversing Decades of Cultivation'.
125. Rinat, 'Swamps to Be Reflooded, 80 Years Later'.
126. Robertson, 'The Neoliberalization of Ecosystem Services'.
127. Tessler, *A History of the Israeli-Palestinian Conflict*, p. 177.
128. Bar-Gal and Shamai, 'The Jezreel Valley Swamps—Legend and Reality'.
129. Katriel, 'Sites of Memory', p. 7.
130. Sufian, *Healing the Land and the Nation*, p. 346.
131. Cronon, 'A Place for Stories', p. 1348.

132. Liebman and Don-Yehiya, *Civil Religion in Israel*.
133. Cited in Sufian, *Healing the Land and the Nation*, pp. 4–5.
134. Faris, *Ordinary Enchantments*, p. 7.
135. Freud, *The Uncanny*, p. 148.
136. Ibid., p. 124.
137. Ibid., pp. 124, 132.
138. See Punter and Byron, *The Gothic*, p. 54; Sugars and Turcotte, *Unsettled Remains*.
139. See Smith and Hughes, *Ecogothic*.
140. Freud, *The Uncanny*, p. 129.
141. Ibid., p. 129.
142. Cowan, *The Slave in the Swamp*, p. 14; Giblett, *Postmodern Wetlands*, p. 13.
143. Shalev, *The Blue Mountain*, p. 250.
144. Ibid., pp. 118, 123, 234, 232, 287, 336.
145. Giblett, *Postmodern Wetlands*, p. 45.
146. Shalev, *The Blue Mountain*, p. 352.
147. Oz, 'In a Faraway Place at Another Time', pp. 255–65.
148. Ibid., p. 255.
149. Oz, 'Digging', p. 106; 'Lost', p. 152.
150. Shalev, *The Blue Mountain*, p. 316.
151. Levy, *The Punishment of Gaza*, pp. 20, 23.
152. Parmenter, *Giving Voice to Stones*, p. 32.
153. Zerubavel, 'Revisiting the Pioneer Past', pp. 212, 216.
154. Azaryahu, 'Water Towers', p. 332; Katriel, *Performing the Past*; Zerubavel, 'Revisiting the Pioneer Past', p. 212.
155. Shalev, *The Blue Mountain*, p. 19.
156. Ibid., p. 19.
157. Ibid., p. 242.
158. Ibid., pp. 242, 281.
159. Ibid., pp. 328, 281, 329.
160. Ibid., pp. 281, 329.
161. Ibid., p. 332.
162. Ibid., p. 352.
163. Ramras-Rauch, *The Arab in Israeli Literature*, p. xi; Peleg, *Orientalism and the Hebrew Imagination*, ch. 3.
164. Boym, *The Future of Nostalgia*, ch. 4.
165. Ibid., p. 41.

166. Ibid., pp. 41, 44–5.
167. Ricœur, *Memory, History, Forgetting*, pp. 70, 78–9.
168. Ibid., p. 85.
169. Shalev, *The Blue Mountain*, p. 337.
170. Ibid., p. 276.
171. Ibid., p. 278.
172. Ibid., p. 330.
173. Azaryahu, 'Water Towers'.
174. Shalev, *The Blue Mountain*, pp. 1, 236, 241, 369.
175. Ibid., pp. 332, 337, 370.
176. Alatout, '"States" of Scarcity'.
177. Shalev, *The Blue Mountain*, p. 350.
178. Ibid., p. 377.
179. Ibid., p. 285. The cemetery is frequently described as an act of revenge. See pp. 27, 119, 264.
180. Ibid., p. 377.
181. Buell, *The Environmental Imagination*, p. 82.
182. 'Going Green: Israeli Military Chooses Solar Energy over Diesel'.
183. Weizman, *The Conflict Shoreline*, p. 15.
184. Mintz, *Translating Israel*, p. 42.
185. Ibid., p. 42.
186. 'Hula Lake Park – Birding in Israel'.
187. 'The Hula Valley'.
188. Nitzan and Bichler, 'From War Profits to Peace Dividends', p. 61. On debates over Israel's historical socialism, see footnote 60 on p. 33 of the Introduction.
189. Jameson, 'On Magic Realism in Film', p. 311. See also WReC, *Combined and Uneven Development*, p. 21.

3

'CURRENT LIQUIDISATIONS LTD.': ISRAEL'S 'MEDITERRANEAN' IDENTITY IN AMOS OZ'S *THE SAME SEA*

As we must make the Negev fruitful, so we must turn to profit the multitudinous sea. – David Ben-Gurion[1]

The sea allows an obfuscation of the violence that the territorial story cannot avoid. – Hannan Hever[2]

In the lead-up to Israel's hosting of the 2019 Eurovision Song Contest a video advertisement circulated on social media that said a great deal about how Israel currently wants to be seen by the international and, crucially, European, community. Produced by Visit Israel, the video begins with a reminder of Israel's 2018 Eurovision win as a male and female presenter in evening dress announce 'twelve points' to Tel Aviv and 'douze points' to Jerusalem. It then shifts abruptly to a beach location as an upbeat R&B track fades in and the two presenters are surprised, but apparently pleased, to find themselves in swimwear from the waist down. A troupe of smiling, youthful (and thin, able-bodied and almost entirely white) Israelis dance, sing and beckon to us on the sandy Tel Aviv beach under a cloudless sky, next to – and in the case of the women, often in – Tel Aviv's crystal-clear sea, fountains and outdoor pools. The camera rushes between the dancers and the buildings of Tel Aviv's famous white shoreline, gleaming in the Mediterranean sunlight. Tel Aviv's luxury Dan Hotel, with its famous rainbow façade, provides the centrepoint of the beachfront vista and a colour scheme for the clip, echoed in the dancers' bright costumes and the font in the final slide, which urges us to 'book your trip now'. While the video names Israel as a country of two capitals, Tel Aviv and Jerusalem, the latter appears only briefly. We are left in no doubt that the true star here is Tel Aviv and its Mediterranean coast.

With its sun, sea, sand and conspicuous rainbows, the advert is an example of the attempted reorientation of Israel's image undertaken by the Israeli government since 2006 as part of the 'Brand Israel' campaign, discussed in this book's introduction. Hosting Eurovision was a triumphant coup for this project, allowing Israel to assert its place not at the periphery of Europe but at its heart, and to demonstrate its adherence to the progressive 'European' value of gay inclusion.[3] At the same time, the advert is a descendant of an older Israeli discourse, that of *Yam Tikhoniut*, also referred to as 'Mediterraneanism' or 'the Mediterranean option'. Mediterraneanism, or the idea of Israel as a geographically and culturally 'Mediterranean' country, emerged in the 1980s and rose to mainstream prominence during the Oslo era of the 1990s. Mediterraneanism is now largely forgotten outside academic contexts, but remains crucial to understanding the role of the sea in Israeli culture, politics and identity from the 1990s onwards.

In this chapter I consider the portrayal of the Mediterranean Sea in Amos Oz's novel *The Same Sea* (*Oto Ha-Yam*), translated by Oz's favoured translator Nicholas de Lange.[4] The novel was published in Hebrew in 1999, dating its inception to the height of the popularity of the Mediterranean idea. It is endorsed by Alexandra Nocke and David Ohana, major academic advocates of Israel's 'Mediterranean' identity, as a characteristically 'Mediterranean' novel for apparently reflecting Israel's 'Mediterranean' reality.[5] While Oz is one of Israel's best-known novelists, *The Same Sea* is something of an outlier among his works in terms of content and style, which may explain why it has been relatively overlooked by critics. Set between Israel's coastal cities of Bat Yam, Tel Aviv and various locations in South East Asia, *The Same Sea* avoids the traditional 'Zionist places' of Oz's other works including the kibbutz, Jerusalem and Israel's 1950s development towns.[6] Its style also differs sharply from Oz's usual psychological realism, written in an experimental mode that moves between times and places, poetry and prose, and narrators, including interjections by an unnamed narrator who seems to be Oz himself.[7]

As a result of these contrasts in subject and style, the few reviewers and critics who have discussed *The Same Sea* have tended to see it as a departure from the political contexts that typically shape the reception of Oz's work. *Guardian* journalist Jonathan Freedland described *The Same Sea* as 'avowedly, a work of art, not politics – a break from the din of the conflict, and a journey into the quieter, more elusive terrain of the heart'.[8] This reception of Oz's turn to the sea echoes the way that the Mediterranean idea is often seen as a move away from the fraught politics of the land to something potentially more productive. This move is echoed in the cover image of the novel's English edition. It features the back of a young, white male covered by a white towel from the waist down, seemingly presenting *The Same Sea* as a classy beach read.

In this chapter I show that *The Same Sea* manifests both the possibilities of Mediterraneanism and the evasions ultimately at its core. In this sense I agree with Nocke and Ohana that *The Same Sea* is a characteristically 'Mediterranean' text, but for rather different reasons. I show that an orientation towards the Mediterranean Sea is decidedly not, as Ohana describes it, a 'post-ideological' Israeli identity that departs from earlier Zionist attachments to the land.[9] Instead, the Mediterranean operates in Oz's novel as 'a frontier of capitalism and colonial expansion', as the sea so often does.[10] Israel's turn to the sea is continuous with the Zionist project of establishing exclusive Israeli sovereignty over both land and water, asserting Israel's territorial 'roots' through mapping 'routes' that naturalise Israel's presence as part of a long-term regional history.[11] Yet rather than representing a new integration into the region, Israel's Mediterranean affiliation operates to exclude another 'imaginative geography', the Orient, in the form of both Israel's Arab and Muslim neighbours and citizens and Diaspora Judaism.[12] A Mediterranean orientation in fact takes Israel back to Europe. Oz's formal experimentation is not, as Freedland reads it, a retreat from the political, but key to the novel's politics. Oz's hydrological motifs of flows and circulations illuminate the effects of Israel's post-Oslo economic boom both at home and on the global peripheries.[13] In doing so, they highlight the ultimate nature of Mediterraneanism as a discourse that, like Oslo, served to boost Israel's economy and its relationship with the countries of the core but contained no real potential for peace. It is telling that Mediterraneanism was never adopted by Palestinians.

The idea of Israel as a 'Mediterranean' country has primarily been debated in social science and cultural studies contexts.[14] Its literary manifestations have received relatively little attention. This may be explained in an Anglophone context by the tendency of readers to receive Israeli and Palestinian works through the framework of the conflict, as noted in the previous chapter. By explicitly seeking to go beyond this framework and stage what Alan Mintz calls the 'sun-drenched actuality of Israeli society' – regardless of whether we agree on this as Israel's actuality – Mediterraneanism is less intelligible to an Anglophone readership.[15] Several Israeli authors have engaged with the Mediterranean idea, including the poets Erez Biton and Natan Yonatan and the novelists Shulamit Hareven and A. B. Yehoshua. In this chapter I focus on Oz because of his reputation as Israel's 'national novelist' and particularly as a representative of the Israeli Left. Oz is the most translated Israeli novelist, with works in forty-six languages, and he received many awards, including the Israel Prize, the Goethe Prize (Germany) and the Prince of Asturias Award (Spain). Before his death in 2018 Oz was frequently mooted as a candidate for the Nobel Prize for Literature. *The Same Sea* is the engagement with Israel as a 'Mediterranean' country to have received the most international attention, widely circulated despite its unusual subject matter because of Oz's existing international stature. Oz's interest in the idea of Israel as a Mediterranean country, meanwhile, would appear to lend credibility to suggestions that it might serve as a cultural counterpart to formal peace negotiations.[16] At the same time, the contradictions in Oz's leftist commitments reflect the tensions and ultimate failure of Mediterraneanism.

The wider critical context for this chapter is the renewed attention to the sea in the arts and humanities represented by the Blue Humanities and its sister discipline, Oceanic Studies. Over the past ten years there has been an increasing interest in the sea within the arts and humanities that has mirrored a more established 'maritime turn' in the social sciences, notably in Geography.[17] The Blue Humanities and Oceanic Studies have shown the capacity for a turn to the sea to offer, as Hester Blum writes in an influential *Atlantic Studies* editorial, 'new critical locations from which to investigate questions of affiliation, citizenship, economic exchange, mobility, rights, and sovereignty'.[18] Criticism on the sea has shown that it is much more than merely a metaphor or an 'empty' space to be crossed on the way to land, providing the foundation for explorations of human and nonhuman experiences at, with and in the sea and a reminder of the wide-reaching impacts of the transformation of the ocean, as Rachel Price writes, into 'a final frontier for privatized extractivism'.[19] The move towards the sea is often framed as a move away from the nation, as in Blum's reference to 'land- and nation-based perspectives' as the twin opposites of an oceanic orientation.[20] It is also seen in Herman Wittenberg's assertion that the sea, as 'a liquid and connective space of flux and flow, detached from the divisive politics of the land, could be a space of alternative imaginative investment' that 'undoes topographies of power'.[21]

It is certainly true that starting from the ocean has provided new ways to conceptualise transnational communities and connections. This can be seen in the work of Paul Gilroy, and Marcus Rediker and Peter Linebaugh in Atlantic history, the writing of geographers Philip Steinberg and Kimberley Peters on the sea as a space for subversive political and cultural practices, or Teresa Shewry's account of the potential for literary imaginings of the ocean as a utopian space to yield responses to climate change that avoid despair or naturalising the inevitability of capitalism's triumph.[22] In an Israel/Palestine context the sea has famously been a site for the forging of transnational connections in the journeys of the International Solidarity Movement 'Freedom Flotillas' to Gaza, connections that were violently challenged by the Israeli state in 2010 when the IDF killed nine peace activists on board the Mavi Marmara.[23] As this incident suggests, oceanic space is also rigidly stratified in the service of national and military ends, functions that can be obscured in literary contexts by what Elizabeth DeLoughrey calls the appeal of an 'easy poetics' of flow and fluidity.[24] In this chapter I show that Israel's turn to the sea is continuous with earlier nation-building projects associated with the land. In doing so I offer a note of caution for the Blue Humanities, calling for a recognition of the extent to which imagery of flow, liquidity and connection can reinscribe national interests.

The Origins of Israel's 'Mediterranean' Identity

Mediterraneanism emerged in Israel in the early 1980s, rising to prominence during the period of the Oslo Accords in the 1990s. It was popular among academics, politicians and the Israeli public, as well as featuring in the marketing of products, books, music and television programmes.

Mediterraneanism foregrounded Israel's coastal location and seeming ethnic diversity as core components of a bold, pluralistic and outward-looking Israeli culture. A Mediterranean outlook seemed to offer an identity appropriate to the post-Zionist era in which, as discussed in the previous chapter, earlier narratives of Israeli identity appeared to be in terminal decline. A turn to the sea seemed to reflect the optimistic Oslo climate, suggesting the potential for conflict resolution through a move away from the fraught politics of the land. The European Union, too, saw potential in the idea of a unified Mediterranean, setting up the Barcelona Process in 1995, relaunched in 2008 by then French President Nicolas Sarkozy as the Union for the Mediterranean with its pillars of 'peace, security and prosperity'. Much like the peace process, however, the benefits of Mediterraneanism have been unevenly distributed, while the Union for the Mediterranean has produced less of a fluid space of connection and more a solidifying wall of Fortress Europe.[25] As its incorporation into an advert for tourism to Israeli highlights, the ultimate value of Israel's Mediterranean reorientation has largely been economic, serving to reaffirm Israel's cultural proximity to Europe rather than to demonstrate any substantive Israeli commitments to cultural reciprocity with Palestinians or the surrounding region.

Part of the appeal of Mediterraneanism is its promise of a 'post-ideological' Israeli identity.[26] Where the Zionist movement once sought to create the Jewish people anew in the land of Israel, advocates of Mediterraneanism argue that the country now has another identity. As Ohana writes, Israel is made up of 'people who, for sixty years now, have constituted a society on the eastern shore of the Mediterranean Sea. Their new identity is not ideologically based; it is constructed out of geography and culture.'[27] For Ohana this is merely a matter of describing an observed Israeli reality. While earlier accounts of Israeli identity seemed ideologically tainted and artificial in the post-Zionist era, the seashore represented the exact opposite of dated Zionist narratives of building the land, furnishing it with considerable appeal. It is a symbolically outward-looking space, with connotations of leisure, relaxation and, as a site of exposed bodies, social liberation. Ohana described the seashore as taking a prime role from this point onwards in the 'geography of collective redemption' because of its capacity to stand in for 'the new liberated Jewish existence' and demonstrate 'the normality of the life lived by the Jews'.[28] If the seashore seems materially distant from older Zionist narratives of building the land and nation, Ohana's comments suggest that it ultimately plays a similar role in 'normalising' Jewish life in Israel compared with 'abnormal' life in the Diaspora. A turn to the sea affirms a sense of ahistorical Israeli 'nativeness' to the land of Israel/Palestine in a way that is continuous with the earlier Zionist project of remaking the Jewish body through planting trees and draining the swamps. This process is, of course, hardly 'post-ideological', enacting the same effect that Zionism sought to achieve.

One change that Mediterraneanism initially seemed to offer was a new recognition of Israel's Mizrahi Jewish communities and of Mizrahiyut identity. Israel's Mizrahi citizens originate from Israel's local geographical region, the Middle East and North Africa, but have long been marginalised in Israel's Ashkenazi-dominated national culture.[29] As Nocke notes, mainstream Israeli interest in Mizrahi culture, particularly music, increased significantly in the 1990s, paralleling the rising Israeli curiosity about Arab culture more widely after the Oslo peace negotiations.[30] The increasing visibility of previously stigmatised Mizrahi culture seemed to indicate a greater Israeli openness towards the surrounding region as part of the Mediterranean phenomenon. Indeed, this aspect of Israeli culture in the 1990s forms a primary aspect of Nocke's claims for Israel as a 'Mediterranean' country.[31] Commentators who professed suspicions about cultural appropriation and concessions to silence Mizrahi dissent were, however, closer to the mark.[32] The 'Mediterranean' trend for Mizrahi music lent an appearance of inclusivity to Israeli culture while failing to translate into any actual material benefits for Mizrahi communities.[33]

Academic advocates of Israeli Mediterraneanism often stress its intellectual credentials with reference to the work of the major twentieth-century French historian Fernand Braudel.[34] Braudel was a member of the Annales school, a group of French historians founded in 1929 that centred on Lucien Febvre and Marc Bloch. The Annales approach emphasised a 'total' perspective on history that focused on deeper social and structural shifts over time rather than political events. Braudel adopted a similar approach towards what he called the *longue durée* in his most famous work, *The Mediterranean and the Mediterranean World in the Age of Philip II* (1949).[35] This monumental, two-volume project situated the history of the Mediterranean in the sixteenth century in the context of long-term, large-scale processes of geography and climate, offering an account of their impacts on the development of human culture in the region that brought together the micro scales and temporalities of everyday life with slow, geological change. Developing what he called '*géohistoire*', Braudel argued that the Mediterranean basin was a single unified space, with shared ways of life produced by geographical conditions and constant commercial exchange across small journeys over the ocean. While Braudel's project is sometimes criticised for its apparent environmental determinism, his mapping of the interactions between human social life and environmental factors in the rise of capitalism laid the groundwork for fields including environmental history, Mediterranean Studies, world history and world-systems analysis.

Uses of Braudel in the context of claims for Israel's Mediterranean identity tend, however, to take from his work an ahistorical, romanticised notion of Mediterranean geo-cultural unity rather than any analysis of structural trends in the development of capitalism. Ohana, for instance, offers the following:

> The Mediterranean option offers a dialogue, not a confrontation. It proposes a voyage, a slow and reflective cultural journey rather than a civil war in which, as in all wars, there must be only losers. It is a journey from the shores of Israeli identities to their mental and intellectual sources, the landscape of *mare nostrum*. It is a journey with, not a flight from, the Israelis' immediate neighbours, the Arabs and Palestinians. It is a journey to the space where everything was born: western and eastern civilization, monotheism and Hellenism, the polis and the Renaissance, the Old and the New Testaments.[36]

In this account, a Braudelian regional framework inscribes modern-day Israel into a longer history outside the framework of its comparatively recent conflict with the Palestinians, with Israel's purported ancient Mediterranean 'roots' and notions of slow maritime voyages obscuring the violent and much more recent history of Israel's creation. Also pertinent is Ohana's description of Mediterraneanism as 'a journey with, not a flight from' Israel's Arab and Palestinian neighbours. This claim is undermined by his primarily European cultural frame of reference, notably his predetermining use of the Latin *mare nostrum* (our sea), a phrase commonly found in Israeli notions of the Mediterranean which reinscribes the terms of discussion as European ones, a tendency that is worth examining further.

References to Italian and Greek culture are common in accounts of Israel's 'Mediterranean' identity, with the alternative regional formations of the Levant (or Mashriq, as it is referred to by Arabic speakers) and Maghreb conspicuous by their absence.[37] This emphasis on Italy and Greece over, for example, Morocco or Libya, is not unique to Israel but derives from an older European Mediterranean imaginary. The idea of the Mediterranean as a unified region first rose to prominence in late-eighteenth-century narratives of Northern European travellers on the Grand Tour. These countries were favoured in this context because of their associations with the purported origins of European civilisation and culture and the region's alleged 'golden age', with Mediterranean travel thought to allow Northern Europeans to access 'Mediterranean' qualities such as 'joyfulness, spontaneity, harmonious existence and artistic inspiration'.[38] The vagueness and stereotyping of this Mediterranean imaginary has not escaped critics; the term 'Mediterraneanism' was initially coined in the 1980s by anthropologist Michael Herzfeld as a critique of essentialism in studies of the region.[39] More significantly, however, this older, Europeanised Mediterranean was often set by its advocates against an imagined hostile and uncivilised Muslim Middle East, reproducing another regional formation, Edward Said's 'Orient'.[40] Braudel's work was structured according to the same division between mutually exclusive realms: for Braudel, the Islamic world was not 'fully "Mediterranean"' and its 'proper' geographical place was in the desert.[41] This aspect of Braudel's work anticipates the exclusion of Arab and Muslim Mediterraneans in Israel's Mediterranean imaginary. This shared exclusion across Israeli and European Mediterraneanisms underscores the extent to which the notion of a unified Mediterranean serves more as a way of avoiding the region and turning back to Europe than engaging with Israel's geographical reality.

In working to exclude the local while professing to do the opposite, Israeli Mediterraneanism bears intriguing resemblances to the depiction of California in tourist literature as a 'Mediterranean' region from the late nineteenth century onwards. This discourse often centres on California as an 'improved' or, more accurately, sanitised version of the actual Mediterranean. In one publicist's words, California offered 'the climate of the tropics without its perils', or without discomfiting encounters with the local poor and racial or religious otherness.[42] This Mediterranean imagery has been widely used. As Mike Davis writes: '[f]or more than a century, this Mediterranean metaphor has been sprinkled like a cheap perfume over hundreds of instant subdivisions, creating a faux landscape celebrating a fictional history from which original Indian and Mexican ancestors have been expunged'.[43]

Davis' observations on Los Angeles seem easily applicable to Israel's 'Mediterranean' identity. In both cases 'the Mediterranean' is deployed as a familiar and marketable commodity which attracts tourist dollars and external investment while concealing local histories of settler-colonial violence.

Israel and the Sea

The idea that Israel's identity could be defined in relation to the sea might come as a surprise given the long history of Zionist attachments to the land. Zionism is often described as premised on a rejection or, as Hannan Hever writes, a 'repression' of the sea.[44] The relationship between Israel and the sea is typically understood as limited to the history of 'Aliyah Bet', or the clandestine Ashkenazi Jewish migration from Europe to Palestine in the 1930s and 1940s. In this case, the sea is a mere route to the longed-for land and the dangerous maritime voyages extend the existential uncertainty of life in the Diaspora.[45] This is, however, a partial picture of early Zionist perspectives on the sea. In the pre- and early state period, imagining Jewish relationships to the sea provided a way to establish a 'native' Israeli identity that was parallel to the practices associated with the land. Moshe Shamir's 1951 novel *With His Own Hands*, for instance, famously opens with the line 'Elik was born from the sea', suggesting a Hebrew *creatio ex nihilo* in the land of Israel.[46] Members of the Canaanite and Revisionist movements turned to the sea in efforts to establish the ancient roots of the Jewish people in Palestine, attempting to recover supposed ancient Hebrew and Phoenician maritime traditions that are invoked frequently by advocates of Israel's modern 'Mediterranean' identity.[47] As noted in Chapter 1 in relation to Smilansky's character Lazar's skills in swimming and sailing, the Palestine Maritime League and Hakibbutz Hameuchad movement promoted the need for Jewish connections to the sea, showing that land and sea were both viewed as playing a part in the renewal of the Jewish people and of Palestine.[48]

The role of both land and sea in Zionist plans for a Jewish future in Israel/Palestine was made explicit by David Ben-Gurion. Ben-Gurion is the Zionist leader most associated with settling the land and making the desert bloom, but it is often forgotten he thought of the 'conquest of the soil' and 'conquest of the sea' as complementary.[49] For Ben-Gurion the value of the sea was both pragmatic and ideological. He described Israel's Mediterranean coastal location as 'a fact of economic, political and strategic moment'.[50] As indicated by this chapter's epigraph, Ben-Gurion believed the sea to be a major potential source of income, filled with exploitable natural resources.[51] The discovery of large natural gas fields off the coast of Gaza and the increasing importance of desalination in Israel's water supply may have proved him right.[52] What was more, the Mediterranean provided something that the land could not: a 'bridge' to the world, particularly to Europe.[53] Maritime connections would allow Israel to 'preserve [its] connection with the centres of culture in the west', while 'returning to the east'.[54] These were important culturally and ideologically for Zionist leaders as part of maintaining Israel's 'European' identity, but also politically and economically given Israel's tense relationship with its Arab neighbours on land.[55] The 'conquest of the sea' would allow the Jewish people to travel the world and attest to Israel's success in building the land, including by trading its commodities.[56] Israel's turn to the Mediterranean, then, is continuous with this longer history of nation-building usually associated with the land and by no means 'post-ideological'. While building the land involves looking inwards, turning to the sea allows Israel to demonstrate its hold on the land to the world.

Amos Oz and Mediterraneanism

Oz's writing is known for engaging with earlier periods of Israeli history associated with building the land, particularly, as seen in novels including *Elsewhere, Perhaps* (*Makom Aher*, 1966) and *A Perfect Peace* (*Menuhah Nekhonah*, 1982), the kibbutz movement. A turn to the Mediterranean Sea might seem surprising in this context. Oz's interest in Mediterraneanism was not immediate; he admitted to having initially dismissed it as an academic construct.[57] He later began to refer the Mediterranean idea as 'the real Israel'. His comments in a 2009 interview with the *Jewish Chronicle* are typical:

Some 70 or 80 per cent of Israelis live on the coastal plain. They are very Mediterranean. Secular to the bone. Noisy, passionate, materialistic, hedonistic, selfish. Coastal plain Israel – containing the bulk of the Israeli population – is like Piraeus, like Naples, like Barcelona. A warm-hearted, noisy Mediterranean community.[58]

It is worth noting that Oz's examples of 'Mediterranean' cities are in Greece, Italy and Spain, reproducing the exclusion of the Arab and Islamic Mediterranean common to claims of Israel's 'Mediterranean' identity. Oz juxtaposes this 'real' Israel with '[t]he Israel you see in the media', which he characterised as a disparate and implausible grouping of fanatical settlers, cruel soldiers and a minority of intellectuals, like Oz himself.[59] He also contrasts the modern Mediterranean Israel with early Zionist aspirations 'of an Austria-Hungary in the heart of the Middle East' and 'the dream of reviving the biblical kingdom of David and Solomon, or replicating the Eastern European shtetl'.[60] As for other advocates of the 'Mediterranean option', for Oz Mediterraneanism represented Israel's reality rather than the ideological impositions he saw as characteristic of earlier Zionist discourse or the stereotypes of the international media.

Mediterraneanism, as noted above, has been presented as a cultural counterpart to formal peace negotiations. Oz's turn to Mediterraneanism as a well-known 'leftist' writer is therefore significant, underscoring its association with peacemaking for readers within and outside Israel. Oz had a long association with the Israeli left, frequently acting as its spokesperson. He opposed the occupation of Gaza and the West Bank from early on, helped to found the Israeli organisation Peace Now in 1978 and participated in the drafting of the unofficial Geneva Accords in 2003.[61] He authored a number of non-fictional books on the conflict and published regularly on Israeli and Palestinian politics in the international press, particularly during times of crisis. As Anna Bernard notes, Oz's international stature derives in large part from his reputation as a determined advocate of the liberal values of reason, moderation and humanism in the fraught context of the ongoing conflict.[62] These qualities transfer to the idea of Israel as a Mediterranean country by virtue of Oz's support. The legitimating effect of Oz's endorsement of Mediterraneanism is heightened by his confession of initial scepticism; we assume that this was a position he considered carefully.

Oz's leftist image is, however, not clear-cut. The Israeli poet Yitzhak Laor criticised how Oz was 'taken for granted as a man of peace'.[63] Oz, Laor notes, was never as much of an outsider within Israel as he tended to claim and 'has always been a favourite son of the Israeli establishment, not least the Army'.[64] The habit of calling for recognition of the suffering and loss shared by both sides that endeared Oz to European and American audiences also rendered his views rather less progressive. After the 1967 war Oz became known for describing the conflict as 'a clash between right and right' on the model of a Greek tragedy.[65] He positioned himself as a supporter of 'disappointing compromise' as the ultimate solution to the conflict, which for him was the inevitable partition of the land into two states (this is also the position of Peace Now).[66] While this approach seems commendable in embodying the liberal virtue of 'balance', it presents what Said described elsewhere as a 'false symmetry' between two opponents with a dramatically unequal balance of power and international support.[67] What is more, in spite of his reputation as a liberal voice, Oz described Palestinians at times in terms that differed little from the stereotype of the Palestinian 'terrorist'.[68] He railed against Yasser Arafat, calling him 'a colossal tragedy for both peoples' and claimed that '[t]he Palestinian people are suffocated and paralysed by blind hate'.[69] While Oz favoured Mediterraneanism for representing Israel's reality and countering binary media stereotypes, he seemed unconcerned at times about replicating this image of the Palestinians. Such a combination of ostensibly 'progressive' sentiments with belligerent incitement and virtually unquestioning support for the actions of the Israeli state is, as Laor notes, indicative of the contradictions of a liberal Zionist position.[70] Oz's attraction to Mediterraneanism, then, suggests that its associations with peace are not as straightforward as they may seem.

Oz continued to profess his support for the Mediterranean idea in interviews towards the end of his life.[71] Indeed, in his later years he left his former desert home of Arad for an apartment in Tel Aviv with a sea view.[72] Still, his literary engagement with Mediterraneanism was brief. It began with the concluding chapter of his 1982 travelogue *In the Land of Israel*, was reiterated in the 1993 preface to its English translation and gained fictional form only in *The Same Sea*.[73] In Oz's many works since, the most prominent settings are the more traditional locations of Jerusalem and the kibbutz. This return may be the result of Oz revisiting formative experiences in old age, beginning with his 2002 memoir *A Tale of Love and Darkness*. We might also see it as an acknowledgement of changing political times, notably Israel's hardening shift to the right. While the Mediterranean remains crucial to the image it presents internationally, as seen in the advert discussed at the start of this chapter and the widely circulated 2017 images of Benjamin Netanyahu strolling on the Tel Aviv shore with Indian Prime Minister Narendra Modi, it is rare to find Israel's Mediterranean location cited today as a route to regional peace.[74] Oz's return to these settings perhaps represented a pragmatic move in terms of book sales, tapping into nostalgia for Israel's past and facilitating an escape from the violence of the present.

Mediterraneanism as 'Geographical Reality'

I now turn more closely to *The Same Sea* and Oz's literary engagement with Mediterraneanism. Advocates of Mediterraneanism often cite lived experience as the main evidence for Israel's Mediterranean identity.[75] *The Same Sea* appears to reflect this in the appearance of the Mediterranean Sea as a constant background to characters' everyday lives, evoking a sense of location. This begins with the novel's first lines: 'Not far from the sea, Mr Albert Danon/lives in Amirim Street, alone, He is fond/of olives and feta'.[76] The sea is also frequently referred to in relation to the passing seasons. This gives a sense of geographical permanence, as in the lines: 'The winter is passing. The sea remains', and 'the sea is talking about autumn already'.[77] The sense of Mediterraneanism as lived experience in the novel is reinforced through associations between the sea and stereotypical elements of Mediterranean culture, climate and diet. This occurs notably in the memories of home recalled by Albert's son Enrico David (Rico) while away backpacking in South East Asia, which he undertakes, like many Israelis, after compulsory military service. From Tibet, Rico recalls Israel in a sequence of associative sensory memories as 'A ruin. A church. A fig tree. A bell/A tower. A tiled roof. Wrought-iron grilles. A lemon tree./The smell of fried fish. And between two walls/a sail and a sea rocking.'[78] These lines suggest a generic Mediterranean climate and culture, while we might read the church as aligning Israel with a Christian Mediterranean history rather than a Muslim one. Their brevity, meanwhile, discourages further thought about the nature of the 'ruin' or the original planters of the 'fig tree'; the location of former Palestinian villages can be identified by the presence of fruit trees, while Palestinian homes are often narrated as ancient 'ruins' in Israel's national parks.[79] A peaceful Mediterranean imaginary, then, may well work here to occlude more recent historical violence, a notion I discuss in greater detail later.

A sense of Israel's Mediterranean location is also underscored by characters' holidays elsewhere in the Mediterranean, with Albert and his wife Nadia visiting Crete before Nadia's death from cancer. Crete and Israel are united in the novel by descriptions of a smell of saltwater that foregrounds their shared location on the Mediterranean coast. Gardening at home in Bat Yam, Albert '[i]nhales the smell of the sea from afar, salt, seaweed, the warm dampness', while the sea features in Nadia's recollections of their holiday in Crete:

> where night fell so slowly and the salt smell mingled with the tang of the pines and we drank wine with ewes' milk cheese while the shadow of the mountains spread right across the plain but the mountains themselves were still illuminated in the distance by a light that promised peace would come[80]

The lack of punctuation in these lines suggests the richness of Nadia's memories of her travels across the sea as they rush back and her attachment to Crete, while the implied ease of Israeli maritime across the Mediterranean contrasts strikingly with more familiar accounts of movement in the region, notably Israel's hard borders on land with its Arab neighbours. The closing reference to 'a light that promised peace' suggests a sense of reconciliation not only for Nadia with her illness, but also the political outcome that might come from Israel's own 'holiday' in the Mediterranean.

This repeated combination of familiar, stereotyped elements of Mediterranean life in the novel leads Nocke to claim that the Mediterranean offers Oz a means of depicting Israel's 'rootedness in the region, the way of life, and state of mind'.[81] In this sense, Nocke writes, Israel's Mediterranean identity is for Oz merely 'a geographical reality linked to Israel's physical location' detached from any 'ideological agenda'.[82] The apparent acknowledgement of Israel's 'real' place in these lines contrasts sharply with the dramatic alterations of the environment earlier in Israel's history discussed in previous chapters, motivated by a version of Zionism that sought to transcend 'natural limits' and transform the landscapes and waterscapes of Israel/Palestine. Mediterraneanism seems instead to be a reconciliation with Israel's actual geographical place. It is not, however, a 'post-ideological' reality. Oz's emphasis on Israel's Mediterranean roots elides its history as a relatively new nation-state, created in 1948 and with its roots not only in nineteenth-century European antisemitism but in European models of nationalism and colonialism. This representation of a supposed history of Mediterranean connections enables a projection of Israel's continuity into the future, seemingly largely separate from its Arab citizens and neighbours.

Mediterraneanism and the Left

Through the character of Rico, Albert and Nadia's backpacking son, Oz puts forward a critique of the Israeli left which presents Mediterraneanism as a 'mature' outcome for Israel. In many ways Rico represents a typical left-wing Israeli youth. He is disillusioned with Israeli society and 'thought the world/was in a bad way'.[83] He reads widely on politics in a scattergun fashion and his shelves are littered with 'piles' of 'books,/pamphlets, papers, publications, on all sorts/of wrongs: black studies, women's studies, lesbians and gays, child abuse, drugs, race,/rain forests, the hole in the ozone layer, not to mention/injustice in the Middle East'.[84]

Rico attends a 'left-wing rally' on an unspecified issue with his girlfriend Dita.[85] He neglects to tell his parents where he is going and comes home late. In doing so, Albert pleads, he is 'making it worse' for his mother as she is dying of cancer.[86] As Laor notes, it is telling that Oz gives no information about the rally other than that Rico attended while his mother was seriously ill.[87] Rico's attendance at the rally is portrayed as a selfish evasion of family commitments, functioning as an implicit critique of the Israeli left.[88] This is underscored by Rico's departure on a seemingly endless family-funded backpacking trip while Albert is still grieving. Dita's attempts to comfort Albert make the misguidedness, even narcissism of their leftist commitments explicit. She tells Albert: 'Now you're giving him guilt feelings;/after all, it's not his fault she's dead. He has a right/to a life of his own.'[89] Dita's references to 'rights' and, later, Rico being 'entitled to try to find himself', suggest the hypocrisy of their concern for an unlimited number of social justice issues while shirking care responsibilities within their personal relationships in favour of an individualistic notion of self-fulfilment.

Rico spends the duration of the book, save for flashbacks, backpacking around Nepal, Tibet, Bangladesh, Bengal and Sri Lanka. While Rico is a long way from the Mediterranean, his narrative is crucial to the novel's engagement with Mediterraneanism. Backpacking, or *tarmila'ut* in Hebrew, has been an Israeli institution since the 1980s. Israeli backpackers are typically middle class, secular and Ashkenazi, with wealthy and well-educated parents.[90] In this sense they mirror the elite youth of Northern Europe, Australia and South Africa who participate in the related ritual of the 'gap year'. In both contexts backpacking functions as a 'rite of passage' between two life phases that indirectly enables socialisation into the home society on return.[91] The key difference between Israeli backpackers and other 'gap year' tourists is that Israelis tend to embark on their travels after completing their military service, to the extent that Israeli backpacking is also sometimes referred to as the 'postarmy trip'.[92] Their travels, then, function as a reward for enduring the privations of army life at the same time as playing a role in reconciling their military and civilian identities in their adult roles in Israeli society.

Rico's backpacking and return can be read as a trajectory through which Oz explores Israel's own 'mature' identity seemingly beyond a history of conflict. It mirrors a recurring narrative of Oz's novels noted by Bernard, in which an alienated protagonist struggles to feel at home in a society which he (or, less frequently, she) feels has very different values.[93] The climax of these novels is often a moment at which the protagonist's desires are revealed as somehow impracticable, with narrative closure achieved when the protagonist disregards his or her ideals and comes to 'realise the values of the domestic and the quotidian', leading to his or her reabsorption within a community.[94] Through Rico's journey Oz suggests that 'maturity' is the recognition that 'finding oneself' ultimately involves a reconciliation with Israel's Mediterranean locus. At the same time, Rico's travels in distant lands are crucial to Israel's modern identity: they position Rico – and, implicitly, Israel – as part of a cosmopolitan, worldly elite, paradoxically reaffirming Israel's affinity with Europe and its settler colonies even as the novel ostensibly situates Israel in its geographical region. What is more, Rico's ability to travel overseas demonstrates that his home is secure and not in need of constant defence. In these senses, Rico's postarmy trip is as crucial to securing Israel's hold on its territory as his military service.

Rico decides to return home on reaching the Sri Lankan coast, where the sea provides a symbolic and material connection to Israel's Mediterranean shores and reminds him of his home. His journey to the sea is repeatedly described in hydrological metaphors that suggest a sense of quasi-religious destiny and inevitability.[95] While in the mountains, Rico feels 'the sea is calling' and Oz compares Rico's downwards route to the path of a river which eventually becomes calm on merging with the ocean, writing: 'all the rivers flow into the sea, and the sea is silence silence silence'.[96] This line borrows from Ecclesiastes 1:7, replacing the well-known final clause of 'and the sea is not yet full' and shifting the meaning of the line from a motto of constant movement and change to stability, perhaps even peace. A comment from the narrator makes this link more explicit, generalising from Rico's wandering to a collective Israeli 'we': 'the young man who went off to the mountains to seek the sea that was there all the time outside his own home. We have wandered enough. It is time to make peace.'[97]

In this line, 'wandering' has multiple associations: Rico's travels, the history of Israelite 'wandering' in the desert and the stereotype of Jewish 'wandering' in the Diaspora, and a national 'wandering' after the creation of Israel as the country seeks to establish its identity. Making 'peace' after 'wandering' points towards acceptance of a local environment, represented in these lines by the sea, but it is impossible not to read this section, particularly given the declarative final sentence, as a resolution to avoid future exilic 'wandering' through political 'peace'. The frequent associations between Rico's mother Nadia and the sea, as in the line where Rico is 'mistakenly searching in the mountains for his sea-tossed mother', underscore this sense of the 'natural' and 'mature' belonging of both Rico and Israel to a home by the sea.[98]

The sense of a Mediterranean affiliation as 'maturity' is reinforced through frequent comments on writing style interspersed throughout the book. Oz refers a number of times to simple observation as a writing strategy, twice repeating advice from a favourite teacher that '[i]f you stop talking sometimes/maybe things will be able to talk to you' and receiving a tip from Albert on writing newspaper comment pieces: 'try to write in a quiet way if you can'.[99] Albert contrasts this practice with a wider political climate in which 'there is so much noise ... the whole country is full of screaming, incantations, amulets, trumpets, fifes and drums'.[100] As the book goes on Oz appears to model 'writing in a quiet way' primarily through repeated descriptions of the sea at different times of day, writing '[a]ll over the sea the moon spreads a quicksilver web which it draws in and heaves up to itself. That is what I'm talking about.'[101] In these moments Oz seems to offer quiet observation of Israel's geographical and climatic realities on the Mediterranean coast as an alternative to the chaotic, unproductive discourse he presents as dominating Israeli politics. In this sense the novel seems to indicate that Mediterraneanism might offer a 'mature' orientation and a way forward in resolving the conflict.

A Mediterranean Peace?

As noted at the start of this chapter, claims of Israel's Mediterranean identity are frequently presented in wider political, literary and academic discourse as a potential asset in peace negotiations, seen as foregrounding ancient histories of regional connection and seeming to emphasise dialogue over antagonism. References to peace recur throughout Oz's text. Some are indirect, like those above, and some more explicit, as in the section titled 'The Peace Process'.[102] The experimental form of *The Same Sea* can be read as part of this apparently conciliatory move. The novel is split into short fragmentary chapters which alternate between prose and poetry and jump between places and times. These fragments are narrated by a number of characters, living and dead, as well as a narrator, who appears as a character bearing considerable resemblance to Oz. Oz has described these techniques as part of the novel's 'metapolitical significance', claiming that '[i]t is a novel that erases, deliberately, every boundary'.[103] The formal structure of Oz's novel seems to mirror its emphasis on sea crossings and regional connection across the Mediterranean, in which the nurturing of regional affiliations promises the breaking down of communal boundaries. The novel, however, ultimately reproduces a stereotypical image of Palestinians that situates them as a threat to a Mediterranean collective rather than an equal participant.

The section titled 'The Peace Process' draws heavily on Orientalist imagery, with Oz envisioning a journey through an unnavigable and inhospitable desert in 'Hadhramaut . . . southern Arabia'.[104] Hadhramaut, a region of modern-day Yemen, is described by Oz as '[s]hifting sands, wilderness, the haunt of foxes'.[105] Oz proposes that '[m]aybe the peace process will open [this place] up to us', suggesting the increased mobility of Israeli tourists within the Middle East which followed the Oslo Accords and, less positively, the Orientalist trope of the East as a gateway to be 'unlocked'.[106] The unnavigability of Oz's desert indicates the futility of entering into this Middle Eastern space, while its aridity illustrates, according to a Eurocentric environmental imaginary which (falsely) views areas with low rainfall as degraded, the political unproductivity of negotiations and a metaphorical drying-up of dialogue and solutions.[107] The Arabic etymology of the place name Hadhramaut – 'death', (موت, *maut*), 'came/attended', (حضر, *hadara*), often understood as 'death has come' or 'death was present' – indicates extreme pessimism about peace negotiations, suggesting that the 'Peace Process' may in fact have dangerous consequences for Israelis.

Oz's association between the Palestinians and the desert recalls the earlier figuring of the settlement of Palestine by Zionist leader and first President of Israel Chaim Weizmann as a battle of the 'forces of civilization' against 'the forces of destruction, the forces of the desert'.[108] This passage, then, far from moving away from 'ideological' framings, replicates older Zionist discourses to produce an image of Palestinians as stubborn, 'landlocked' and a potential threat, aligned with the most stigmatised forms of nonhuman nature, as with the swamps discussed in the previous chapter. This contrasts sharply with the representation of Israelis elsewhere in the text as liberated from ethnic conflict and confrontation through associations with flowing waters, cooling breezes, soft light and rich, nutritious Mediterranean foods. This contrast is illuminated by Oz's remarks to Nocke, in which he bluntly declares his indifference to whether Mediterraneanism can ease Israel's relations with the Arab world. He states:

> if it proves to be a good bridge between Israel and the Arab world – wonderful. If not, I never thought Israel had to adjust to the region. . . . If it does not work the Arab neighbours have to learn to live next door to someone [who is, AN] different.[109]

In this comment, Oz's intransigence is clear, even if he imputes this quality to Arabs instead (Palestinians, significantly, are not mentioned).

The sense that Mediterraneanism ultimately serves as a means of smoothing over conflict while producing the appearance of an open and harmonious society is underscored by Oz's representation of Palestinians. There are no fully realised Palestinian characters in *The Same Sea*, as is often the case in Oz's work. However, some Palestinians do appear in Rico's recollection of a childhood bus journey to Jaffa with his mother. Oz describes a vivid and chaotic scene populated by intimidating figures. On the way, Rico and Nadia observe a minor road accident: 'a donkey cart/had overturned. Smashed watermelons on the asphalt,/a blood bath.'[110] The 'donkey cart' suggests underdevelopment compared to Nadia and Rico's reliable and modern bus, an impression heightened by a reference to 'an unfinished building and dunes of sand' that suggests the encroachment of the desert on the city.[111] This image echoes the association of Palestinians with the desert discussed above, also famously found in Tel Aviv's foundation myth of being built from the dunes next to the squalor of Jaffa.[112] Its evocation here suggests the potential for the threat of an Arab resurgence from Jaffa to overwhelm its neighbour, Tel Aviv (the opposite has, in fact, been the case, with Jaffa absorbed into the 'Tel Aviv-Yafo' municipality as a quaint and exotic tourist destination).[113] The 'smashed watermelons' imagined as a 'blood bath' underscore the threat of unpredictable violence, reinforced by Oz's description of the mouth of a woman who yawns at Nadia as 'a grave, empty and deep'.[114] The short lines and non-rhyming verse of this passage mirror Rico's partial perception of the events through the window of a moving bus and present an Orientalist vision of Palestinian society as without rational order. In this scene Palestinians are literally kept outside Israeli space by the windows of the bus, affirming a suspicion that Oz's interest in the Mediterranean is not about reconciling with Israel's actual Middle East location, but about shutting it out.

The role of Mediterraneanism as a means of excluding the 'Orient' becomes clear in the novel's allusions to Eastern Europe. As Gil Z. Hochberg points out, the 'othering' of both Jews and Arabs in Europe from the eighteenth to the twentieth century was 'directly linked to their shared, albeit different, status as Orientals'.[115] As noted earlier, the Zionist project of creating the Jewish people anew in the land of Palestine involved replacing 'Oriental' traits seen as rooted in Eastern-European Jewishness. This project was haunted by a fear of Israelis becoming 'Arab-like' once more, a preoccupation which accounts for the significance attached by Zionist leaders like Ben-Gurion and Herzl to retaining Israel's ties with Europe.[116] In *The Same Sea*, Albert similarly distinguishes between Israel and Eastern Europe when he admonishes Nadia for telling Bulgarian folk stories to Rico:

> There aren't any forests or goblins here. We came to this country to put all that behind us, to live on yoghurt and salad with an omelette, to settle down, to change, to defend ourselves when we have no alternative, to banish the old troubles, to be cured of the ancient horror, to sit under the vine in the garden . . .[117]

Albert's juxtaposition of symbols of the Mediterranean diet – yoghurt, salad, omelettes, vines – with a form of 'Eastern superstition' represented by 'forests or goblins' indicates that Mediterraneanism in *The Same Sea* operates as a means of separating Israeli Jewish identity from 'Oriental' Jewishness, as well as from histories of antisemitic violence. Nadia's telling of folk tales brings to light the fearful prospect of a 'reversion' to the Jewishness of the Eastern European shtetl which Zionism was meant to have suppressed, suggesting the multiple kinds of 'Orient' to which Mediterraneanism offers an alternative.

Aspects of the novel initially suggest that a Mediterranean orientation might contain a challenge to Israel's Ashkenazi-dominated national culture. These are, however, ultimately unfulfilled.[118] Both Albert and Nadia are Sephardi Jews, from Sarajevo and Sofia respectively, cities of the Balkans which, as a Greek clairvoyant visited in Jaffa by Albert tells him, 'belong/both to the west and to the east', much as Mediterraneanism appears to show that Israel does.[119] The setting of Bat Yam indicates a similar concern with Israel's internal racial politics. Bat Yam possesses the dubious accolade of being the most densely populated city in the Tel Aviv metropolitan area and is often associated with high levels of crime and unemployment.[120] It is home mostly to lower-middle-class Mizrahi Jews and, with other cities on Tel Aviv's periphery, such as Holon, is often stigmatised as Tel Aviv's 'other'.[121] Oz's choice of Bat Yam as a location for a 'Mediterranean' novel seems to suggest more of a commitment to Mediterraneanism as an ethnically inclusive discourse than if he had chosen the more obvious Tel Aviv. In contrast to Tel Aviv's seeming glamour, wealth and much-vaunted modernist architecture, Bat Yam is 'the undesirable "national average"': unexciting, poorly planned, but an appropriate site for a depiction of everyday Israeli reality.[122]

All elements of potentially disruptive ethnicity in the novel are, however, eventually contained. Nadia stops telling her Balkan folktales before her death. Another Bosnian character is Europeanised and Ashkenazified through his love of Italian opera, of which he is described as an 'addict'.[123] Next to nothing of Bat Yam's history is apparent from the text, meaning that its connotations are hidden to most non-Israeli readers. The clairvoyant Stavros Evangelides provides perhaps the most telling example of Mediterraneanism as a heavily partial vision of a multicultural Israel. Evangelides' Hebrew is described as 'simple but correct,/with a slight Arab accent'.[124] This Greek with an 'Arab accent' highlights the way in which Oz's Mediterraneanism operates as a form of substitution in which Southern Europe is as close as we want to get to Israel's actual geographical location in the Middle East.

Oz's religious and mythological framework reinforces a sense of his Mediterranean as premised on the exclusion of anything Arab or Muslim. *The Same Sea* relies heavily on biblical allusion and references to Greek myth, to the extent that its translator, de Lange, appends four pages of notes on Oz's biblical imagery at the end of the novel. Oz creates a meshwork of Mediterranean cultural reference points that are either Jewish, Christian or associated with the symbolic home of European culture, Ancient Greece. In doing so he excises all evidence of Arab and Islamic Mediterraneans, such that Israel's purported Mediterranean affiliations say less about an 'authentic' sense of belonging to the local region and more about an Israeli desire to exclude the 'Orient'. In this way *The Same Sea* fits within a wider tendency of Oz's novels identified by Bernard: they do 'not simply project a separatist demographic imaginary' but 'do so paradoxically and obliquely', in this case through imagining a Mediterranean identity that assimilates all racial or religious difference and erases historical and ongoing Israeli violence against Palestinians.[125] Mediterraneanism is framed as a move away from Israel's own history of nationalist antagonism, but the more pertinent distancing would seem to be from Israel's Arab citizens and neighbours.

'Current Liquidisations Ltd.'

Oz's novel is not wholly positive about Israel's new-found Mediterranean orientation and the post-Zionist era in which it emerged. His depiction of the displacement of Israel's earlier, ostensibly socialist identity by the post-Oslo arrival of multinational capital is highly ambivalent.[126] By 1995, following the Oslo Accords and the end of the Arab boycotts, Israel had a rapidly growing economy with a per capita GDP comparable to that of the UK.[127] This boom is often described as the 'peace dividend'. *The Same Sea* betrays anxiety about consumer culture, cultural homogenisation brought about by the arrival of multinational corporations, and Israel's complicity in the externalisation of the social and ecological costs of growth to the countries of the global periphery. Hydrological metaphors play a crucial role in Oz's critique, with metaphors of the global ocean rendering visible the connections between Israeli affluence and devastation of the world's peripheries, represented by the Sri Lankan coast. At the same time, Oz's profession of 'First World guilt' over the effects of globalisation serves again to reaffirm Israel's affiliation with the countries of the world's core, while his relocation of the negative consequences of Israeli growth on maritime cultures and marine ecologies on the opposite side of the world elides its impact on Palestinians and on Israel/Palestine's Mediterranean coastline closer to home.

The sea itself is frequently described in Oz's novel in metaphors of financial transactions. This is not unusual; as Christopher Connery notes, the ocean is 'capital's favoured myth-element'.[128] In this case these associations underscore the centrality of the sea, in multiple ways, to Israel's contemporary economy. Oz describes the sea as holding a 'joint bank account' with the desert, making an 'advance payment on the autumn' and as 'smooth tonight, chilly, shining darkly, a sea like the black glass nameplate of a respectable firm, with lines of gleaming gold writing, a pricey, highly polished sea, Current Liquidisations Ltd.'.[129] These repeated associations echo Ben-Gurion's earlier prediction that '[t]he sea is no waste of waters, as many think, but a sealed store of infinite treasures'.[130] Oz's description of a 'gleaming gold', 'pricey, highly-polished sea' and ironic invocation of 'respectability' highlights the potentially underhand processes at work in Israel's post-Oslo economic boom, which promises considerable wealth, Oz suggests, but dubious moral consequences.

The activities of Dita's lover, Giggy Ben-Gal, provide the strongest sense of the changing economic significance of the sea and its role in Israel's financial relationship with Europe. Ben-Gal travels back from Brussels – home of the European Parliament and symbolic heart of Europe – to the small town of Binyamina, south of Haifa, to inspect 'an orange grove that was dying because it didn't pay to irrigate it'.[131] It might, Ben-Gal considers, be wise to 'snap up today at the price of farmland what tomorrow would be prime building lots in a sought-after district'.[132] The land is potentially valuable because of its proximity to the sea, as an announcement by Ben-Gal's firm highlights: 'Ben-Gal & Partners have purchased a new plot to build luxury apartments and duplexes and commissioned a ninety-second promotional film . . . your dream home, penthouse with sea view'.[133]

The location of Binyamina is significant. The town was founded in 1922 as a citrus colony and was one of the settlements which made the Mediterranean coastal plain into Palestine's centre of citrus production.[134] It is named after Baron Edmond Benjamin de Rothschild, member of the European Jewish banking dynasty, who made significant donations towards the establishment of agricultural settlements in Palestine in the late nineteenth and early twentieth centuries.[135] The orange, specifically the 'Jaffa orange', was a crucial national symbol for the early-twentieth-century Zionist movement and, later, Israel, in the first decades of the state. In spite of the existence of a thriving Palestinian citriculture industry prior to the creation of Israel the orange came to be seen, as Bardenstein notes, as a 'quintessentially Israeli agricultural export'.[136] The orange became the symbol abroad of the success of the Zionist project of restoring the connection between Jewish people and the land through 'Hebrew labour'. It was celebrated in art, posters and propaganda films, and in the orange uniform and orange-shaped hat of 1960s El Al air stewardesses, while Shelley Egoz writes that the orange grove, or pardess, was 'romanticized beyond any other agricultural landscape'.[137] Tel Aviv's nickname, 'the Big Orange', indicates both the centrality of the orange in the Zionist project and, through its echo of New York's 'Big Apple', the vibrancy and youthfulness of Israel's newly revived Jewish culture.

Ben-Gal's purchase of neglected citrus plantations in Binyamina at a bargain price indicates the decline of Labour Zionism's founding national narratives of agricultural settlement, working on the land and rebuilding the nation. In repurposing this 'symbolic landscape', a term I take from Egoz, he is a counterpart to Baruch in Shalev's *The Blue Mountain*.[138] However, where Baruch is driven by pioneer feuds that refuse to die, Ben-Gal's motive ten years later is pure profit. Ben-Gal's activities echo a real phenomenon taking place in Israel in the 1990s as orange groves on the coastal plain began to be destroyed for housing construction.[139] The groves were no longer needed as Israel's economy turned towards sectors such as property development and tourism: the iconic national commodity is no longer an orange but a sea view. Israel's economic transition was summarised most aptly by a representative of the airline easyJet on the inauguration of their route from London to Tel Aviv in 2009: 'Tel Aviv has always been famous for its oranges. Now the orange planes of easyJet will give thousands more people the chance to enjoy the sweet taste of Israel's 24-hour city.'[140]

The increasing role of tourism and foreign investment in Israel's economy is seen through Dita's part-time job. We learn that 'Dita Inbar in her orange uniform, with a name-badge on the lapel, / works three nights a week as a receptionist in an expensive seaside hotel', processing 'tourists, investors, philanderers, foreign airline pilots in uniform / and teams of tired stewardesses. Forms. Credit Cards'.[141] We later learn that this hotel is Tel Aviv's Hilton with the mention of the Hilton brand, one of the largest chains in the global hotel market, illustrating Israel's post-Oslo attractiveness to multinational corporations, just as Dita's 'orange uniform' recalls older Israeli economic priorities.[142] Dita's night-time work, meanwhile, indicates the 24-hour nature of the economic system into which Israel has belatedly entered. The hotel acts as a node in the international circulation of a transient and anonymous population of workers, travellers and visitors with more nefarious ends whose impact on Dita is merely registered through the parallel, repetitive circulation of international capital: 'Forms. Credit Cards.' Intriguingly, Dita encounters the 'Narrator' staying in the hotel after a lecture, who bears a resemblance to Oz in a number of ways, including, like Oz at the time, living in Arad and having written a novel called *To Know a Woman*.[143] In writing himself into the text at this point Oz self-consciously suggests his own ambivalence about the status of literature as a commodity within the world marketplace, a knowing declaration of complicity that ironically increases his capital within this market.[144]

Oz's depiction of multiple 'circulations' of people and capital recalls Zygmunt Bauman's concept of 'liquid modernity'.[145] Bauman proposes that speed, rather than space, is now the crucial element in securing economic and cultural power, while our era has been witness to the 'liquefaction' of social bonds.[146] This social 'liquefaction' is evident from Dita's interpersonal interactions with hotel visitors – themselves Bauman's 'extraterritorial elite' – which involve only financial transactions.[147] Bauman argues that in 'liquid modernity' the 'solid' modernity of industrial, 'heavy' capitalism has been replaced by the 'light' capitalism of deregulation and liberalisation.[148] These processes are mirrored in the decline of Israel's orange industry and the more recent opening up of Israel's markets to international capital, signified by the Hilton and its 24-hour transactions. Oz's metaphors of flow integrate Israel ambivalently into Bauman's 'liquid' world.

The decline of Israel's earlier 'socialist' orientation is linked in *The Same Sea* to a rise in consumer culture and an increasing homogenisation and privatisation of public space. Oz's seedy would-be film producer Dubi Dombrov laments the effects of 'commercialisation, which in fact, let's be clear, is destroying everything here'.[149] Elsewhere in the novel the effects of this are seen in a changing urban environment: 'In south Bat Yam they're building a new mall, they've closed a grocery shop and opened a fashion boutique or a bank, dedicated a garden to Yitzhak Rabin with a fountain and benches'.[150] The replacement of a grocery shop, a reminder of Israel's agricultural tradition that provides necessary goods for sustaining the body, by interchangeable symbols of affluence, disposable income and urban homogeneity, a boutique and bank, deepens our sense of the negative impacts of Israel's new affluence on its society.

The mention of Rabin is similarly significant. Rabin was Israel's Prime Minister from 1974 to 1977 and again from 1992, when he was the leading Israeli politician behind the Oslo Accords. In 1995 he was assassinated by a right-wing Israeli, an event that was recent news at the time of the book's writing. Rabin's memorialisation at the centre of an image of commercialisation might seem incongruous and perhaps ironic, since the image appears to suggest the death of earlier unifying Zionist narratives in the face of the homogenising forces of global capital. This is certainly a fear in Oz's 1966 novel *Elsewhere, Perhaps*, in which Oz depicts Israeli society under threat from two outside forces: consumer capitalism and the Diaspora.[151] However, by the time *The Same Sea* was written the forces of capitalism no longer triggered Israeli anxieties about national integrity. Instead, as Eric Zakim writes, '[t]he late twentieth-century arrival of global capital has been met as national affirmation', representing, as it did, the fulfilment of the old Zionist desire for

Israel to be 'normal'.[152] In Oz's novel, the threats posed to Israel by globalisation paradoxically serve to strengthen Israel's national position through aligning its concerns with those of countries of the economic core, from which it solicits and receives economic, military and political support. On top of this, if Israel is threatened by the homogenising effects of globalisation it is implicitly no longer subject to existential threats to its continued survival. In this sense, this scene of malls and banks would seem to have achieved Rabin and Zionism's goals.

The Globalised Ocean

As well as expressing ultimately nationally affirming anxieties about the impact of neoliberal globalisation at home, Oz conveys concern about its effects abroad through Rico's travels in South East Asia. Rico ends his journey in 'a remote fishing village in the south of Sri Lanka' in the fictional 'Gulf of Kirindi'.[153] In spite of its 'remote' location, the village is thoroughly integrated into processes of international capitalist extractivism as a fish export site.[154] The expansion of an export-oriented fishing industry, particularly through the growth of aquaculture, has been promoted by South Asian governments including Sri Lanka's in recent decades, funded by loans from the International Monetary Fund (IMF) and World Bank as part of the 'Blue Revolution'. Given the history of IMF and World Bank lending to poorer countries in the 1970s and 1980s, in which loans were offered on the condition of acquiescence to socially and ecologically devastating 'structural adjustment programmes', their involvement marks a reason for caution. Indeed, the incorporation of South Asian fishing communities into global commodity chains has had devastating effects. As Mariarosa Dalla Costa and Monica Chilese have documented, the easing of access for transnational corporations to the natural resources of the global periphery has destroyed the basis of coastal subsistence economies, making it harder for fishing communities to find their own food and pushing fishermen and their families further into poverty and malnutrition.[155] Industrial aquaculture farms release waste and drugs into the water, while the loss of mangrove forests to shrimp farming on a mass scale causes coastal erosion and species loss.[156] These processes damage ecosystems and harm the ability of coastal communities to support themselves. Little of the income generated by the expansion of industrial aquaculture production in the world's peripheries made its way to local communities as promised; it is primarily used to service existing debt.[157]

Rico's experiences show the extent to which the advent of intensive fishing has entrenched the international control of local industries and accelerated the transfer of capital out of the Sri Lankan economy. Rico, an Israeli, works as a nightwatchman in a refrigeration plant belonging to a Belgian company, with a shifty Austrian engineer as a colleague.[158] He mentally translates his wage in Sri Lankan rupees into the global currency of the US dollar, reflecting the composition of the Sri Lankan fishing industry in which 55 per cent of workers are outsiders.[159] His overnight work parallels Dita's receptionist duties in Tel Aviv, illustrating the 24-hour operation of the capitalist world-system and the low-paid workers on which it depends across the core and periphery. Meanwhile, Oz's descriptions of the coast itself manifest the environmental degradation caused by capitalism's externalisation of its costs of production in the search for continuing accumulation, which ultimately exhaust the source of its own capacity to produce.[160]

The Sri Lankan coast is described as a nightmarish vision of seemingly all-encompassing, irreversible environmental damage. Oz writes: 'all around the derelict plant mangy dogs/are barking, skinny dogs shrieking then sinking to a whimper, as a murky sun/chokes through the screen of haze: an opaque sunrise that resembles/a diseased, inflamed eye'.[161]

The 'screen of haze' and 'opaque sunrise' suggest a wider ecological context for the 'derelict plant' and its 'mangy dogs' in the effects of anthropogenic climate change. The degraded condition of the landscape is closely associated with social disintegration. The only Sri Lankan character who features at any length is an unnamed 'abandoned' boy, aged 'six or possibly eight', depicted as an abject figure.[162] The boy 'somehow belongs to the fishery' and has 'been abused by other watchmen', neglect which is linked repeatedly to the degraded environment in which he lives.[163] He 'sleeps by day in some disused cooling compartment and at night among bearded pipes sticky with solidified engine oil', moving '[i]n and out of the dark gaps between refrigerators', while his continued survival is attributed to his having 'managed to float up to the surface of the swamp'.[164] The boy's 'belonging' to this environment portrays him as a secondary victim of the forces of neoliberal globalisation which have despoiled the Sri Lankan coast so dramatically. He is, in Bauman's terms, the 'human waste' of liquid modernity.[165]

Oz's stark description of both the child and the environment initially seems to represent a brave and self-implicating stance. He even seems prepared to countenance a comparison between present-day Israel and European colonialism that would usually be unpalatable. Rico chooses a postcard featuring the incongruous image of a British imperial officer stationed in Sri Lanka when it was the British colony of Ceylon, a choice that implies a direct line from resource extraction in the world's peripheries from the colonial era to the present.[166] This is a legacy in which, Oz suggests, Israel is implicated, as the other side of Israel's rapid economic growth and the luxury hotels, sea view apartments, banks and boutiques in Tel Aviv and Bat Yam.

The 'flowing' form of *The Same Sea*, which switches frequently between different geographical locations and narrative perspectives, is crucial to the novel's portrayal of the unevenness produced by the capitalist world-system. In this point I draw on the work of the Warwick Research Collective, who argue that literary registrations of combined and uneven development manifest this phenomenon through aesthetic techniques including implausible encounters, nonlinear structures and combinations of genres.[167] This style allows Oz to place descriptions of Israeli consumer culture directly next to accounts of environmental disasters in the world's peripheries, rendering visible the unseen connections between the two. For instance, the description of the changing Israeli urban scene from grocery shops to shopping malls is immediately followed with: 'In Bangladesh there has been more flooding: the monsoon has washed away bridges, villages and crops. Not here.'[168] In a novel which suggests in its title that the Indian Ocean and Mediterranean Sea are 'the same sea', Oz highlights the extent to which contemporary Israeli affluence is dependent on the production of underdevelopment elsewhere within the same world-system fuelled by circulating 'flows' of capital and commodities. This adds another dimension to Oz's description of the book as one that 'erases, deliberately, every boundary'.

Oz encourages Israeli readers to feel sympathy and outrage about conditions in the countries experiencing the negative side of their country's development, while his references to 'malls' and 'boutiques' may prompt guilt about their own consumer behaviour. Yet if Israel is complicit in the harms of neoliberal globalisation alongside countries of the world's core it is implicitly itself a stable nation, apparently no longer reliant on external support. Oz's expressions of Israeli guilt over conditions observed by Rico simultaneously serve as the kind of 'national affirmation' noted by Zakim, producing the country's 'normality' by aligning its problems with those of Europe and America. His invocation of historical colonialism in Sri Lanka in relation to industrialised fishing can be read in this sense as a self-exculpating strategy, eliding colonial dimensions of Israel's actions in the present on a shore much closer to home.

Returning Home

The Mediterranean on Israel's shores, like the Indian Ocean, is a space of fractures and frontiers as much as flows and a site of political and ecological violence. None of this is apparent in *The Same Sea*. For instance, Oz's externalisation of the negative effects of Israeli development ignores the fact that this has been premised on an active 'de-development' of the Palestinian economy, as previously noted. A major means through which this de-development has been enacted is Israel's denial of Palestinian access to the sea. Israel has devastated the Gazan fishing industry and the livelihoods of the people who rely on it through imposing restrictions on the distance Palestinians can travel from shore, which vary month by month and are policed by live Israeli fire.[169] Palestinian fishermen can only access the waters closest to shore, risking overfishing and the danger of catch being contaminated by Gaza's polluted waters. Over 100 million litres of sewage gushes daily into the Mediterranean from Gaza's overstretched and under-maintained infrastructure, while the sea has been a site for joint Israel-US tests of missiles now degrading on the ocean floor.[170] The Mediterranean has also been harmed by Israeli militarism in Israel's bombing of Lebanon's Jiyyeh power plant during the countries' 2006 conflict, which caused a massive oil spill in the Eastern Mediterranean that was worsened by continued bombing that prevented clean-up operations.[171] While Palestinians are prevented from leaving Gaza by sea, members of the international community are prevented from entering; notoriously so, in the case of the Mavi Marmara killings. A Mediterranean beach was the site of perhaps the most widely reported incident of the 2014 Gaza war, in which four children were killed by an Israeli air strike.[172] This is not a Mediterranean we would recognise from Oz's text.

The wider Mediterranean is, Serenella Iovino writes, 'a suffering and exploited sea'.[173] The dispersed, confetti-like plastic debris of its 'Garbage Patches' may not be as immediately visible as the industrial toxicity of Oz's Sri Lankan shoreline, but is deadly nonetheless, particularly for marine wildlife. As one of the world's busiest shipping routes, particularly for oil transportation, the Mediterranean is more like a congested highway than a site of the leisurely voyages described by Oz and Ohana, subject to frequent oil spills, both accidental and deliberate.[174] It also receives untreated sewage, heavy metals such as lead and mercury, and the persistent organic pollutants (POPs) produced in industrial manufacturing including the manufacture of pesticides.[175] Ironically, the Mediterranean's basin structure and extended water residence time, which in Oz and Ohana's works operates as the implicit oceanographical basis for imaginaries of regional connection and exchange, exacerbate the environmental harm caused by plastics and pollutants, turning the region into an accumulation zone in which harmful chemicals persist and increase in concentration over longer periods of time.

The role of the Mediterranean as a site of violence has been nowhere more apparent in recent years than in the ongoing refugee crisis, in which the sea has become witness to Europe's disregard for those seeking asylum on its shores. In many cases those making the journey across the sea are fleeing conflicts in which Europe is implicated; the most common nationality of land and sea arrivals in 2019 was Afghan.[176] While numbers of deaths have fallen since the height of the Mediterranean refugee crisis in 2015 and the story has fallen out of media focus, the International Organisation for Migration's Missing Migrants Project records 686 deaths in the Mediterranean in the first half of 2019, indicating that journeys continue on a mass scale.[177] These deaths, and the rigid European border policies that produce them, undercut the Israeli and European claims of cosmopolitanism and inclusivity which take Mediterranean coastlines as their basis. The Mediterranean is certainly a space which tells us about European and Israeli values, but perhaps not in the ways these countries would like it to.

Conclusion

Oz is often hailed locally and internationally as Israel's 'national novelist', meaning that *The Same Sea* is the novel through which Mediterraneanism achieved its greatest international visibility. Mediterraneanism is often presented as a peacemaking discourse which might facilitate dialogue between Israel and its neighbours on the grounds of ancient geographical and cultural connections. Oz's leftist reputation heightens the appeal of Mediterraneanism in this respect, while common metaphorical associations of water with connection and flow similarly make a turn to the sea seem like a turn away from the divisive politics associated with the land. In this chapter I have argued that, in contrast to its popular image, Mediterraneanism operates as a way of consolidating Israel's ownership of both the land and sea. It does so partly through claiming Israel's historic origins in the symbolic home of European civilisation, but also through presenting an image of Israel which is attractive and marketable in Europe and which encourages political, economic and military support based on cultural similarity. Mediterraneanism, despite apparently presenting an ethnically diverse and regionally integrated Israel, ultimately serves to shut out a different region, the Orient. Oz uses hydrological metaphors to self-consciously highlight the flipside to Israel's economic boom in underdevelopment elsewhere in the world. However, in doing so, he reaffirms Israel's belonging to Europe and the West and externalises the social and ecological consequences of Israeli policy in the Mediterranean region. In this chapter I have offered reason to be cautious about the emancipatory potential often attached to the sea, showing that representations of the sea can easily be incorporated into exclusionary nationalist discourses.

The previous two chapters focused on a period in which Israel seemed to be moving towards a 'post-Zionist' culture with prospects of peace on the horizon. Yet even in the immediate wake of the Oslo Accords, Israel continued to pursue its policies of closure and settlement expansion. Said's description of Oslo as a 'Palestinian capitulation' has since proven accurate.[178] While the Oslo era saw the emergence of an oceanic imaginary of regional connection, its effects on land can also be understood in liquid terms. As Eyal Weizman writes, Oslo transformed the Occupied Territories into an 'archipelago' of zones under different degrees of Israeli military control, with different degrees of citizenship existing 'adjacent to, within or over each other'.[179] The military has governed by 'modulating flows' of capital, commodities and vital resources – not least, water – between checkpoints and the Wall that have allowed Israel to dominate from a distance, as seen in the discussion of

Barghouti in Chapter 1.[180] In the following chapter I turn to this latest period, examining Israel's use of water and the destruction or incapacitation of water infrastructure as mechanisms of control in its wars on the West Bank and Gaza since 2002. In this chapter metaphors of flow and connection recur to express the relationship between the individual body and the national collective. Through a discussion of 'hydraulic citizenship' I show that in these contexts water becomes the dividing line between those who are included as subjects of Israeli moral consideration and those who are not.

Notes

1. Ben-Gurion, 'The Navy, Israel and the Sea', p. 312.
2. Hever, 'The Zionist Sea', p. 32.
3. See Puar, *Terrorist Assemblages*; Schulman, *Israel/Palestine and the Queer International*.
4. Oz, *The Same Sea*.
5. Nocke, *The Place of the Mediterranean*, p. 148; Ohana, *The Origins of Israeli Mythology*, p. 193. See also Ohana, *Israel and Its Mediterranean Identity*.
6. I take this phrase from Grumberg, *Place and Ideology*, p. 6.
7. Bernard, *Rhetorics of Belonging*, p. 96; Cleary, *Literature, Partition and the Nation-State*, p. 146.
8. Freedland, 'Cease Fire'.
9. Ohana, 'Foreword', p. xiii.
10. Cohen, 'Literary Studies on the Terraqueous Globe', p. 657.
11. I borrow this phrasing, used in a rather different context, from DeLoughrey, *Routes and Roots*.
12. Said, *Orientalism*, p. 49.
13. In doing so I draw on Warwick Research Collective (WReC).
14. For favourable perspectives on Mediterraneanism, see Nocke, *The Place of the Mediterranean*; Ohana, *The Origins of Israeli Mythology*; Ohana, *Israel and Its Mediterranean Identity*. For critical perspectives, see Hochberg, '"The Mediterranean Option"'; Del Sarto, 'Israel's Contested Identity and the Mediterranean'; Shavit, 'The Mediterranean World and "Mediterraneanism"'.
15. Mintz, *Translating Israel*, p. 137.
16. For example, Ohana, *The Origins of Israeli Mythology*, p. 224.
17. On the 'turn' to the sea in Literary Studies, see Bystrom and Hofmeyr, 'Oceanic Routes'; Yaeger, 'Theories and Methodologies'. In Geography, see Peters and Anderson, *Water Worlds*.

18. Blum, 'Introduction: Oceanic Studies', p. 152.
19. Price, 'Afterword: The Last Universal Commons', p. 45.
20. Blum, 'Introduction: Oceanic Studies', p. 152.
21. Wittenberg, 'Editorial: Coastlines and Littoral Zones in South African Ecocritical Writing', pp. 2–3, 5.
22. Gilroy, *The Black Atlantic*; Linebaugh and Rediker, *The Many-Headed Hydra*; Steinberg and Peters, 'Wet Ontologies, Fluid Spaces', p. 1; Steinberg, 'Of Other Seas', p. 158; Theresa Shewry, *Hope at Sea*.
23. Kosmatopoulos, 'On the Shores of Politics'.
24. DeLoughrey, 'Toward a Critical Ocean Studies for the Anthropocene', p. 22.
25. Chambers, *Mediterranean Crossings*, p. 68; Kausch and Youngs, 'The End of the "Euro-Mediterranean Vision"'.
26. Ohana, 'Foreword', p. xiii.
27. Ibid., p. xvi.
28. Ohana, *The Origins of Israeli Mythology*, p. 192.
29. On Israel's Arab Jews, see Shohat, 'The Invention of the Mizrahim'.
30. Nocke, *The Place of the Mediterranean*, pp. 54–5.
31. Ibid., p. 62.
32. Regev and Seroussi, *Popular Music and National Culture in Israel*, pp. 230–1.
33. Ibid., pp. 230–1. Hochberg notes that the Mediterranean idea has frequently been articulated in opposition to Mizrahiyut, as a way to go beyond its apparently unproductive 'identity politics'. Hochberg, '"The Mediterranean Option"', pp. 49–51.
34. Nocke, *The Place of the Mediterranean*, p. 26; Ohana, *Israel and Its Mediterraneam Identity*, pp. 5–6.
35. Braudel, *The Mediterranean and the Mediterranean World*.
36. Ohana, *The Origins of Israeli Mythology*, p. 225.
37. An alternative, related tradition sometimes invoked in discussions of Israeli Mediterraneanism is that of 'Levantinism', a positive reformulation of a previously stigmatised notion of the Levant primarily associated with the mid-century Egyptian-born Israeli author Jacqueline Kahanoff. On Kahanoff and Levantinism, see Hochberg, '"Permanent Immigration"'; Ohana, 'The Mediterranean Option in Israel'; Slyomovics, 'Who and What Is Native to Israel?'.
38. Chambers, *Mediterranean Crossings*, p. 33; Giaccaria and Minca, 'The Mediterranean Alternative', p. 350; Hochberg, '"The Mediterranean Option"', p. 43.
39. Herzfeld, 'The Horns of the Mediterraneanist Dilemma'.
40. Armstrong, 'Braudel's Mediterranean', p. 633; Said, *Orientalism*.

41. Armstrong, 'Braudel's Mediterranean', p. 633; Braudel, *The Mediterranean and the Mediterranean World*, p. 187.
42. Cited in Deverell and Flamming, 'Race, Rhetoric and Regional Identity', p. 118.
43. Davis, *Ecology of Fear*, pp. 11–12.
44. Hever, 'They Shall Dwell by the Haven of the Sea', p. 51.
45. Herbert, 'A View of the Sea', p. 191.
46. Shamir, *With His Own Hands*, p. 1; Nocke, *The Place of the Mediterranean*, p. 13.
47. Ohana, *The Origins of Israeli Mythology*, pp. 188–90; Hever, 'The Zionist Sea', p. 65.
48. Azaryahu, 'The Formation of the "Hebrew Sea"', p. 262.
49. Cited in Azaryahu, 'The Formation of the "Hebrew Sea"', p. 259.
50. Ben-Gurion, 'The Navy, Israel and the Sea', pp. 312, 310.
51. Ibid., pp. 312, 310.
52. Antreasyan, 'Gas Finds in the Eastern Mediterranean'.
53. Cited in Azaryahu, 'The Formation of the "Hebrew Sea"', p. 259.
54. Cited in Ohana, *The Origins of Israeli Mythology*, p. 186.
55. Ben-Gurion, 'The Navy, Israel and the Sea', p. 310.
56. Ibid., p. 313.
57. Nocke, *The Place of the Mediterranean*, pp. 147–8.
58. Jacobs, 'Amos Oz'.
59. Ibid.
60. Ibid.
61. Ibid.
62. Bernard, *Rhetorics of Belonging*, p. 91.
63. Laor, *The Myths of Liberal Zionism*, p. 73.
64. Laor, 'The Tears of Zion', p. 54.
65. Oz, 'The Meaning of Homeland', p. 91.
66. Ibid., p. 91.
67. Said, 'The Burdens of Interpretation and the Question of Palestine', p. 33.
68. On this stereotype, see Bernard, 'Another Black September?'. See also Shaheen, *Reel Bad Arabs*.
69. Cited in Laor, *The Myths of Liberal Zionism*, pp. 42–3.
70. Ibid., p. 43.
71. Ivry and Estrin, 'Amos Oz, 74 Years Old and a National Treasure'.
72. Ibid.
73. Oz, *In the Land of Israel*.
74. AFP, 'Beach Stroll by Modi'.

75. Nocke, *The Place of the Mediterranean*, pp. 145–8; Ohana, *The Origins of Israeli Mythology*, p. 193.
76. Oz, *The Same Sea*, p. 1.
77. Ibid., pp. 190, 97.
78. Oz, *The Same Sea*, p. 5.
79. Pappé, *The Ethnic Cleansing of Palestine*, ch. 10.
80. Ibid., p. 88.
81. Nocke, *The Place of the Mediterranean*, p. 149.
82. Ibid., p. 148.
83. Oz, *The Same Sea*, p. 3.
84. Ibid., p. 3.
85. Ibid., p. 3.
86. Ibid., p. 3.
87. Laor, 'It's Wild. It's New. It Turns Men On', p. 23.
88. Oz, *The Same Sea*, p. 3.
89. Ibid., p. 3.
90. Cohen and Noy, 'Introduction: Backpacking as a Rite of Passage in Israel', p. 23.
91. Ibid., pp. 3, 6.
92. Haviv, 'Next Year in Kathmandu', p. 46.
93. Bernard, *Rhetorics of Belonging*, p. 98.
94. Ibid., p. 99.
95. Tuan, *The Hydrologic Cycle and the Wisdom of God*.
96. Oz, *The Same Sea*, pp. 18, 130.
97. Ibid., p. 148.
98. Ibid., p. 72.
99. Ibid., pp. 111, 145.
100. Ibid., p. 143.
101. Ibid., p. 193.
102. Ibid., p. 73.
103. Farnsworth, 'Coping with Conflict'.
104. Ibid.
105. Oz, *The Same Sea*, p. 73.
106. Stein, *Itineraries in Conflict*, ch. 1.
107. On the stigmatisation of aridity, see Linton, *What Is Water?*, pp. 122–5; Tuan, *The Hydrologic Cycle and the Wisdom of God*, p. 144.
108. Cited in Cleary, *Literature, Partition and the Nation-State*, p. 244.

109. Nocke, *The Place of the Mediterranean*, p. 149.
110. Oz, *The Same Sea*, p. 5.
111. Ibid., p. 5.
112. Mann, *A Place in History*, p. 74.
113. LeVine, *Overthrowing Geography*, ch. 8.
114. Oz, *The Same Sea*, p. 5.
115. Hochberg, *In Spite of Partition*, p. 8
116. Ibid., p. 13.
117. Oz, *The Same Sea*, p. 176.
118. Laor, 'It's Wild. It's New. It Turns Men On', p. 23.
119. Oz, *The Same Sea*, p. 19.
120. Cohen, 'Territorial Stigma Formation in the Israeli City of Bat Yam', pp. 119–21.
121. Ibid., pp. 114, 118.
122. Ibid., p. 114. For a critical perspective on Tel Aviv's modernist and specifically Bauhaus architectural heritage, see Rotbard, *White City/Black City*.
123. I adapt this point from Laor, who mistakenly attributes the love of opera to Albert. Laor, 'It's Wild. It's New. It Turns Men On', p. 23.
124. Ohana, *Israel and Its Mediterranean Identity*, ch. 6; Ohana, 'Mediterranean Humanism'; Oz, *The Same Sea*, p. 19.
125. Bernard, *Rhetorics of Belonging*, p. 97.
126. On Israel and socialism, see footnote 64 in the Introduction.
127. Aruri, *Dishonest Broker*, p. 104.
128. Connery, 'Pacific Rim Discourse', p. 56.
129. Oz, *The Same Sea*, pp. 143, 69, 150.
130. Ben-Gurion, 'The Navy, Israel and the Sea', p. 311.
131. Oz, *The Same Sea*, p. 196.
132. Ibid., p. 196.
133. Ibid., p. 186.
134. Karlinsky, *California Dreaming*, p. 18.
135. Pappé, *A History of Modern Palestine*, p. 39.
136. Bardenstein, 'Threads of Memory and Discourses of Rootedness', p. 14.
137. Ibid. pp., 14–17; Egoz, 'The Pardess', p. 181. See also *Jaffa: The Orange's Clockwork*.
138. Egoz, 'The Pardess'.
139. Ibid., p. 175.
140. 'Tel Aviv Gets Bus Publicity Drive in UK'.

141. Oz, *The Same Sea*, p. 85.
142. Ibid., p. 131.
143. Ibid., p. 85.
144. Brouillette, *Postcolonial Writers in the Global Literary Marketplace*, p. 1.
145. Bauman, *Liquid Modernity*.
146. Ibid., pp. 13–14.
147. Ibid. , pp. 13–14.
148. Ibid., pp. 5, 128.
149. Oz, *The Same Sea*, p. 61.
150. Ibid., p. 186.
151. Cleary, *Literature, Partition and the Nation-State*, pp. 157–8.
152. Zakim, 'Palimpsests of National Identity', p. 49.
153. Oz, *The Same Sea*, pp. 153, 168. This may be a reference to Sri Lanka's Kirindi Oya, a river that terminates in the Bundala National Park. The Kirindi Oya is currently threatened by illegal sand mining.
154. Ibid., p. 153.
155. Dalla Costa and Chilese, *Our Mother Ocean*, p. 76.
156. Ibid., pp. 77–8.
157. Islam, *Confronting the Blue Revolution*, ch. 3.
158. Oz, *The Same Sea*, p. 186.
159. Bergquist, 'Sustainability and Local People's Participation in Coastal Aquaculture', p. 787.
160. Moore, 'Ecology, Capital, and the Nature of Our Times', p. 110.
161. Oz, *The Same Sea*, p. 169.
162. Ibid., p. 168.
163. Ibid., p. 168.
164. Ibid., p. 169.
165. Bauman, *Wasted Lives*.
166. Oz, *The Same Sea*, p. 174.
167. WReC, *Combined and Uneven Development*, p. 17.
168. Oz, *The Same Sea*, p. 186.
169. '2018: Plight of Gaza Fishermen'.
170. 'Seawater Pollution Raises Concerns of Waterborne Diseases and Environmental Hazards in the Gaza Strip'; Zitun, 'Israel Test Fires Target Missile in Mediterranean'.
171. Hmaidan, 'Sands Are Running out for Lebanon's Ecosystem'.
172. Beaumont, 'Israel Exonerates Itself over Gaza Beach Killings of Four Children Last Year'.

173. Iovino, 'Introduction: Mediterranean Ecocriticism', p. 13.
174. Ibid., pp. 31–2.
175. 'State of the Mediterranean Marine and Coastal Environment', pp. 44–8.
176. 'Mediterranean Situation'.
177. 'Missing Migrants Project'.
178. Said, 'The Morning After'.
179. Weizman, *Hollow Land*, p. 7.
180. Ibid., p. 11.

4

WATER WARS: INFRASTRUCTURES OF VIOLENCE IN SAYED KASHUA'S *LET IT BE MORNING*

Gaza's electricity, sewage and water plants are bombed to smithereens, where the West Bank is ever so tightly wound in the web of Israeli infrastructural administration. – Laleh Khalili[1]

The targeting of Palestinian water infrastructure is a major feature of Israel's periodic assaults on the West Bank and Gaza. From Operation Defensive Shield (2002), through Operation Summer Rains (2006), Operation Cast Lead (2008–9), Operation Pillar of Defence (2012), to Operation Protective Edge (2014), devastation to water infrastructure prolongs the impact of attacks on civilian populations and in Gaza is barely repaired before the next bombardment begins. The lack of clean water, combined with cramped living conditions for refugees sheltering in public buildings, heightens the risk of infectious disease in the immediate aftermath of warfare and has disastrous long-term effects on health and environment.[2] Infrastructural destruction is similarly devastating to the Palestinian economy.[3] The existence of this practice allows us to add a qualifier to discourse on 'water wars'. As Mark Zeitoun writes, '[w]hile water may rarely be the sole motive for war it is often a victim and target of it'.[4] As this chapter's epigraph, written in the wake of the 2014 Gaza War, indicates, Palestinians in the West Bank and Gaza experience water as a 'victim and target' of war in different ways with the same outcome of acute manufactured crisis. The Israeli authorities' obstruction of new infrastructure in the West Bank, systematic neglect of water infrastructure in the Palestinian neighbourhoods of East Jerusalem, threats to disconnect Palestinian communities in Israel and refusal to provide water infrastructure and other services to 'unrecognised' Bedouin villages can be seen as further aspects of this 'water war'.[5]

In this chapter I turn to Israeli Palestinian author Sayed Kashua's 2004 novel *Let It Be Morning* (*Vayehi Boker*) to bring to light the crucial connections between water infrastructure and citizenship that make its disconnection and destruction so potent as a form of warfare. I begin by outlining the longer history of Israeli infrastructural warfare within what Stephen Graham calls the 'new military urbanism' and examining the material and representational challenges involved in producing infrastructural hydrofictions. I then focus on Kashua's novel, published in Hebrew in 2004 and translated into English in 2006 by Miriam Shlesinger. *Let It Be Morning* depicts the fallout when the water supply of a Palestinian village in Israel is abruptly cut off by the Israeli military. Kashua's novel, I argue, shows the fundamental role played by water in producing the material and symbolic inclusion within a national collective captured by Nikhil Anand's concept of 'hydraulic citizenship'.[6] The identity of Kashua's protagonists as Palestinian citizens of Israel is crucial to the novel's capacity to illuminate these connections, as a population whose access to Israeli citizenship and its privileges has only ever been limited and conditional.

Kashua is a prominent figure in contemporary Israeli culture. He is known for his popular novels *Dancing Arabs* (*Aravim Rokdim*, 2002), *Let It Be Morning*, *Second Person Singular* (*Guf Sheni Yahid*, 2010) and *Track Changes* (*Akov Achar Shinuyim*, 2017), his hit television show, 'Arab Labor' (*Avoda Aravit*, 2007 – present), and his column for the Israeli newspaper *Haaretz*. He has won awards including Israel's Prime Minister's Prize in Literature and the Bernstein Prize. However, his future role in Israel is uncertain. In July 2014, in the days before the launch of Operation Protective Edge, Kashua announced in his column that he was leaving Jerusalem for the United States – where he remains – because he could no longer tolerate hostility towards Arabs in Israel.[7]

While Kashua is widely known in Israel, there is little scholarship on his work. This seems in part due to a scholarly reluctance to engage with popular literature; his writing is sometimes criticised for its plot-driven narratives and 'journalistic' style.[8] A more significant factor may be Kashua's identity and that of his protagonists as Palestinian citizens of Israel, a group also known as 'Israeli Palestinians' or, often more pejoratively, 'Israeli Arabs'.[9] Palestinian citizens of Israel fail to fit into the two supposedly ethnically and territorially exclusive groups imagined as the primary actors in the conflict. They are frequently mistrusted by both Israelis and Palestinians, viewed in Israel as a potential 'fifth column' and suspected by Palestinians of being traitors or collaborators.[10] This uncertain status makes it harder to place Kashua's work within the binary narratives that structure mainstream understandings of Israeli and Palestinian culture in an international Anglophone context.

Kashua is known for dealing with the paradoxes of Israeli Palestinian identity through dark humour and irony. *Let It Be Morning* has primarily been read as another iteration of this theme, exposing Israeli racism and the tragicomic attempts of Israeli Palestinians to 'pass' in a society which rejects anything viewed as 'Arab'.[11] The disconnection of water in *Let It Be Morning* is dealt with in passing, portrayed as one element among many in a constructed crisis scenario through which Kashua explores identity.[12] In this chapter I read Kashua's novel in relation to Israel's use of infrastructural warfare as a military strategy. Doing so shows that water is not an incidental, replaceable plot point but plays a central role in the novel, serving as the main cause of the deterioration of relations between villagers and the catalyst for their eventual realisation that they are genuinely under threat. *Let It Be Morning* illuminates a dimension of infrastructural warfare and experiences of water crisis in Israel/Palestine and beyond that is often neglected. While campaigning on water often emphasises its capacity to unite across difference through a shared biological human need, 'water crises', as Farhana Sultana and Alex Loftus note, 'can exacerbate socially constructed differences and power relations'.[13] Kashua's representations of water crisis and Israel's racial politics are deeply entangled, with his portrayal of a community on the margins bringing the country's demographic anxieties starkly to light.

Infrastructural Warfare

I begin with an account of the term 'infrastructure'. As Patricia Yaeger writes, 'infrastructure' encompasses a wide range of 'equipment, facilities, services, and supporting structures needed for a city's or region's functioning', including such places and networks as '[a]irports; communications systems; computer grids; highways; gas, electric, and water systems; mass transit; public toilets; sewers; streets; waste management'.[14] 'Infrastructure' incorporates the vast, varied and often out of sight networks that sustain places of inhabitation, particularly cities, in which use and management of infrastructure is most intense.[15] However, infrastructures are not merely physical structures. They are socio-political assemblages, produced by and productive of social, political and legal norms that shape urban life and influenced by the more-than-human in ways that exceed human intention.[16]

This intrusion of the more-than-human can be seen in the interdependence of infrastructures. Almost all infrastructure depends on electricity. For instance, electricity is crucial to the supply of fresh water to homes and removal of 'grey water' (water from sinks, showers and washing machines) and sewage, providing the pressure to pump water through the system, up hills and tower blocks. Many homes in the West Bank and Gaza have water storage tanks on their roofs because of the unreliable supply, and Palestinian and settler homes in the West Bank are easily distinguished by the presence of Palestinians' rooftop tanks in contrast to the neat, European-style red-tile roofs of settlements. Infrastructural interconnection creates the conditions for failures or attacks to 'cascade' through the system via the 'distributive agency' of nonhuman actants, causing unpredictable and, in the case of Palestine, long-term effects.[17]

Stephen Graham describes infrastructural warfare as part of the strategy of 'urbicide', or 'political violence intentionally designed to erase or "kill" cities'.[18] One of the key features of urbicide is 'the systematic devastation of the means of living a modern urban life', which, crucially, means infrastructure.[19] This became increasingly significant in Israel/Palestine after the Second (or Al-Aqsa) Intifada as Israeli military strategy shifted to urban space as the domain of conflict. As Eyal Weizman writes, 'Operation Defensive Shield' in 2002 transformed the West Bank into 'a giant laboratory of urban warfare at the expense of hundreds of civilian lives, property, and infrastructure' under the direction of then Prime Minister Ariel Sharon, the key architect of Israel's strategies of urban warfare.[20] This shift is part of the wider phenomenon Graham identifies as the 'new military urbanism', in which state militaries since the Cold War have increasingly focused on urban space and exchanged technological and strategic expertise for fighting a perceived shift to urban insurgency.[21]

The destruction of infrastructure in warfare is not new. The Second World War saw strategic bombing of cities and civilian infrastructure. In the first and second Gulf Wars the United States sought to 'switch cities off' as a supposedly 'humanitarian' form of war, framed as putting pressure on leaders, destroying morale and reducing casualties.[22] The incapacitation of Iraq's electricity infrastructure in the first Gulf War in fact caused at least thirty times more deaths than the actual fighting, showing that 'humanitarian' destruction of infrastructure operates as a form of public relations management.[23] The term 'urbicide' also has a longer history. It first rose to prominence in the Bosnian War of 1992–5 after its use by a group of Mostar architects to describe the intentional targeting of Bosnia's built environment by Serbian and Croatian forces. Around the same time, Marshall Berman used the term independently in connection with the redevelopment of his home town of New York City. Berman extended the term to encompass what he argued was a general fear and phenomenon of urban destruction throughout human history, indicating, again, the longer history of this strategy.[24]

Just as urbicide is not a new phenomenon on the world stage, it has a longer Israeli history. The 1948 war involved the destruction of Palestinian urban centres and villages to force their inhabitants to leave and prevent them from returning.[25] As such, the devastation of the Palestinian built environment in the cycle of intensive bombardments to which Israel has subjected Palestinians with an almost predictable regularity since Operation Defensive Shield can be understood as an 'intensification of an old policy'.[26] Contemporary Israeli urbicide takes place in a significantly altered context, however, in which the aim of offensives is not so much to gain territory as to control populations. It is also worth noting that in Israel/Palestine, as elsewhere, infrastructural warfare is not limited to state actors. Israeli cities have been a target of Palestinian attacks, notably in a series of suicide bombings on Israel's public transport in the early 2000s. The first Fatah attack in 1965, meanwhile, targeted Israel's National Water Carrier, completed just a year before, echoing attacks against infrastructure in early 1960s apartheid South Africa.[27] Water takes on a significant material and symbolic role in the context of the destruction of infrastructure, fundamental as it is to urban life. As Swyngedouw writes, 'controlling the flow of water implies controlling the city, as without the uninterrupted flowing of water, the city's metabolism would come to a halt'.[28] The removal of water threatens chaos and, potentially, catastrophe.

Military attacks on objects necessary for the survival of civilian populations are prohibited in international humanitarian law, including Article 57 of the Geneva Convention.[29] However, intention to destroy civilian infrastructure is difficult to prove. The integration of infrastructure within the urban fabric means that it is often impossible to establish whether damage was caused by deliberate or 'merely' indiscriminate violence.[30] Besides, as Weizman notes, 'in Gaza ruins are piled on ruins, and it isn't easy to tell them apart'.[31] Matters of intention have taken on a heightened importance in Israel since the publication of the Goldstone Report in 2009, which, until it was retracted in 2011 by Judge Richard Goldstone, alleged that both Israel and Hamas had committed war crimes during Operation Cast Lead with Israel deliberately targeting Palestinian water infrastructure.[32] Yet the scale of the destruction is difficult to dispute. As Jan Selby wrote of Operation Defensive Shield in 2002:

> As with every other area of Palestinian life, water supply services were gravely affected. Pipes were ruptured by tanks and trenches, water spilling down the streets; pumping stations and wells ran out of diesel fuel or lost their electricity supplies; roof-top water tanks were deliberately shot at by Israeli troops; and under curfew, local engineers were often unable or too frightened to undertake necessary repairs. In Nablus, around 30,000 people went without piped water for 11 days in a row. In Ramallah, at least 25,000 people lost their supplies for several days. In Jenin, amidst the piles of corpses and bulldozed sewerage pipes, children screamed for water and drank sewage. Oxfam estimated that, as of 4 April, 400,000 people in Ramallah, Nablus, Qalqilya, Bethlehem and Tulkarm were without access to running water.[33]

Operation Cast Lead (2008–9) had a similarly devastating impact on Palestinian water infrastructure, particularly in Gaza. Over 30 km of water networks were damaged or destroyed, along with 11 wells, 6,000 rooftop tanks and 840 household water connections, causing 10,000 people to be without access to the water network for eight months after the attacks.[34]

During Operation Protective Edge (2014), damage to water and sanitation facilities was extensive and technicians were killed while undertaking repairs.[35] Almost a year later, in April 2015, 120,000 people in Gaza remained dependent on water tankers and the per capita water consumption was less than half of the 100 litres per day recommended by the World Health Organization.[36] In these cases the muddled line between deliberate and 'indiscriminate' violence serves a useful purpose as part of the strategy of abusing international humanitarian law known as 'lawfare'.[37]

Infrastructural violence in the West Bank typically takes a less visible form. Water shortages are engineered in the West Bank using legal and bureaucratic mechanisms deriving from the 1995 Oslo II Interim Agreement. Framed as a means to increase Palestinian autonomy and facilitate cooperation, the Agreement was ultimately an exercise in 'dressing up domination as co-operation', serving to divest Israel of the responsibilities and burdens of occupation while allowing it to maintain control over pricing and supply.[38] The Joint Water Committee, created to encourage cooperative management, operates as an instrument for extending Israel's 'facts on the ground' by providing a veto over improvements to the Palestinian network unless these offer permission to construct new settlement infrastructure.[39] Water installations built without a committee permit are likely to be destroyed, including infrastructure built by international donors and NGOs.[40] These practices indicate the role of targeting water infrastructure in Israeli warfare and Israel's 'occupation regime'.[41]

The targeting of infrastructure is a form of what Rob Nixon calls 'slow violence'. In contrast to the immediate and hyper-visible display of military assault, slow violence is 'neither spectacular nor instantaneous, but rather incremental and accretive', making its effects felt at a range of temporal scales.[42] The death and suffering caused by infrastructural disconnection and destruction largely takes place after the event and out of sight.[43] One of the 'slow' consequences of the destruction of water infrastructure is an increased frequency of water-associated disease – disease caused by inadequate sanitation or water-borne pathogens – including hepatitis A, typhoid and acute diarrhoea. The World Health Organization cites inadequate water supply and access as a factor in over a quarter of reported disease in Gaza and the primary cause of death in Gazan children.[44] The slowest form of violence caused by these periodic assaults may yet be the contamination of Gaza's aquifer by sewage, toxic rubble, and the remnants of chemical weapons Israel is alleged to have used during attacks.[45] The destruction of water infrastructure, in short, causes maximum damage with a minimum of the visibility that might lead to prosecutions under international humanitarian law.

The 'slow' consequences of damage to water infrastructure are not just its environmental and health impacts, but its implications for Palestinian governance and statehood. Water is often understood as the circulating 'lifeblood' which sustains urban life. As Matthew Gandy writes, 'the history of cities can be read as a history of water'.[46] The destruction of water infrastructure thus represents the destruction of the urban foundations of any future Palestinian state and an attempt to undermine the legitimacy and authority of Palestine's ruling parties through diminishing their ability to provide for a people.[47] Infrastructural warfare keeps Palestinians in a state of responding to emergency rather than able to plan for the long term. As such, this practice forms part of the process of 'politicide' identified by Baruch Kimmerling in his 2003 account of the legacy of Sharon.[48] 'Politicide' is 'a wide range of social, political, and military activities whose goal is to destroy the political and national existence of a whole community of people and thus deny it the possibility of self-determination.'[49] By incapacitating water infrastructure, this type of warfare incapacitates a symbol of potential Palestinian statehood: the city, the locus of a country's cultural, economic and political life.

Infrastructural Warfare in Palestinian Literature

In spite of its prominence as a military tactic, infrastructural warfare is typically in the margins of Palestinian writing. For instance, in her 2011 novel *Out Of It*, British Palestinian author Selma Dabbagh refers to the 'mile-long walks for water' endured by some Gazans, if not the novel's middle-class protagonists.[50] Even their supply runs short, however, and is 'too intermittent to be shared'.[51] They supplement this with bottled water, causing household litter with its own ecological impacts: 'a battalion of water bottles that spread out across the kitchen floor'.[52] The military metaphor of 'battalion' hints at the origin of water shortages, to which Dabbagh refers directly in describing the messy aftermath of a hit on an overground water pipe. She writes: 'A water pipe next to the road had been hit and there was water everywhere in the streets, a brown rush of it sloping around the potholes'.[53] Allusions to damaged water infrastructure also occur in Nour Al-Sousi's short story 'Canary', in Refaat Alareer's 2013 edited collection *Gaza Writes Back*.[54] Its events are triggered by the shooting of a young boy while he and his brother return home to a Gazan refugee camp from fetching water delivered by an United Nations Relief and Works Agency (UNRWA) truck.[55] Often, we are told, '[t]he camp did not have fresh water for days' and the boys face a lengthy queue, waiting 'for an hour or so' before they 'stagger' home with their heavy loads.[56] The story shows the adult responsibilities that children in Gaza are forced to take on to provide the basic material means of survival for themselves and their families. Here this necessity has tragic consequences.

In Dabbagh's and Al-Sousi's texts water shortages appear in passing within a broader picture of Gazan life in the face of Israeli warfare and the blockade, yet are not a narrative focus. In one way this is typical of water in literature, which is rarely the focus of attention, yet its absence is surprising since we might expect water to come to the fore in contexts of crisis. It would be misguided, of course, to expect Palestinian literature to merely catalogue each aspect of life under occupation, operating as a medium for transmitting 'cultural information' to supplement news broadcasts.[57] However, water is not just an aspect of Palestinian life: it is a matter of life and death. Shortages of water are readily noticed and restrict and reshape day-to-day activities in major ways. The destruction of water infrastructure is an issue of national significance and water rights are a prominent feature of Palestinian national demands. Palestinian literature has tended to self-consciously examine issues of national significance, whether in attempts to build a Palestinian community in the absence of a shared national home, or to inform an international readership often ignorant of the Palestinian situation.[58] This tendency is amplified in literature in translation, produced for an audience who view Palestine through the prism of the conflict with Israel. As such, the expectation that infrastructural warfare might feature more prominently as a literary theme does not seem unfounded.

Material conditions may offer some answers. We might expect Gazan literature to be especially likely to feature this topic given the intensity and frequency of Israel's devastation of its water infrastructure. However, publishing in Gaza is subject to acute material constraints. Books and paper for printing are restricted from entering Gaza under Israel's blockade, while writing fiction on a computer may not seem the best use of electricity that arrives for just a few hours a day.[59] Unstable material conditions are also not conducive to sustained creative work. Discussing restrictions on the production of Palestinian literature more generally, Anna Bernard cites Edward Said, commenting after the 1982 Lebanon War on the paucity of Palestinian literature. Said writes:

> I recall during the siege of Beirut obsessively telling friends and family there, over the phone, that they ought to record, write down their experiences . . . Naturally, they were all far too busy surviving . . . The archive speaks of the depressed conditions of the Palestinian narrative at present.[60]

While the situation of Palestinian literature has since improved, Said's observation remains relevant.[61] Living under what Arabic literature blogger M. Lynx Qualey describes as a 'thousand and one upheavals', it is no coincidence that Gazan writing is overwhelmingly dominated by the short story form.[62]

It is worth noting that the relatively recent appearance of infrastructural warfare in its current systemic and intensified form may mean that it takes longer for works dealing with this topic to emerge. It is useful here to turn to Anthony Carrigan's insights into temporality and narrative form in the context of postcolonial disaster studies. While Palestine's water crisis is not a disaster in the traditional sense of a 'natural' event that 'ruptures' or 'inverts' everyday life, it nonetheless bears comparison with events such as Hurricane Katrina or the 2010 Haiti earthquake in the sense that its frequent framing as a 'natural disaster' disguises the social origins of the subsequent catastrophe.[63] Disasters, as Carrigan notes, drawing on Haitian author Dany Laferrière, tend to be followed by 'different waves of representation'.[64] Forms such as testimony, memoir, poetry and painting typically emerge first, with longer forms like films and novels following later.[65] The 'slow' nature of the novel, in terms of reading, writing and, we should add, publication, leads Carrigan to conclude that '[o]ften the best disaster novels are not produced until at least a generation after a catastrophic event'.[66] As such, we might say that the 'slow' violence of infrastructural warfare obstructs the necessarily 'slow' work of literary representation. Still, with Carrigan's timetable in mind we might expect to see more Palestinian representations of infrastructure in future, following

Atef Abu Saif's *The Drone Eats with Me* (2015), which includes references to the difficulty of accessing water in the 2014 war.[67]

A final reason for the absence of infrastructural warfare from Palestinian literature in English is how difficult this damage, and particularly its scale, is to represent. While water is constantly visible in everyday practices, its infrastructure is mostly unseen, part of vast networks of urban infrastructures that are, as Maria Kaika and Erik Swyngedouw write, 'largely hidden, opaque, invisible, disappearing underground, locked into pipes, cables, conduits, tubes, passages, and electronic waves'.[68] In the UK we have little sense of the considerable labour and technologies involved in rendering water drinkable and delivering it to our taps. It is true that water infrastructure in the West Bank and Gaza is much more visible than in the European and American contexts discussed by Kaika and Swyngedouw. Cyclical bombardments and systemic underinvestment have led to the reliance on improvised arrangements including water delivery trucks, rooftop tanks and overground water pipes, like that destroyed in Dabbagh's novel.[69] Yet much infrastructure in the West Bank and Gaza still remains out of sight, meaning that when destroyed it is not available as what Weizman calls a 'visible ruin' which might be capable of communicating 'the facts of domination and violence' to observers elsewhere.[70] This problem is amplified in the case of infrastructure not built because of denied permits, or which exists but is overstretched, or works only irregularly.

The 'visible ruins' that circulate most widely in the aftermath of Israeli attacks are images of destroyed Palestinian houses, which possess a greater affective force than images of destroyed infrastructure.[71] The house has a particular meaning in Palestinian culture, making its ruination carry an additional symbolism and affective power. As Said writes: 'Each Palestinian structure presents itself as a potential ruin. The theme of the formerly proud family house (village, city, camp) now wrecked, left behind, or owned by someone else, turns up everywhere in our literature and cultural heritage.'[72] The image of the ruined house, then, confirms exile and displacement as characteristic components of Palestinian identity, providing an emotive reminder for Palestinians and international readers of the impossibility for Palestinians of returning home. By contrast, underground pipes torn up by a D9 bulldozer, or domestic pipes, rooftop tanks and reservoirs destroyed by aerial shelling, are 'invisible ruins'. Their disappearance is contained only implicitly in the image of the devastated house or street, even while they are equally, if not more essential to Palestinian life. The closest news articles and NGO reports get to depicting damage to Palestinian water infrastructure is the familiar, clichéd image of a child turning on an empty tap, or clutching fizzy drinks bottles refilled with water from an UNRWA truck.[73]

One rare and novel representation of the effects of infrastructural warfare on water access came, surprisingly, out of the 'Ice Bucket Challenge' in August 2014 during Operation Protective Edge. Participants were nominated by friends on social media to film themselves tipping a bucket of freezing water over their heads, then share their video online and nominate others. The 'challenge' had the purported aim of raising loosely defined 'awareness' of amyotrophic lateral sclerosis (ALS), known in the UK as motor neurone disease, and fundraising for research. The meme was adapted into a 'Rubble Bucket Challenge' by Jordanian comedian Mohamed Darwaza and launched by Gazan student Maysam Yusef before being popularised in a YouTube video by Gazan journalist Ayman al-Aloul. The most famous participant was Mohammed Assaf, a Palestinian pop singer and 2013 winner of *Arab Idol*. Al-Aloul comments: 'We looked for a bucket of water, however the use of water is more important than to empty over our heads. And even if the water is available it is difficult to freeze it.' The Gazan adaptation offered a bitterly ironic yet upbeat visual juxtaposition of Palestinian water and electricity shortages with the immense 'infrastructural privilege' of the millions of Western social media users drawn into the summer's craze of wasting water in the name of charity.[74]

Infrastructures of Citizenship: Sayed Kashua's *Let It Be Morning* (2007)

Sayed Kashua's *Let It Be Morning* is a rare example of a Palestinian text with water infrastructure as the narrative focus. The protagonist and narrator is an unnamed Israeli Palestinian journalist who works for an unnamed Hebrew-language newspaper in Jerusalem, where he has lived for ten years.[75] The novel begins with the journalist moving back to his home town, a similarly unnamed Israeli Palestinian village, with his unnamed wife and baby daughter.[76] The lack of names reflects Kashua's preference, as Gil Z. Hochberg notes, for engaging with two collectives – 'Arabs' and 'Jews' – in order to emphasise the absurdly 'prescribed reality' of stereotyped identities which his characters are forced to inhabit.⁷⁷ While the narrator dislikes his home town for what he sees as its traditionalism and small-mindedness, he says that he returned because of increasing hostility towards Arabs in Israel. He states that 'it had become uncomfortable just to walk down the street' and that racist graffiti, declaring 'ARABS OUT = PEACE AND SECURITY', had appeared on his apartment building.⁷⁸ As with many of Kashua's novels, *Let It Be Morning* contains autobiographical elements, including the narrator's occupation and position between Israeli Palestinian and Israeli Jewish worlds. Regular readers of Kashua's work tend to take the novel's setting as Kashua's home town of Tira, once a village but now an Arab city in the Triangle region of Israel, in which his novels *Dancing Arabs* and *Second Person Singular* are explicitly set. The narrator's retreat from Jerusalem, meanwhile, darkly foreshadows Kashua's own later departure.

The village turns out not to be the safe haven the narrator was expecting. Not long after his return it is unexpectedly encircled by IDF tanks.⁷⁹ No one is allowed to enter or leave, and electricity and water supplies are cut off, along with communication with the outside world.⁸⁰ A Hebrew reader familiar with Kashua's work would have a heightened sense of the magnitude of this undertaking, knowing that Tira is a city of 25,000 people (I use 'village' to reflect Kashua's use of כפר ערבי, '*kfar Arab*', or Arab village, a term which also reflects the characters' provincial mentalities).⁸¹ Still, as loyal citizens of Israel the villagers are unable to contemplate the fact that the siege might be anything other than a mistake by the Israeli authorities.⁸² After an unspecified period – not long enough for villagers to have died of thirst or hunger, but long enough for shortages to have led to chaos and violence – a 'historic peace treaty' is signed and the siege lifted.⁸³ As the consequences of the treaty gradually dawn on the villagers they respond with disbelief.⁸⁴ The treaty will involve a transfer of territory and populations which anticipated hard-right former defence minister Avigdor Lieberman's 2004 'peace plan', which Lieberman continues to promote. Israel's larger settlements will be 'permanently annexed to the State of Israel', Jerusalem will be divided, the Old City put under UN control and the predominantly Israeli Palestinian areas of Wadi Ara and the Triangle, including the village, transferred to the Palestinian Authority.⁸⁵ 'I think we're Palestinian now', the shocked narrator tells his wife.⁸⁶

The impact of the roadblock is felt mainly through the loss of domestic water supplies. The absence of water in the home highlights the countless routine practices that rely on its availability and points towards the force of infrastructural warfare in bringing war into 'the sphere of the everyday, the private realm of the house'.[87] This disruption of water supplies occurs after the village's electricity is cut off. As the narrator recalls, the villagers are told that 'the water pumps had stopped functioning when the power was cut, and that there was unlikely to be any water in the pipes by tomorrow morning'.[88] This domino effect shows the potential vulnerability brought about by the overlapping and mutually dependent nature of modern urban infrastructures and the rapid and cumulative demodernisation which infrastructural warfare can – indeed is designed – to produce. Power cuts are in fact a common way in which water shortages are indirectly engineered in the West Bank and Gaza, particularly in Gaza, where Israel's attacks on the territory's only power plant in 2006 marked the start of an ongoing electricity crisis exacerbated by tensions between Hamas and the Palestinian Authority.[89] In June 2019 Gazans received electricity for an average of ten hours a day, an average that fluctuates wildly and had dropped to as little as four hours a day the previous year.[90] These acute power shortages mean that Gazans typically receive piped water for only short periods of the day, every few days. This is a state of affairs which Kashua's novel implicitly evokes, transposed to the different context of a community who are, supposedly, citizens of the State of Israel. I unpack the implications of this allusion in greater detail below.

In *Let It Be Morning* villagers are left dependent on the limited water in their rooftop tanks, which the narrator tells his family 'is for drinking only' rather than washing, cleaning, or its many other domestic uses.[91] He institutes careful changes to his daily personal routines, which he suddenly realises are water-intensive, stating: 'I'm sweating and I feel sticky. For a moment I consider getting in the bath, but I decide to wait. Mustn't waste water now. When I urinate, I don't even flush the toilet.'[92]

Later, as the house sewage system starts to fail, the narrator instructs his family to avoid using the toilet altogether: 'all peeing will be done in the yard'.[93] When the tank supply runs out, the family relies on bottled water and 'fruit juice and carbonated drinks' which the narrator stockpiled before other villagers realised a crisis was underway.[94] The narrator eventually decides that the water should be reserved for the children and that adults should consume the other remaining drinks.[95] Lack of water prompts wider changes to family routines beyond drinking and washing, restricting modes of food preparation and foods available to eat. 'No more cooking with water', the narrator rules, '[a]nd let's not even think of tea or coffee'.[96] The rice and flour gathered by the narrator before the crisis become useless without water and the family's usable food supplies dwindle.[97] Even with shrinking food supplies the narrator insists that '[f]ood is less of a problem than water'.[98] He says: 'I try not to think about water, because it only makes me thirstier.'[99] Thinking about water would force the narrator to recognise the threat posed by the siege: without water, a human body can survive for less than a week.

The starkness of the water crisis which ultimately emerges is heightened by the contrast with the high levels of water use in the early stages of the roadblock when its implications for water supply are not yet apparent. Kashua describes the narrator's wife's unchanged morning routines on the second day – using the toilet, brushing her teeth and making tea – all of which require water.[100] She pours away old water from the kettle because '[s]he doesn't like using water left in the kettle from yesterday'.[101] In doing so, the narrator's wife shows the extent to which she takes water for granted. Even when the family becomes aware of the shortage, they are slow to adapt. The narrator's father rejects a glass of water fetched by his wife for not being cold enough and 'spills it out' onto the floor, suggesting a routine wastefulness (and patriarchal manner) that is difficult to shake.[102] The narrator's mother continues to make tea, having to be reminded by the narrator: 'please, go easy on the tea, and for heaven's sake don't start cleaning the house like our idiot neighbours'.[103] The forced alteration of the family's practices and their difficulties in adapting mark a major shift in how water is imagined in the novel. It changes from 'something self-evident, an apparent triviality, located simply at the mouth of the tap', in Swyngedouw and Kaika's words, to a substance which can no longer be taken for granted.[104] Instead of magically appearing from the tap, water is always mentioned in relation to the container in which it is held – the tank, or plastic bottles. The irregular water supplies disrupt the 'comfort and security, both material and symbolic', which, Roger Silverstone notes, bodies require.[105] These, he notes, are usually sought 'in the repetitiveness of the everyday, its very familiarity and predictability'.[106] The removal of the possibility for comfortable repetition represents both bodily and psychological disruption for Kashua's villagers.

This disruption of water supplies represents something greater than a disturbance in the ability of villagers to wash, cook or quench their thirst. It undermines what Nikhil Anand would call their 'hydraulic citzenship', or 'substantive membership in the city's [or country's] water distribution regime'.[107] Water infrastructure provides a material and symbolic connection between individual bodies and the national body politic, serving, as Bakker notes, as a key 'emblem of inclusionary citizenship'.[108] This symbolic significance helps to explain the controversy and mass resistance generated by government proposals for water privatisation and taxation, from Bolivia's 'water war' in 2000 to recent protests in Ireland. The association between water access and national inclusion is typically traced to movements for the production of 'sanitary cities' in nineteenth-century Europe.[109] The extension of water infrastructure was seen as one of the hallmarks of modernity, with new projects demonstrating technological capability and serving as monumental concretisations of hopes for future social 'progress' and emancipation.[110] Infrastructural projects were viewed as testaments to the power of 'man' to 'conquer' and 'civilise' unruly nature, and to use it to serve the relatively new idea of the 'public good'.[111] This process is mirrored in the mega-hydraulic projects undertaken in postcolonial states after independence, seeking to prove their status on a world stage.[112] In Europe at this time even banal infrastructural sites such as pumping stations were often highly visible and elaborately decorated, celebrating their social significance.[113] The frequent appearance of Marianne, icon of the French Republic, on top of fountains built after the French Revolution underscores the link between water access and egalitarian ideals of citizenship.[114]

Water infrastructure does not just provide for a country's citizens: it produces them. The extension and administration of water infrastructure forms part of what Foucault called 'governmentality', or techniques of government intended 'to shape conduct in certain ways in relation to certain objectives', otherwise summarised as 'the conduct of conduct'.[115] This is closely related to Foucault's concepts of 'biopolitics' and 'biopower', in which power is conceived as the management of the life of a population rather than the capacity to deprive a population of goods, services or life.[116] In nineteenth-century

Europe the construction of water infrastructure combined with new cultural codes of bodily conduct and self-discipline to (paradoxically) produce the ideal free, liberal subject capable of transcending base, animal instincts and exercising the virtue of self-government.[117] The material nature of infrastructure, meanwhile, disguises its biopolitical character as a 'technology of rule'.[118] In this way, as Patrick Joyce notes, 'the hygienisation of the city was accompanied by processes making for the individuation of the self' that produced the liberal citizen.[119]

If water infrastructure makes citizens, they can just as easily be unmade. In this sense hydraulic citizenship always contains the possibility of its undoing. In *Let It Be Morning* the sudden exclusion of the village from Israel's water network materially enacts the villagers' exclusion from the privileges and guarantees of Israeli citizenship. Crucially, their status is downgraded so swiftly because their inclusion within Israel's national collective had only ever been limited and provisional, even if the villagers refuse to admit it. Israeli Palestinians exist in a difficult position, fully accepted neither by Israeli nor Palestinian society. Descending from around 160,000 Palestinians who remained within the territory that became Israel in 1948, Israel's Palestinian citizens constitute 20.8 per cent of the country's population. Many were internally displaced and classified by the Israeli state as 'present absentees', a paradoxical category that allowed Israel to claim ownership of their land and property (Mahmoud Darwish is a famous example).

Palestinians in Israel are ostensibly Israeli citizens. However, until 1966 they were subject to military rule and since then have often been treated as a potential threat, in part because they provoke Israeli anxieties over the Jewish future of the state. Israeli Palestinian communities have high rates of poverty, unemployment and domestic violence, while the areas they live in – predominantly Wadi Ara and the Triangle – have suffered from systematic neglect and underinvestment. The divisions between Israeli Palestinian and Jewish Israeli society intensified during the Second Intifada, when Israeli Palestinian communities staged widespread solidarity demonstrations in villages of northern Israel. In what has become known as the 'October 2000 events', these protests were violently suppressed by the Israeli police with tear gas, rubber-coated steel bullets and live fire, killing thirteen demonstrators and injuring many more. In spite of an investigation by the Or Commission, no officers were charged and the Police Internal Affairs Bureau claimed to have found no evidence of criminal conduct.[120] These events brought the persistent exclusion of Israeli Palestinians from Israeli society sharply into view.

The October 2000 events were recent news when Kashua was writing *Let It Be Morning*. They appear in the opening of the novel, when Kashua's narrator states that reporting on the shootings marked an irrevocable shift in his sense of his position in Israeli society. He recalls:

> Like me, the demonstrators had always thought of themselves as citizens of Israel, and never imagined they would be shot at for demonstrating or for blocking an intersection . . . Two days of demonstrations had been enough for the state to delegitimise its Arab population, to repudiate their citizenship.[121]

As Hochberg notes, it is no accident that Kashua chose to begin the novel with a reminder of October 2000.[122] These events presented a stark example of the key concern that animates Kashua's novel, 'the fictive transformation of Israeli Arabs "back into" Palestinians'.[123] Hochberg misses, however, the fundamental role of the village's disconnection from their water supply in this transformation.

Kashua's novel tracks the villagers' gradual loss of their Israeli citizenship, culminating in the loss of water as its ultimate expression. Early on, the narrator believes that his phone not working is due to a 'technical problem' and comments that this 'happens all over the country', emphasising the village's inclusion within Israel.[124] This belief is widespread, apparent in the villagers' reluctance to use words like 'curfew' or 'closure' that would link events to Israeli practices in the West Bank and Gaza, preferring to talk about a 'roadblock'.[125] As the narrator realises before other villagers that something else is happening, he articulates his suspicions in terms of a breakdown in the 'rules' of citizenship, stating: 'they don't see the events as a blatant breach of normal relations between citizens and their country'.[126] Finally, as sewage streams around the village, there is no piped water and people 'continue behaving normally' the narrator becomes more explicit, even scornful, declaring: 'I can't help feeling unspeakably sorry for them when I see how much they believe in their citizenship.'[127] As in much of Kashua's work there is irony here, given that the narrator believed in his citizenship until recently. Both his heightened awareness of Israeli racism and his sense of superiority to other villagers derive from his having lived in Jerusalem and worked with Israelis. At the same time as the narrator's comments demonstrate the revocation of the villagers' Israeli citizenship, they simultaneously make an implicit case for his own. His desire for inclusion persists even when shown to be impossible.

Kashua's representation of the removal of water illustrates the extent to which citizenship is never a given, but is produced through continual acts by state and citizen.[128] In this context, washing, cooking or watering plants become what Michael Rubenstein, drawing on Benedict Anderson, describes as 'repetitive moments of communion with the state'.[129] This allows us to recognise the full significance of the narrator's remark that '[p]eople barely have enough to drink. Every trace of a normal modern life has disappeared'.[130] When these practices of 'normal modern life' are disrupted in Kashua's novel, they turn from ritualised everyday performances of hydraulic citizenship into an embodied encounter with the village's rejection from the Israeli national collective. In the West Bank and Gaza, similarly, efforts to use water can become encounters with Israeli biopower and the incapacitated Palestinian governments at the most personal level. As Strang points out, many practices involved in using water are connected to intimate bodily processes including 'ingestion and expulsion, contact and immersion'.[131] A lack of water, felt through embodied uncleanliness and thirst, becomes one of the most intrusive ways in which, as Julie Peteet writes in a different context, '[t]he daily inscription of power on the unwilling bodies of Palestinians' takes place.[132] Given the close connection between practices of hygiene and personal identity, this can be deeply damaging. What is more, as I discuss below, a perceived lack of cleanliness can heighten an individual or population's vulnerability to violence.

The stark change in the village's status is encapsulated in a polluted fountain at its entrance.[133] The fountain, the narrator tells us, was once 'dedicated with much pomp and circumstance' by the mayor and was intended 'to welcome the Saturday shoppers into the village', these being Jewish Israelis who travelled to the Arab towns assuming (falsely, the narrator notes with irony) that prices will be cheaper.[134] As noted above, fountains often carry historical connotations of egalitarian politics, serving as reminders of state commitments to public water supply and shared public space. In Kashua's novel the fountain affirms the villagers' Israeli citizenship through displaying the water that they are able to waste, unlike Palestinian towns in the West Bank subject to inflated Israeli pricing and the 'infrastructural administration' described by Khalili in the epigraph to this chapter. The claim on Israeliness represented by the fountain serves an economic purpose, reassuring Israeli shoppers on their arrival through visual similarity between the village and Israeli towns that while they may be in an Arab area, they haven't travelled too far from home.

Following the siege, the fountain stops working and quickly becomes neglected. The narrator tells us: 'The water seems dirtier than ever. Cans and cigarette butts and other trash thrown in . . . floating on the water.'[135] This rapid deterioration, caused by villagers trapped at the entrance waiting to leave, indicates the provisional status of the village's Israeli identity. It provides a reminder that the privileges of citizenship, including mobility in and out of the village, are reserved for Jewish Israelis only. The dirty fountain is another of Kashua's ironies. While its filthy state is produced by Israeli aggression, it appears as the result of the villagers' lack of environmental concern. In doing so, it marks them as lacking in a quality seen as part of a modern 'Israeli' sensibility (even if this is regularly not borne out in Israeli practice). The fountain signifies the villagers' 'reversion' to a fundamental 'Arab-ness', legitimating their separation from the communities afforded protection by Israeli citizenship and heightening their vulnerability to violence.

The disconnection of water becomes proof for the initially sceptical villagers that the roadblock is a genuine threat. When the narrator proposes that they might be facing a shortage his family responds with disbelief. He comments: 'Mother stares at me as if I've gone mad. As if the idea that we could run out of water [as well as food] has never occurred to her.'[136] For the narrator, threats to water as well as food mark these events as distinct from what has come before. He describes fears of running out of food during 'the October War, Land Day, during the first Gulf War, at the beginning of the Intifada', but adds that 'nobody ever thought in terms of running out of water. . . . There were never any real shortages. This war is different from all the others.'[137] The loss of water becomes a fundamental material enactment of the exclusion of Israeli Palestinians from the realm of Israeli citizenship, which the village's residents had previously taken for granted because it seemed to offer an easy and more prosperous life.

It is telling that the narrator decides as the village is being bombarded that his family should take shelter in the bathroom. He is uncertain of his reasons, saying that 'for some reason I figure that is the safest place in the house'.[138] This assumption seems reasonable on a practical basis. The room is on the ground floor and allows the narrator and his wife to protect the baby as much as they can by covering her in the bath.[139] At the same time, the bathroom is a space which 'protects' the narrator and his family symbolically and psychologically in providing reminders of Israeli citizenship. This can be understood through returning to the history of urban hydrological development in Europe. The installation of bathrooms in private British homes proliferated in the late nineteenth and early twentieth centuries. Advocates of the 'sanitary city' saw the construction of separate bathrooms – or, at least, toilets – in working-class homes as a crucial aspect of the project of moral reform, contributing to the production, in reformer Henry Roberts' phrase, of a 'well-ordered family'.[140] The bathroom provided an 'intimate interface' between private and public spheres, in which bodies were regulated according to strict cultural codes.[141] The narrator's decision to hide his family in the bathroom represents an attempt to 'shield' himself with a link to the infrastructural connection which had, until now, provided evidence of their citizenship and adherence to its norms.

The family's relief after the end of the siege is shown primarily through actions in the bathroom, underscoring its role as a connection to the Israeli body politic. The narrator takes a long shower, which is, unusually for Kashua, described over almost a page. The short sentences of this passage emphasise the impression of a savoured, sensory encounter. At the end of the account, the narrator states: 'After every part of my body that I clean, I rest a little, lift up my head and let the water run down my face and over my closed eyes. I open my mouth and let the water in.'[142]

In his careful, detailed account of systematically washing each part of his body before a moment of silent appreciation, the narrator's shower evokes religious rituals of immersion including Christian baptism, Jewish *mikveh* and Islamic *ghusl* in which bathing represents a process of regeneration, transition and removal of sin.[143] His wife, too, delights in the possibility of showering again, declaring: 'How I've missed water . . . I'm going to spend at least two hours in the shower'.[144] The tensions between the narrator and his wife which have persisted throughout the novel finally dissipate as the two shower together.[145] It is easy to understand the experience of feeling dirty as physically unpleasant and in some cases potentially dangerous. Still, the relief of the narrator and his wife at being able to shower again, combined with Kashua's uncharacteristically lengthy description of the narrator's shower, suggests a greater significance to the restoration of a water supply. We can understand this through briefly considering the cultural and political meanings of dirt.

Dirt, in Mary Douglas' famous definition, is 'matter out of place'.[146] The presence of dirt, or fear of its presence, prompts strong emotions and elaborate cultural practices, yet many of our practices to 'remove' dirt have no real effect.[147] Douglas argues that we can understand these responses in terms of dirt's capacity to disturb a system and disrupt the symbolic boundaries through which society is ordered under regular circumstances.[148] With this in mind, the narrator's inability to shower can be read as holding a number of symbolic meanings. First, it produces a visceral, embodied experience of a broader breakdown of social life. It can also be seen as producing a particular kind of helplessness, closer to infantilisation, given the strong cultural connection between adulthood and the ability to manage the body through hygienic practices. This aspect of being unable to wash may be particularly troubling for the narrator since his own sense of masculine adulthood is under stress even prior to the siege. His position as 'head' of and provider for his family is undermined by the loss of his job and return to his parents' house, in a process that mirrors the wider effects of Israeli rule on Palestinian masculinity.[149] The restoration of water supplies simultaneously restores the narrator's sense of adult and masculine autonomy, affirmed through sex with his wife in the shower. Crucial here, however, are the connections between dirt, cleanliness and the notion of the human, particularly with regard to the notion of race.

Water and the State of Exception

To understand these connections, I now turn to Italian political theorist Giorgio Agamben's work, particularly his *Homo Sacer: Sovereign Power and Bare Life* (1995). Agamben has been cited with increasing frequency over the past fifteen years in academic and non-fictional interpretations of Israeli warfare and occupation.[150] His work is similarly pertinent in the context of water, while Ronit Lentin's recent critical approach to using Agamben in an Israeli Palestinian context in the light of theories of racialisation offers further insight.[151] Agamben takes the term *homo sacer* from ancient Roman law, in which it describes an individual who has committed a crime so grave they have been exiled from the polis.[152] The *homo sacer* is a figure who can be killed with impunity, but is also impure, so cannot be killed in rituals that require human sacrifice.[153] This person is reduced to what Agamben calls 'bare life', for which he uses the Greek term *zoē*, meaning the 'simple fact of living common to all living beings (animals, men, or gods)'.[154] Agamben distinguishes *zoē* from *bios*, 'the form or way of living proper to an individual or a group', meaning a kind of 'qualified life' which affords the legal status and political recognition of being included in a political community.[155]

For Agamben, the capacity to suspend the law from certain individuals or groups as part of what he calls, after Nazi jurist Carl Schmitt, a 'state of exception' is the fundamental basis of sovereign power.[156] As well as Schmitt, Agamben draws on Foucault's notion of biopolitics and conceptualisation of state power as the management of life. In contrast to Foucault, however, Agamben argues that this has been the foundation of sovereign power since ancient times.[157] The modern period is distinguishable by a reorientation in which bare life, originally at the 'margins' of politics, has become the 'hidden foundation' of the entire political order with its ultimate expression in the concentration camp.[158] In this period we see an increasing declaration of states of emergency, which for Agamben is not new but integral to what has always been the logic of sovereignty. Israel itself has been in a 'state of emergency' for the entirety of its existence. Its legal basis is the British Mandate's Defence (Emergency) Regulations, renewed by the Knesset every year since 1948.[159] These make provision for acts including the use of military tribunals to try civilians, indefinite administrative detention, and, pertinently in the case of Kashua's novel, isolating territories and imposing curfews.[160] This indefinite 'state of emergency' served as the basis for the military rule of Israel's Arab citizens until 1966 and allows Israel to suspend laws at will in the apparent service of state security.

In Kashua's novel, the encirclement of the village by IDF tanks and removal of crucial state services of electricity and water mirrors Agamben's account of the ability of the state to suspend the law from certain populations, in this case Palestinian citizens of Israel subject to Israel's 'state of emergency'. The villagers have not merely lost their hydraulic citizenship but are at risk of a more extreme expulsion from the Israeli national collective through being rendered 'bare life', to which anything can be done with impunity, including the deprivation of the basic necessities for the reproduction of the body. Dirt plays a further role here as part of the exclusion of the villagers from the national collective. Agamben writes that *homo sacer* has frequently been associated in legal traditions with a confusion of boundaries between human and animal, particularly a 'monstrous' wolf-human hybrid positioned outside the borders of the city.[161] Through their dirty bodies and surroundings the villagers are positioned both outside the nation and on the fringes of the human, unable to perform hygienic practices that mark their symbolic distance from the animal and affirm their position (in a humanist logic) as morally considerable subjects.

Kashua's novel is filled with references to the village's stench, associating the villagers with animality and a failure to adhere to the requirements of liberal citizenship.[162] The dirty fountain becomes part of a landscape of filth including 'piles of garbage' with rotten meat and dairy as the village fills with an inescapable 'putrid smell'.[163] The villagers battle to keep their own excrement at bay as the sewage system fails, with Kashua's narrator attempting to block the pipes connecting his domestic system to that of the village to stop the community's waste from rising up into his home.[164] To do so, he must plunge his arms into stinking sewage, an act so disgusting that he vomits into a ditch and unwillingly covers himself further in bodily wastes. The villagers are unable to suppress the reminders of their animal bodily functions that had been controlled through domestic water infrastructures.[165] The village's dirty bodies and streets reinforce an imagined Israeli 'connection between pollution and terror', producing Israeli Palestinian communities as internal sites of threat to the order of the 'hygienic', 'civilised' nation.[166]

Ronit Lentin has recently extended Agamben's work in an Israeli context by considering race, largely neglected by Agamben and in analyses of Israeli and Palestinian politics. Her work illuminates the villagers' fear of the loss of water and the communal tensions it provokes, which end in stark violence. Drawing on critics including Patrick Wolfe, Alexander Weheliye and David Theo Goldberg, Lentin identifies race as crucial to Israeli practices of rule and provides examples, particularly from legal contexts, of what Goldberg describes as 'racial Palestinianization'.[167] In considering race alongside Agamben Lentin returns to Agamben's source, Foucault, who understood racism as establishing 'a relationship between my life and the death of the other' in which the death of the other 'will make life in general healthier: healthier and purer'.[168] This understanding, Lentin notes, is absent in Agamben's reading of Foucault, yet is crucial to reading Agamben in an Israeli context.[169] In this context, Israeli government practices 'construct racialized categories through population management technologies of segregation and exclusion' such as Israel's separation wall, the separate legal regimes to which Palestinians and settlers in the West Bank are subject, and, pertinently for this chapter, the military and bureaucratic regimes of water deprivation.[170] This process allows the flourishing of Israel's Jewish citizens within and beyond the Green Line 'at the expense of the Palestinian other(s)', as well as of Ethiopian and Mizrahi Jews racialised as 'other' who are similarly positioned beyond and beneath the Ashkenazi norm in Israel's hierarchy of racial classification.[171]

Lentin's work allows us to understand a dimension of Kashua's novel that might otherwise strike readers as curious. While the historical and continuing antagonisms between Palestinian citizens of Israel and Palestinians in the West Bank and Gaza are well known, readers of *Let It Be Morning* might nevertheless expect Palestinian citizens of Israel experiencing a mirror of the water shortages in the Occupied Territories to express solidarity with their residents. Yet the water crisis depicted by Kashua exacerbates the villagers' articulations of their difference from Gazan and West Bank Palestinians and heightens their cruelty to Palestinians trapped in the village during the roadblock. Illegalised West Bank and Gazan workers in the village – derogatorily referred to by villagers as '*Daffawiyya*' and '*Gazawiyya*' – become the subject of intense persecution, culminating in two of their deaths.

The villagers' lack of solidarity with Palestinians experiencing water shortages is all the more striking given water's metaphorical connotations. Water is often framed as the essence of human existence, as in the slogan 'water is life', used in campaigns by Oxfam, WaterAid and recently in protests by the Standing Rock Sioux Tribe against the Dakota Access Pipeline. This sense of water as the foundation of human life provides the basis for a popular coding of water as 'a substance that carries common "humanity"' and unites groups across difference through a shared biophysical need.[172] The apparent ethical compulsion of claims of a universal human need for water seems to be a particularly potent version of Judith Butler's argument that common bodily vulnerabilities afford possible grounds for solidarity.[173] Butler writes that 'the apprehension of another's precarity is implicitly an apprehension of our own' and that this apprehension imposes an 'ethical obligation'.[174] Yet this is nowhere in Kashua's novel. In fact, the apprehension of precarity deepens the villagers' hostility towards the Palestinian workers and each other. Reading these moments more closely can tell us more about the racial dynamics of Israeli rule.

The onset of the siege brings about increasing assertions by the villagers of their difference from Palestinians. For instance, the narrator and other villagers initially assume that if the roadblock is not a mistake it must be part of a search for a Palestinian terrorist cell or suicide bomber.[175] This suggestion affirms the difference between the loyal villagers and presumably extremist Palestinians disrupting peaceful Israeli Palestinian life. The articulations of Israeli Palestinian superiority brought about by the roadblock are an intensification of the villagers' existing perception of their difference from Palestinians in the West Bank and Gaza. The narrator's brother-in-law, Ashraf, for instance, tells the narrator as they drive past Palestinian day labourers in the village square hoping for work, '[d]on't feel sorry for them . . . Now they're begging, but deep inside they're convinced that every Israeli Palestinian is a traitor and a collaborator'.[176] Ashraf portrays Palestinians as a threat to Israeli Palestinians through a refusal to get past nationalist grudges, distinguishing Palestinians from his community through using the pronoun 'them'. In doing so, he separates Palestinians from 'us' and presents them as an amorphous and depersonalised mass. 'Us', for the narrator, crucially includes the IDF, whom he describes as 'our soldiers'.[177]

Loyalty to the IDF is widespread in the village. One neighbour jokes that the IDF might have 'confused us with Tul-Karm', a city in the West Bank, a comment which provokes laughter from others.[178] This joke indicates that the town's residents view unexplained military actions as a fact of life in the West Bank, while the possibility of this state of affairs being the subject of a joke illustrates their lack of regard for the lives of Palestinians and trust in the Israeli military. However, the implication that the two places might be confused at all suggests that the villagers' position is less secure than it seems. This technique of destabilising a claim at the moment of its articulation recurs in Kashua's work as part of his wider preoccupation with the instability of identity categories.[179] The reference to Tulkarm, a West Bank city captured by Israel in 1967 and transferred to the Palestinian Authority after the Oslo Accords, in fact foreshadows the novel's ending. The villagers have more in common with Tulkarm than they realise.

While the early phase of the closure prompted some villagers to 'imitat[e] well-known Palestinian scenes', as the narrator cynically describes the initial protests at the funeral of a contractor and two workers, killed trying to charge the barrier, this is short-lived.[180] Ultimately the villagers abandon any gestures of solidarity or protest and declare their resentment at the perceived injustice of being subjected to military tactics used in the West Bank. One claims: 'we're not like them, we can't last long'.[181] In one sense this complaint emphasises a paradoxical vulnerability of the Israeli Palestinian village. The village's deep integration into Israeli systems of money, electricity, food, water has created an infrastructural dependence that has ultimately become a risk. The narrator points out that '[t]his isn't Jenin, everything here is Israeli'.[182] The village, he indicates, is unable to survive being cut off from Israeli society and is under total Israeli control.

These claims that Palestinians in the West Bank are better able to endure siege conditions are, however, clearly untrue. As discussed at the start of this chapter, Palestinians in the West Bank and Gaza have been subjected to infrastructural warfare with devastating effects. West Bank Palestinians remain under the control of Israeli 'infrastructural administration', forced to buy back water from aquifers under their own lands at inflated prices from Israel's water company Mekorot. As a result, they are vulnerable to being disconnected in the same way as Kashua's villagers. The narrator's mention of the West Bank city of Jenin is also significant. While the narrator mentions only the place name, the 'Battle of Jenin' during Operation Defensive Shield in 2002 was recent history when *Let It Be Morning* was published in 2004. Its name would have evoked these events for Hebrew readers of the time and international readers familiar with Israeli and Palestinian politics. The Battle of Jenin was an eight-day assault launched in Jenin refugee camp that was a prototype in the development of infrastructural violence. It was launched by

Sharon following a series of Palestinian suicide attacks inside Israel, ostensibly to remove Palestine's 'terrorist infrastructure'.[183] However, the attack went far beyond what may have been 'justifiable' for this purpose. The IDF flattened large areas of the camp using armoured bulldozers, helicopters and tanks, while soldiers battered their way through the walls of Palestinian homes with sledgehammers to create new routes.[184] Jenin's 14,000 residents went without food, water and electricity, while at least fifty-two were killed and 4,000 made homeless.[185] In its visible and invisible devastation, the Battle of Jenin can be seen as both 'spectacular' and 'slow' violence.

Given these recent events, the narrator's presumption that Palestinians find it easier to survive attacks seems dismissive in the extreme. This belief seems grounded in a lack of knowledge about the realities of Israeli attacks and a dehumanising belief in the hardier nature of West Bank and Gazan Palestinians. In drawing lines of separation on the basis of imagined differential capacities of the biological human body, the narrator and villagers draw a racial distinction between themselves and Palestinians in the Occupied Territories. It is a racial distinction in the sense identified by Weheliye, 'not as a biological or cultural classification but as a set of socio-political processes of differentiation and hierarchization, which are projected onto the putatively biological human body'.[186] In doing so, Kashua's characters position themselves as more worthy of Israeli state protection and Palestinians in the Occupied Territories as the 'natural' objects of Israeli rule, undermining any possibility for solidarity on the basis of a shared biological human vulnerability to water shortages.

The villagers' lack of knowledge about the realities of occupation is underscored in a later comment by a neighbour overheard by the narrator. The neighbour remarks: 'What are they trying to do, kill us by dehydration? Even on the West Bank they never did that.'[187] In this comment the neighbour emphasises the injustice of the village's current situation through a comparison with the West Bank, seen as the locus of the most extreme forms of military violence. The narrator, too, struggles to believe that Israel would use the removal of essential material provisions as a military strategy, stating: 'it's inconceivable that any army or country in the world would let people collapse that way, let little children die of hunger and thirst before their own eyes'.[188] The 'slow' impact of infrastructural warfare in reducing access to water supplies to dangerous levels indicates that death by dehydration is not in fact an unrealistic outcome of attacks on the West Bank and Gaza, while death from water-associated disease is frequent. Indeed, in 1967 Israel's then Prime Minister Levi Eshkol proposed depriving Gazans of water to force them to leave.[189] The Israeli government's 2008 'Red Lines' document, released after public pressure in 2012, prescribed a strict 'humanitarian minimum' of basic food products to be allowed into Gaza under the blockade inaugurated after Hamas took control of the Strip in 2007.[190] While Israel's calorie-counting was ostensibly aimed at keeping Palestinians alive, it can be read as a further aspect of the 'slow' violence of infrastructural warfare. To borrow from Butler, this 'sustain[s] populations on the edge of death' such that the life permitted may seem barely worth living.[191] The villagers' ignorance of such practices in their rush to present their experience as exceptional speaks again to their refusal to acknowledge Palestinians as morally considerable subjects. This may be essential to their own ability to feel secure in their Israeli citizenship, since it shows how easily it might be removed.

Threats of water shortage not only fail to prompt solidarity with Palestinians in the West Bank and Gaza, but ultimately trigger violence towards Palestinian workers trapped in the village by the roadblock. In one dark scene the villagers are persuaded to round up the workers and hand them over to the soldiers. Their reluctance is transformed into assent when the mayor threatens the possibility of interruptions to water and the humiliation of a failing sewage system which would mean 'people would have to start taking a shit outdoors, the way they used to long ago'.[192] The threat of public defecation suggests the return of the 'animal' body that the 'sanitary city' was designed to disguise, forcing the villagers into the humiliating position of divesting themselves of their hydraulic citizenship to fulfil bodily needs. Excrement in villagers' gardens would suggest a 'reversion' to a 'backward' form of life ('long ago'). What is more, this is a form of racialised life; as Sara Ahmed writes, '[t]he other is already seen as dirt, as the carrier of dirt' and as a source of disgust.[193] The threatened 'return' of sewage emphasises the villagers' racial character as 'out of place' within Israel's borders while threatening to push them further down Israel's system of moral considerability.

The decision to 'transfer' the Palestinians is compounded by the villagers' realisation that their access to drinking water is genuinely at risk. Kashua writes: 'But once the mayor explained that there was no choice, that if things went on this way for one more day there would be no drinking water left, they backed down.'[194] The extreme threat of being reduced to 'bare life' through the loss of water encourages the villagers to reduce the Palestinian workers to 'bare life' instead, with their lives sacrificeable for the 'good' of the village collective. The 'sobbing workers' are 'stripped brutally' before the attempted transfer and those who resist are 'kicked hard in the ribs'.[195] Two workers are shot and killed by Israeli soldiers before the villagers realise that the plan was misguided. Kashua describes one of the workers in animalistic terms after he is attacked by the villagers: '[t]rembling all over, practically naked . . . on all fours'. This language heightens the shock at the workers' dehumanisation by a group we might otherwise have considered to be their own people, showing the urgency with which villagers seek to secure their own humanity at the expense of Palestinians.[196]

In rounding up Palestinian workers in the hope of restoring their water and sewage infrastructure the villagers become, as the narrator acknowledges, quasi-agents of the state which has caused their difficulties in the first place.[197] Darker still, as Sadia Agsous notes, is the echo of the *Judenräte* of the Second World War, the Jewish councils established in European ghettos to enforce Nazi German laws whose tasks eventually involved identifying residents for deportation.[198] This allusion to the Holocaust in an Israeli context is highly provocative, perhaps providing justification for critics who view Kashua as a mere controversialist. Kashua's reference to the *Judenräte* is especially inflammatory; Hannah Arendt's criticism of the Jewish councils in *Eichmann in Jerusalem* (1963) led to her effective excommunication from the Jewish community. Yet the allusion is not the antisemitic claim sometimes found in leftist discourse of Jews having moved from victims to oppressors with the establishment of the State of Israel.[199] Instead, Kashua indicts both the Israeli state and the villagers. This scene underscores the sense of water access in Kashua's novel as the fundamental feature not just in producing hydraulic citizenship but in 'racial Palestinization', with the villagers seeking to escape their classification as racially other through their brutal and ultimately fruitless transfer of the Palestinian workers.

Water shortages in the village prompt conflict between villagers too, as tensions created by their unequal position within Israeli society come to the surface. Their behaviour in the face of failing water infrastructure becomes the basis for another provocative comparison, this time with settlers. As the shortages start to become apparent, Kashua's narrator discovers that his water tank, which he had thought half full, is 'completely empty. Someone has stolen our water.'[200] His brother's tank, too, is empty.[201] Following the 'theft', the narrator resolves to steal water himself – if he can find anyone to steal it from – and thereafter regards other villagers with suspicion, thinking of a group of children in the street, '[w]ho knows, maybe they're the ones who stole the water from our tank'.[202] The notion of 'stolen' water evokes Israel's discriminatory water policies and particularly settler water use in the West Bank, regularly framed in activist contexts as 'theft'.[203] The reference to stolen water within an Israeli Palestinian community is absurd, highlighting the extreme divisions produced under Israeli rule by suggesting similarities between villagers and supposedly the worst embodiments of the Israeli occupation.

The novel reaches an ironic climax as the narrator desperately attempts to imagine how the crisis might be overcome. He reflects:

> I try to think of ways of getting hold of more water . . . I wonder what would happen if we dug some water holes in the village. Maybe the groundwater would rise to the surface and give enough not only for us but for everyone.[204]

In this moment the narrator seems briefly to go beyond the individualism that has characterised the villagers' response to the crisis, even if only in his vague thought that a well – a word which he doesn't use, emphasising his lack of knowledge – might help them to find water. He even speculates about Israel's wider water infrastructural network: 'And maybe there are pipes running under our land, leading from the reservoirs and the rivers of the Galilee to the cities in the centre and the desert in the south.'[205] Yet he ultimately concludes his idealistic thoughts with anger, declaring: 'I hope the ones who stole our water die of poisoning!'[206] In these moments we see the benefits and risks of the 'infrastructural privilege' enjoyed by the villagers as part of their hydraulic citizenship. This has served as a form of 'self-defence' and 'active forgetting' that allows villagers to get on with everyday life.[207] It has also left them vulnerable: their water, as the narrator begins to realise, has been redistributed around the country by extensive and hidden infrastructural networks to which it is too late for them to regain access.

Let It Be Morning ends with a rigid separation between Jewish Israelis and Palestinians that reflects Israel's racialised demographic fears. New borders are drawn and a noted university professor commends Israel's government in the conclusion for ensuring that 'the population of the State of Israel has now become almost one hundred percent Jewish. At long last, a truly Jewish state.'[208] The novel itself, however, works to undermine boundaries of nationality and race, producing complicated affiliations. Kashua's works are middlebrow novels, written in a first-person voice and a colloquial and confessional tone.[209] These elements, as Bernard notes, coerce the reader into 'a sense not only of affinity, but of identification' with his characters.[210] This effect is intensified by Kashua's avoidance of names for his characters or, in *Let It Be Morning*, settings, which mostly reads as if it could be set anywhere. The novel's genre similarly encourages a sense of identification. While *Let It Be Morning* is sometimes described as dystopian, Kashua's novels are more accurately understood by Batya Shimony as written in a 'realistic style taken to an absurd extreme', a style that heightens a reader's horror as the plot unfolds.[211] This identification has the potential to play a disarming role for Jewish Israeli Hebrew readers, particularly Ashkenazi readers, luring them into a position they may not usually enter voluntarily. Through being forced into an identification with Israeli Palestinians and, indirectly, Palestinians in the West Bank and Gaza subject to more explicit forms of infrastructural warfare, Kashua reminds his readers of the arbitrariness of the protections afforded in Israel to certain bodies over others.

Conclusion

Infrastructural warfare is a major current strategy of the Israeli military. The destruction and disconnection of water supplies entrenches Israeli control over Palestinian populations, functioning as a form of slow violence with effects on health and environment that persist well after offensives have ended and international media teams returned home. Infrastructure often disappears from view; indeed, its absence is often desired as a sign that it is working.[212] This means that damage to infrastructure is often obscured and not readily available as a subject for literature, while the production of literature on infrastructural warfare is hindered by the unstable conditions of life during and in its wake. Kashua's *Let It Be Morning* is a rare text that puts water infrastructure at its centre, yet this has been neglected in critical readings. *Let It Be Morning* makes the effects of infrastructural warfare visible through illustrating its disruption of the routines of everyday life and showing the capacity for the disconnection of water to enact a parallel disconnection from a national community. The novel illustrates the close connection between water and citizenship as part of hydraulic citizenship, while also illuminating the relationship between water and racialisation. While popular metaphors of water stress its capacity to connect, in *Let It Be Morning* water is integral to the drawing of lines of national and racial purification and to the production of a demographic reality in which Israel – as some within it wish – becomes a solely Jewish state.

I have read *Let It Be Morning* as a hydrofiction, drawing attention to its portrayal of the relationships between water and Israeli state power. It is, however, also a work of 'cli-fi' in a way that has not previously been acknowledged. Kashua evokes a climate-changed world through references to Israel's increasingly extreme patterns of weather, which include a record-breaking heatwave in May 2019 and the severe storm that blanketed Jerusalem in snow during winter 2013. The novel's events take place with a 'heat wave sweeping over the country' during which 'the Water Council is weighing up the possibility of declaring a state of emergency in the water supply' to counter 'the national water shortage'.[213] The shortage persists even after 'the longest and rainiest winter in three decades', suggesting climate fluctuations.[214] This context heightens our sense of the villagers' panic as their taps dry up and the Israeli government's disregard for their lives, yet it does more than this.

A telling moment of confusion occurs as the narrator is watching the Israeli news and sees that the defence minister is considering declaring a 'state of emergency'.[215] He assumes that this must relate to the blockade of the village, which has not yet been publicly acknowledged. In fact, it relates to the threatened water shortage. This moment gives us an indication of the Israeli government's likely militarised response to climate change, treated as a matter for the defence minister rather than for Israel's Ministry of Environmental Protection. This indicates the spread to Israel of a tendency of the US army, which is in fact one of the biggest contributors to climate change.[216] What is more, this discussion suggests a lack of concern for communities already experiencing water shortages induced by Israel's existing 'state of emergency', whose lack of water is caused by Israeli domination and not by 'natural' conditions of climate change. Climate change, Kashua suggests, may intensify water shortages in Israel/Palestine in the future, but infrastructural warfare is causing water crisis right now.

Notes

1. Khalili, 'A Habit of Destruction'.
2. On health and sanitation during and after Operation Protective Edge, see 'Gaza: Initial Rapid Assessment, 27 August 2014', pp. 17–19.
3. The initial cost of damage to water infrastructure during Operation Protective Edge was estimated by the Palestinian Water Authority as over $34 million. Long-term repairs of accumulated damage to water, sanitation and hygiene infrastructure over years of attacks are estimated at $855 million. 'Water Sector Damage Assessment Report', pp. 12, 14–15.
4. Zeitoun, *Power and Water in the Middle East*, p. 4.
5. Beaumont, 'Welcome to Shuafat, East Jerusalem'; Massalha, 'In Suspension', pp. 289–92; Cook, 'The Negev's Hot Wind Blowing'. See also Dajani, 'Drying Palestine'.
6. Nikhil Anand, *Hydraulic City*, p. 7. A related concept, 'hydrocitizenship', was used by the UK research project 'Towards Hydrocitizenship', which ran from 2014 to 2017 and was led by Owain Jones. This use of the term built on the notion of 'ecological citizenship', aimed at cultivating individual and collective behaviours that will lead to a sustainable society. I use Anand's term to express my distinct concern with the relationship between water and the production of citizenship. 'Vision'.
7. Kashua, 'Why Sayed Kashua Is Leaving Jerusalem and Never Coming Back'.
8. Hochberg describes being told by an anonymous reviewer that Kashua should not be analysed by literary critics since he is 'not really a writer . . . [but] a journalist provocateur'. 'To Be or Not to Be an Israeli Arab', p. 71, note 6.
9. Kashua uses the term 'Israeli Arabs'. In this chapter I use 'Israeli Palestinians' to highlight my concern with the politics and paradoxes of national belonging and because of my own outsider position.
10. On the position of Palestinians in Israel, see Peleg and Waxman, *Israel's Palestinians*; Pappé, *The Forgotten Palestinians*.
11. Grumberg, *Place and Ideology*, pp. 151–2; Hochberg, 'To Be or Not to Be an Israeli Arab', p. 76; Rottenberg, 'Let It Be Morning (review)', p. 138.
12. Grumberg, *Place and Ideology*, p. 149; Hochberg, 'To Be or Not to Be an Israeli Arab', p. 77; Rottenberg, 'Let It Be Morning (review)', p. 139.

13. Sultana and Loftus, 'The Right to Water', p. 9.
14. The phrase is from Yaeger, 'Introduction: Dreaming of Infrastructure', p. 15.
15. Ibid., p. 15.
16. Anand, *Hydraulic City*, p. 6; Bennett, *Vibrant Matter*.
17. Bennett, *Vibrant Matter*, p. 21.
18. Graham, *Cities Under Siege*, p. 84.
19. Ibid., p. 84.
20. Weizman, *Hollow Land*, p. 188.
21. Graham, *Cities Under Siege*, p. 153.
22. Ibid., p. xxiv.
23. Ibid., pp. 279–80.
24. Ribarević-Nikolić and Jurić, *Mostar '92 – Urbicid*; Berman, 'Falling Towers'.
25. Pappé, *The Ethnic Cleansing of Palestine*, pp. 91–102; Khalidi, *All That Remains*.
26. Weizman, 'Strategic Points, Flexible Lines', p. 197.
27. Wenzel, 'Amandla! Awethu!'.
28. Swyngedouw, *Social Power and the Urbanization of Water*, p. 2.
29. 'Protocol Additional to the Geneva Conventions of 12 August 1949'.
30. Zeitoun, *Power and Water in the Middle East*, pp. 91–2.
31. Weizman, 'Short Cuts'. Weizman has investigated the destruction of buildings in Gaza as part of the Forensic Architecture research agency at Goldsmiths, University of London. 'Investigations'.
32. 'Report of the United Nations Fact-Finding Mission on the Gaza Conflict'.
33. Selby, *Water, Power and Politics*, p. 2.
34. 'Fact Sheet: How Gaza's Blockade Impacts on Water and Sanitation', p. 2. See also the comments on this in the Goldstone Report. 'Report of the United Nations Fact-Finding Mission on the Gaza Conflict', sec. XIII C, XVII D.
35. 'Gaza Emergency Humanitarian Snapshot'.
36. 'United Nations Seminar on Assistance to Palestinian People'.
37. Weizman, *The Least of All Possible Evils*.
38. Selby, *Water, Power and Politics*, pp. 95, 140–3.
39. Ibid., p. 113. For a recent account of these effects using data from JWC files, see Selby, 'Cooperation, Domination and Colonisation'.
40. 'Fact Sheet: Demolition and Destruction'; 'Israeli Forces Destroy UNICEF-Funded Water Pipeline in Jordan Valley'.
41. Azoulay and Ophir, cited in Weinthal and Sowers, 'Targeting Infrastructure and Livelihoods in the West Bank and Gaza'.

42. Nixon, *Slow Violence*, p. 2.
43. Graham, *Cities Under Siege*, p. 265.
44. Manenti et al., 'Report of a Field Assessment of Health Conditions in the Occupied Palestinian Territory', p. 21.
45. World Health Organisation and United Nations Environment Programme, cited in 'Report of the United Nations Fact-Finding Mission on the Gaza Conflict', p. 268.
46. Gandy, *Concrete and Clay*, p. 22.
47. Graham, *Cities Under Siege*, p. 226. See Massalha's discussion of Mekorot's 1987 disconnection of water to Umm al-Fahem, an Israeli Palestinian city in northern Israel. These were ostensibly for not paying its debts but also served to worsen conditions in the city and undermine its communist leadership. Massalha, 'In Suspension', pp. 289–92.
48. Kimmerling, *Politicide*.
49. Ibid., p. 4.
50. Dabbagh, *Out of It*, p. 22.
51. Ibid., p. 22.
52. Ibid., p. 33.
53. Ibid., p. 47.
54. Al-Sousi, 'Canary'.
55. Ibid., pp. 55–6.
56. Ibid., p. 55.
57. Spivak, cited in Bernard, *Rhetorics of Belonging*, pp. 2–3.
58. Cleary, *Literature, Partition and the Nation-State*, pp. 86–90. See also Alareer, 'Editor's Introduction', p. 26; Jayyusi, 'Introduction', pp. 2–3, 53–4.
59. Hamilton, 'At the Islamic University in Gaza'; 'UNRWA Calls on Israel to Lift Book Blockade of Gaza Schools'.
60. Cited in Bernard, *Rhetorics of Belonging*, pp. 2–3.
61. Ibid., p. 3.
62. Qualey, '"The Book of Gaza"'; Saif, 'Introduction', pp. ix–x.
63. Anderson, *Disaster Writing*, p. 1.
64. Carrigan, 'Introduction: Representing Catastrophe'.
65. Carrigan, 'Compound Disaster, Uneven Recovery'.
66. Carrigan, 'Introduction: Representing Catastrophe'.
67. See, for instance, the diary entry for 12 August 2014, titled 'The Tyranny of Water'. Saif, *The Drone Eats with Me*, pp. 179–82.
68. Kaika and Swyngedouw, 'Fetishizing the Modern City', p. 121.

69. Swyngedouw writes on improvised water infrastructure in Latin America in *Social Power and the Urbanization of Water*.
70. Weizman, *The Least of All Possible Evils*, p. 141.
71. A powerful example is Wiedenhöfer's *The Book of Destruction*, which juxtaposes images of destroyed homes with maimed Gazan bodies.
72. Said, *After the Last Sky*, p. 38.
73. See, for instance, 'Troubled Waters'.
74. Yaeger, 'Dreaming of Infrastructure', p. 17.
75. Kashua, *Let It Be Morning*, p. 18.
76. Ibid., p. 16.
77. Hochberg, 'To Be or Not to Be an Israeli Arab', p. 74.
78. Kashua, *Let It Be Morning*, pp. 7, 17.
79. Ibid., p. 52.
80. Ibid., p. 52.
81. Thanks to Oren Yiftachel for prompting me to look into this.
82. Kashua, *Let It Be Morning*, p. 68.
83. Ibid., p. 260.
84. Ibid., pp. 267–71.
85. Ibid., pp. 261–2.
86. Ibid., p. 266.
87. Weizman and Misselwitz, 'Military Operations as Urban Planning'.
88. Kashua, *Let It Be Morning*, p. 143.
89. 'Act of Vengeance: Israel's Bombing of the Gaza Power Plant and Its Effects'.
90. 'Gaza Strip Electricity Supply'.
91. Kashua, *Let It Be Morning*, pp. 172.
92. Ibid., p. 145.
93. Ibid., p. 169.
94. Ibid., p. 200.
95. Ibid., p. 200.
96. Ibid., p. 200.
97. Ibid., p. 201.
98. Ibid., p. 217.
99. Ibid., p. 217.
100. Ibid., pp. 99–100.
101. Ibid., p. 100.
102. Ibid., p. 182.
103. Ibid., p. 173.

104. Kaika and Swyngedouw, 'Fetishizing the Modern City', p. 135.
105. Silverstone, 'Complicity and Collusion', p. 765.
106. Ibid., p. 765.
107. Anand, *Hydraulic City*, p. 7.
108. Bakker, 'Neoliberalizing Nature?', p. 559.
109. Anand, *Hydraulic City*, pp. 6–7.
110. Kaika and Swyngedouw, 'Fetishizing the Modern City', p. 130.
111. Gandy, *Concrete and Clay*, p. 52; Kaika and Swyngedouw, 'Fetishizing the Modern City', p. 125. A related, earlier example from the Islamic world would be the water fountains often found at crossroads or outside mosques that are constructed by *waqf*, or Islamic endowment, and used for religious and public purposes. Deguilhem, 'The Waqf in the City', p. 949.
112. Nixon, *Slow Violence*, ch. 5.
113. Kaika, *City of Flows*, ch. 1; Kaika and Swyngedouw, 'Fetishizing the Modern City', p. 121.
114. Goubert, *The Conquest of Water*, pp. 81–2.
115. Foucault, 'On Governmentality', pp. 102–3; Rose, cited in Otter, 'Making Liberalism Durable', p. 1.
116. Foucault, *The History of Sexuality Vol. 1*, p. 136.
117. Otter, 'Making Liberalism Durable', p. 5.
118. Ibid., p. 5.
119. Joyce, *The Rule of Freedom*, p. 73.
120. Bennet, 'Police Used Excessive Force on Israeli Arabs, Panel Says'; Bishara, 'Reflections on October 2000'; Raved, 'Case Closed'.
121. Kashua, *Let It Be Morning*, pp. 18–19.
122. Hochberg, 'To Be or Not to Be an Israeli Arab', p. 77.
123. Ibid., p. 77.
124. Kashua, *Let It Be Morning*, p. 59.
125. Ibid., p. 72.
126. Ibid., p. 73.
127. Ibid., p. 176.
128. Anand, *Hydraulic City*, p. 8.
129. Rubenstein, *Public Works*, pp. 9–10.
130. Kashua, *Let It Be Morning*, p. 212.
131. Strang, *The Meaning of Water*, p. 4.
132. Peteet, 'Male Gender and Rituals of Resistance in the Palestinian Intifada', p. 32.

133. Kashua, *Let It Be Morning*, p. 160.
134. Ibid., p. 160.
135. Ibid., p. 160.
136. Ibid., p. 173.
137. Ibid., p. 173.
138. Ibid., p. 185.
139. Ibid., p. 185.
140. Penner, *Bathroom*, pp. 58–9.
141. Gandy, *The Fabric of Space*, p. 6.
142. Kashua, *Let It Be Morning*, p. 254.
143. Tvedt and Oestigaard, 'Introduction', p. xxi.
144. Ibid., p. 255.
145. Ibid., p. 257.
146. Douglas, *Purity and Danger*, p. 44.
147. Ibid., pp. 44–5.
148. Ibid., p. 44.
149. Kashua, *Let It Be Morning*, pp. 43, 136–8. See Johnson and Kuttab, 'Where Have All the Women (and Men) Gone?'; Sa'ar and Yahia-Younis, 'Masculinity in Crisis'.
150. See Gregory, *The Colonial Present*, p. 16; Langley, 'Exceptional States', p. 73; Lentin, *Thinking Palestine*; Shehadeh, *When the Bulbul Stopped Singing*, p. 95.
151. Lentin, *Traces of Racial Exception*.
152. Agamben, *Homo Sacer*, pp. 10, 13.
153. Ibid., p. 12.
154. Ibid., p. 9.
155. Ibid., p. 9.
156. Ibid., p. 13.
157. Ibid., p. 11.
158. Ibid., p. 12.
159. Lentin, *Traces of Racial Exception*, p. 31.
160. Ibid., p. 31.
161. Agamben, *Homo Sacer*, p. 63.
162. See Corbin, *The Foul and the Fragrant*.
163. Kashua, *Let It Be Morning*, pp. 161–3.
164. Ibid., p. 180.
165. References to Palestinians as animals recur in Israeli right-wing discourse. Just before the 2014 Gaza War, for instance, Benjamin Netanyahu referred to the kill-

ers of the teenage settlers kidnapped in the West Bank as 'human animals', declaring that 'Hamas is responsible and Hamas will pay'. Agence France-Presse, 'Israel Vows to Make Hamas Pay for Alleged Murder of Three Teenagers'.
166. Weizman, *Hollow Land*, p. 21. Graham and Mike Davis point out that images of the 'enemy' city in chaos are incorporated into constructions of the homeland under threat, in a form of moral geography which transposes a presumed conflict between 'civilisation and barbarism' onto physical space. Davis, *Planet of Slums*, pp. 205–6; Graham, *Cities Under Siege*, pp. 53–6.
167. Cited in Lentin, *Traces of Racial Exception*, p. 28.
168. Foucault, *Society Must Be Defended*, pp. 255, 257; Lentin, *Traces of Racial Exception*, p. 24.
169. Lentin, *Traces of Racial Exception*, p. 24.
170. Ibid., pp. 24–5.
171. Ibid., p. 8.
172. Strang, *The Meaning of Water*, p. 62.
173. Butler, *Precarious Life*; Butler, *Frames of War*.
174. Butler, *Frames of War*, p. xvi.
175. Kashua, *Let it Be Morning*, pp. 56, 62, 71.
176. Ibid., p. 27.
177. Ibid., p. 127.
178. Ibid., p. 53.
179. Hochberg, 'To Be or Not to Be an Israeli Arab', p. 76.
180. Kashua, *Let It Be Morning*, p. 203.
181. Ibid., p. 144.
182. Ibid., p. 144.
183. Graham, 'Constructing Urbicide by Bulldozer in the Occupied Territories', p. 194.
184. Weizman, *Hollow Land*, ch. 7.
185. Baroud and Abu Turk, *Searching Jenin*; Graham, 'Constructing Urbicide by Bulldozer', pp. 192–213.
186. Weheliye, *Habeas Viscus*, p. 5. This understanding of race is a key source for Lentin and it is through her book that I came to Weheliye.
187. Kashua, *Let It Be Morning*, p. 204.
188. Ibid., p. 196.
189. Cited in Lentin, *Traces of Racial Exception*, p. 45.
190. The document came to public attention in 2009 after a *Haaretz* investigative report by journalists Yotam Feldman and Uri Blau and was released in 2012

after campaigning from the Israeli human rights organisation Gisha. 'Reader: "Food Consumption in the Gaza Strip - Red Lines"'.
191. Butler, *Frames of War*, p. xix.
192. Ibid., p. xix.
193. Ahmed, *Cultural Politics of Emotion*, p. 82.
194. Kashua, *Let It Be Morning*, p. 143.
195. Ibid., p. 158.
196. Ibid., p. 159.
197. Ibid., p. 143.
198. Agsous, 'Hegemonic (Israeli) Time and Minority (Palestinian) Space'.
199. On the Holocaust and the Nakba, see Achcar, *The Arabs and the Holocaust*; Bashir and Goldberg, *The Holocaust and the Nakba*.
200. Kashua, *Let It Be Morning*, p. 195.
201. Ibid., p. 200.
202. Ibid., pp. 196–7, 209.
203. For instance, Baroud, *My Father Was a Freedom Fighter*, p. 178, as well as campaigns by Palestine Solidarity Campaign (2013) and War on Want (2014).
204. Kashua, *Let it Be Morning*, p. 216.
205. Ibid., p. 216.
206. Ibid., p. 217.
207. Rubenstein et al., 'Infrastructuralism: An Introduction', p. 576.
208. Kashua, *Let it Be Morning*, p. 265.
209. Bernard, 'Sayed Kashua'.
210. Ibid.
211. Shimony, 'Shaping Israeli-Arab Identity in Hebrew Words', p. 150.
212. Rubenstein et al., 'Infrastructuralism: An Introduction', p. 576.
213. Kashua, *Let It Be Morning*, pp. 92, 94.
214. Ibid. pp. 8, 94.
215. Ibid. p. 94.
216. Gilbert, 'The Militarization of Climate Change', Marzec, *Militarizing the Environment*.

CONCLUSION

Sahar Khalifeh's novel *The Inheritance* (*Al-Mirath*, 2005) opens with a Palestinian in New York selling 'holy water and holy sand from the holy river' to unsuspecting locals.[1] Under the pretence of being from Jerusalem, when he is in fact from a small West Bank village, he asks a passing woman: 'Is there a baptism in your family? We have many baptisms in ours, we get baptised every day'.[2] A similar vignette appears in Elia Suleiman's 1996 film *Chronicle of a Disappearance* (*Sijill Ikhtifa*), in which the proprietor of a Nazareth souvenir shop named 'the Holyland' fills bottles marked 'holy water' from a tap.[3] Many social, cultural and political meanings of the deceptively 'natural' substance of water collide in these brief scenes. For these characters water is both an object of religious reverence and an unholy commodity, sold under comically false pretences to pious American Christians and gullible foreign tourists. The depiction of Palestinians as tricksters, meanwhile, challenges the 'tragic discourse' through which Palestinian lives are often narrated.[4] Through representations of water Khalifeh and Suleiman undermine clichés about Palestinian experience, affirming Palestinian agency and suggesting a playful rather than reverential relationship to the homeland. Water, in these scenes, intersects with existing understandings of Palestinian life while telling us something new.

The role of water in Israeli and Palestinian literature has largely been overlooked until now. Israeli and Palestinian literatures are widely understood as determined by their relationship to the land. This is perhaps unsurprising given the centrality of the settlement or loss of land in the Israeli and Palestinian national narratives and in the present-day conflict. Conflict over land persists in Israel's ongoing land grabs in East Jerusalem and the West Bank, its control of Palestinian movement over land through the siege on Gaza, the separation wall and the West Bank system of floating checkpoints, and in the as-yet unresolved debates about future borders. Water quality, availability and rights are recognised as major Israeli and Palestinian political issues, yet are largely seen in technocratic terms as problems to be 'solved' by politicians, engineers and hydrologists, with water understood as a mere 'biological fact'.[5] This approach masks the extent to which water is always invested with social and cultural meanings and shapes cultures and subjectivities, in Israel/Palestine and elsewhere. Crucially, water is a material conduit for flows of social power, one that mediates between national projects of statebuilding, war and occupation and the intimate level of embodied life. The project of producing a just and sustainable allocation of resources cannot be separated from understanding the meanings of water. This is where literature becomes necessary.

The examples presented in this book undermine the widespread perception of water in Israel/Palestine as primarily a matter for technical calculation. They show both the role of literature in understanding Israeli and Palestinian environmental politics and the potential for further environmental readings of Israeli and Palestinian writing, a topic that has been underexplored. I have surveyed the meanings of water at crucial points in Israeli and Palestinian history: from the arrival of Zionist 'pioneers' in the early twentieth century to their draining of Palestine's swamps in the 1920s and 1950s; to the displacement of Palestinians in the Nakba and Naksa and the transformation of the Jordan into a symbol of loss; to the emergence of post-Zionism and the Israeli environmental movement in the 1980s; and from Oslo and the Israeli optimism attached to a turn to the sea to the infrastructural warfare of the present. Turning to water allows us to see familiar stories in a different light, showing, for example, that Zionist settlement and building the State of Israel were as premised on establishing the quantities of water in Israel/Palestine and harnessing water to the national cause as they were about settling and remaking the land. These chapters show that water has been as implicated as land in producing versions of the 'new Jew' and in shaping Palestinian identity and experience over the twentieth and twenty-first centuries. My discussion of the hydropolitics of the early Zionist movement, meanwhile, indicates that estimates of water as 'scarce' or 'abundant' are dependent more on political priorities than on 'objective' observation of natural phenomena.

Concern for water is often understood as going beyond the narrow politics of nationhood associated with land. This assumption seems reinforced by water's metaphorical associations with flow and connection across borders, associations that have a material basis in the global water cycle, our permeable skin and the dependence on water common to all humans and across species. The texts in this book instantiate different features of this 'hydrological imaginary', with recurring imagery of flow, surging or aridity. These translate in some cases into the form of the text, as in Oz's journeys with the water cycle across the world in *The Same Sea* and his shifts between narrative voice and poetry and prose, or Shalev's magical realist depiction of the monstrous swamp. At the same time, this book has shown that these meanings of water are not a move away from the politics of land, but remain tied to the projects of nation-building, occupation and war.

The meanings of water are in fact not entirely dissimilar from those associated with the land and the familiar 'terrestrocentric' symbols of Israeli and Palestinian life. Darwish's 'A River Dies of Thirst' presents the Jordan as a feature of the lost land to be mourned just as much as the olive tree or village, while Shalev's representation of the Jezreel swamps in *The Blue Mountain* sits within a wider body of Israeli texts that see reminders of a history Israel would prefer to forget in the country's landscape alongside, for instance, A. B. Yehoshua's and Oz Shelach's representations of Israel's forests.[6] In this sense, the significance of water in Israeli and Palestinian literature is closely intertwined with that of land. The chapters in this book are about land as much as they are about water: claiming it, 'redeeming' it, irrigating it, draining it, or rendering it unliveable through the deprivation of water supplies. This book shows the need for land and water to be thought together in reading Israeli and Palestinian literature as environmental writing and in delineating Israeli and Palestinian environmental imaginaries.

I hope that the case studies in this book will invite future studies of water in Israeli and Palestinian literature. Such work might look to 'virtual water'

(water embedded in food and other commodities), 'grey water' (water from hand basins, showers and baths), or 'black water' (sewage), bringing together the mutually dependent infrastructures of water and electricity and their parallel metaphors of flow and interruption, and life and death. It might pivot on a vertical axis, looking up into the air to consider Orly Castel-Bloom's juxtaposition of extreme weather events with the Second Intifada in *Human Parts* (*Halakim Enoshiyim*, 2003), or downwards to aquifers, wells, springs and cisterns in works by Jabra Ibrahim Jabra, Elias Khoury and Anton Shammas.[7] It might linger on the borders to consider Palestinian experiences of Israeli colonisation alongside those of African refugees in Israel's Negev desert detention camps in Ayelet Gundar-Goshen's *Waking Lions* (*Leha'ir Arajot*, 2014), or Bedouin displaced by the Israeli state in Daniella Carmi's *Goats* (*Izim*, 2011).[8] It might look beyond the borders, considering Ghassan Kanafani's depiction of three Palestinian refugees who suffocate in an empty water tanker while attempting to escape to Kuwait in *Men in the Sun* (*Rijal fi al'Shams*, 1963).[9] Or it might cast off seawards and turn towards the nonhuman inhabitants and users of water, considering David Grossman's weaving together of oceanic ecosystems, salmon migration and Holocaust trauma in *See Under: Love* (*'Ayen 'Erekh: Ahavah*, 1989).[10] While this project focused on texts available in English translation as part of mapping the outlines of a wider theoretical approach, turning to untranslated writing would allow discussion of works including Sami Michael's *Water Kissing Water* (*Mayim Noshkim Le-Mayim*, 2005) and of workers in Israel's water industry (both Michael and his protagonist are hydrologists).[11]

Future work would also find rich material in film and the visual arts. This might include Zionist propaganda films such as *Sabra* (*Tzabar*, 1933) and *They Were Ten* (*Hem Hayu Asara*, 1961), which depict water conflicts between modernising Jewish 'pioneers' and Palestine's native population.[12] More recently, Tawfik Abu Wael's Palme D'Or-winning 2004 film *Atash* (*Thirst*) depicts an Israeli Palestinian family attempting to live in an abandoned military training camp in northern Israel to which the father is obsessed with building a water pipe.[13] The film shows the role of water infrastructure in securing land and mediating gender relations, making much of the movement and sounds of water. In the visual arts we might consider Palestinian graffiti artist Alaa Albaba's 2013–16 series 'Route of the Fish', in which Albaba painted fish in refugee camps, the West Bank and, illegally, Jaffa, to reframe the Palestinian tragedy as having being cut off from the sea rather than the land, or the photographs of Tanya Habjouqa in *Occupied Pleasures* (2015), which frequently use watery settings and activities such as swimming or surfing to portray Palestinian experiences in unexpected ways that go beyond the familiar 'tragic discourse'.[14]

This project builds on a small but growing body of scholarship on Israeli and particularly Palestinian literatures.[15] Israeli and Palestinian writing is, however, largely avoided within Postcolonial Studies, Ecocriticism and the Environmental Humanities, including the Blue Humanities. Writing about Israeli and Palestinian literature is more fraught than ever in the current academic climate, so scholars may be wise to steer clear. Nevertheless, engaging with Israeli and Palestinian literature is not only politically urgent in the light of the region's ongoing injustices but offers the potential to invigorate critical work in these fields more broadly. While Postcolonial Studies has been in the midst of an identity crisis in recent years, reading Israeli and Palestinian literature has the potential to add to a turn in the field identified in 2013 by Timothy Brennan from 'discourse, identity, migrancy and subjectivity . . . to an engaged, activist language of political movements and positions' that revitalises postcolonialism by reconnecting it with anticolonial energies historically and today.[16] Israeli and Palestinian literatures take Postcolonial Studies beyond the 'woefully restricted and attenuated corpus' identified by Neil Lazarus in 2011, while turning to water offers the potential for new methods that combine postcolonialism's insights into settler-colonial cultures with emerging work in world literature on capitalism and world-ecology.[17] Israeli and Palestinian writing also offers one way to sharpen the often fuzzy political commitments of the Environmental Humanities, warning against vague gestures around the 'Anthropocene' and adding to a reorientation of the field led by Indigenous scholars towards a focus on environmental justice.

This book has examined Israeli and Palestinian literature because these countries are at the centre of global discourse on water crisis. However, water crisis is not only an issue in Israel/Palestine. One in three people around the world do not have access to safe drinking water.[18] The Intergovernmental Panel on Climate Change and the United Nations warn that climate change will intensify existing water shortages, while reports of climate migration already circulate frequently in the Anglophone press.[19] At the same time, the Israeli/Palestinian example provides a crucial reminder that vulnerability to climate change depends on existing socio-political inequalities and that attributing migration or war solely to climate risks environmental determinism.[20] It reminds us that the apparent urgency of responding to scarcity can enable an increasing securitisation of water that intensifies existing power asymmetries, 'justifying', for instance, European and American interference in countries identified as most vulnerable, primarily in the Middle East and North Africa.[21] Focusing on climate change as the cause of shortages can naturalise problems that are socially and politically produced, while the common framing of climate change as a universal problem can make marginalised communities appear petty and intransigent when they refuse, as Palestinians have done, to participate in environmental partnerships with their oppressors, or, as Indigenous people in Canada regularly do, to sacrifice more of their land to hydroelectric projects that will power faraway cities. Beginning with Israel/Palestine, then, reflects its centrality in contemporary discourse on water crisis while also offering some crucial caveats.

What might a literary project look like that brought Israeli and Palestinian experiences of water into dialogue with this wider context? Just as petro-critics have shown the connections between American highways, Saudi oilfields and the Niger Delta, hydrocriticism should look to water in world literature, following water's flows around the world and tracking the spread of capital, contamination and expertise, of literary strategies and of modes of resistance. This would follow practices already being undertaken by activists: just as protesters in Flint, Michigan displayed banners stating 'Flint Stands with Standing Rock', literary critics might read for water across borders. We might consider how water provides new ways of imagining the collective, in the shared need for water across nations and species, and in our responsibilities to it and to other water-dependent beings within what Astrida Neimanis calls the 'hydrocommons'.[22] Palestinian poet Lena Khalaf Tuffaha's 2017 poem 'Water and Salt' is one place to start.[23]

Tuffaha's poem addresses a 2014 Palestinian prisoners' hunger strike in which up to 290 prisoners consumed only water and salt for two months in protest at Israel's continued use of administrative detention, or detention without trial.[24] While the hunger strikers are separated into cells, they are connected by water as they mobilise their bodies in struggle. Tuffaha describes their 'current of blood running thin/indigo rivulets pulsing loud beneath parchment skin', with the rhyming structure of these lines echoing the strikers' hearts, beating harder as their fat and muscle shrinks. The hunger strikers 'sip water and salt like sacrament', suggesting that their protest has a spiritual blessing. This reference to water and salt also connects their bodies to Israeli/Palestinian bodies of water including the Coastal Aquifer and River Jordan, damaged by saline intrusion yet still, Tuffaha implies, possessing grace, and to the Dead Sea, one of Israel/Palestine's most unusual and fragile environments. The poem concludes with a watery vision of triumph and destruction in which the prisoners

> assert their 'freedom'
> to wait and wait
> for your checkpoints and your watchtowers
> to be subsumed in a crashing wave
> of water and salt
> you never saw it coming, this cleansing,
> how we have become this ocean.

Representations of the sea in Palestinian literature often evoke displacement and national loss.[25] In Tuffaha's poem, however, the ocean offers a new metaphor for Palestinian collectivity, with Israel's diminishment of Palestinian life and water ultimately undermining its military power through a biblical flood. Given Tuffaha's ambiguous use of the first-person plural, this might also be read as a transnational aspiration for water justice on behalf of communities who have been subordinated along with their waters. Tuffaha suggests that relationships between bodies of water are mediated by other flows of social, political and colonial power, but that water's properties offer ways of imagining these flows being sent in new directions.[26]

In reading water in Israeli and Palestinian literature, this book is primarily a contribution to literary studies, yet has implications beyond this field. Any study of water is necessarily interdisciplinary, a fact that brings methodological challenges, intellectual pleasures and, crucially, political possibilities. Research into water in Israeli and Palestinian literature deepens our understanding of the social and political significance of narratives of scarcity and abundance by showing how these are reinforced or challenged in literary texts. It also illuminates the severe effects of systemic and deliberately induced water shortages in Palestinian communities, showing their psychological as well as physical toll and helping us to see why Palestinian refugees say that water from Israel/Palestine simply 'tastes better', or is 'the most delicious water in the world'.[27] This book has shown that in Israel/Palestine water is never 'merely' water, in the sense of the familiar, quantifiable compound of H_2O. It is far more than that: water is a substance and medium through which social, cultural, geopolitical and economic relations flow, which is as 'cultural' as it is 'natural' and which must be recognised in this complexity in calls for water justice, in Israel/Palestine and beyond.

Notes

1. Khalifeh, *The Inheritance*, pp. 3–5.
2. Ibid., pp. 3–4.
3. *Chronicle of a Disappearance*.
4. Khalili, *Heroes and Martyrs of Palestine*, p. 34.
5. Orlove and Caton, 'Water Sustainability', p. 402.
6. Boast, '"Planted Over the Past"'.
7. Castel-Bloom, *Human Parts*, pp. 3–8; Jabra, *The First Well*, pp. xix–xxi; Khoury, *Gate of the Sun*, p. 98; Shammas, *Arabesques*, pp. 47–8. See Braverman, 'Silent Springs'.
8. Gundar-Goshen, *Waking Lions*; Carmi, *Izim*. For existing work on Israeli culture and the desert, see Omer-Sherman, *Israel in Exile*; Zerubavel, *Desert in the Promised Land*.
9. Kanafani, *Men in the Sun*.
10. Grossman, *See Under: Love*, pp. 89–186.
11. Michael, *Mayim Noshkim Le-Mayim*.
12. These earlier films are discussed in Shohat, *Israeli Cinema*, pp. 39–41.
13. *'Atash (Thirst)*. Wael was born and grew up in Umm al-Fahem, an Arab city in northern Israel that endured regular disconnection of its water in the late 1980s by Israel's water company, Mekorot.
14. Monterescu, 'The Palestinian Trail of Fish'; Habjouqa, *Occupied Pleasures*.
15. See, for instance, Ball, *Palestinian Literature and Film*; Bernard, *Rhetorics of Belonging*; Farag, *Palestinian Literature in Exile*; Abu-Manneh, *The Palestinian Novel*.
16. Cited in Bernard et al., 'Introduction: What Postcolonial Theory Doesn't Say', pp. 3–4.

17. Lazarus, *The Postcolonial Unconscious*, p. 22; WReC, *Combined and Uneven Development*; Deckard and Shapiro, *World Literature, Neoliberalism, and the Culture of Discontent*.
18. '1 in 3 People Globally Do Not Have Access to Safe Drinking Water – UNICEF, WHO'.
19. IPCC Working Group II, 'Freshwater Resources'; 'Water and Climate Change'; Lakhani, '"People Are Dying"'; Relph, 'Indian Villages Lie Empty as Drought Forces Thousands to Flee'.
20. Mason et al., 'Compounding Vulnerability', pp. 42–3; Selby and Hoffmann, 'Water Scarcity, Conflict, and Migration', p. 748.
21. Mason, 'Climate Change, Securitisation and the Israeli-Palestinian Conflict'; Hartmann, 'Converging on Disaster'.
22. Neimanis, 'Alongside the Right to Water', pp. 6, 12.
23. Tuffaha, *Water and Salt*, pp. 37–8.
24. The protest began with 125 participants, rising to 290 participants recorded by the Israel Prison Service. Khoury, 'Palestinian Detainees Reach Deal to End Hunger Strike'.
25. See, for instance, the sense of longing felt by Fawaz Turki when tasting sea salt, Jabra Ibrahim Jabra's reflection on post-1967 disillusionment in the Arab world via a journey around the Mediterranean or Adania Shibli's tragi-comic and Raja Shehadeh's more tragic accounts of the Palestinian separation from the sea. Nofal et al., 'Reflections on Al-Nakba', p. 10; Jabra, *The Ship*; Shibli, 'This Sea Is Mohammad Al-Khatib's'; Shehadeh, *Strangers in the House*, pp. 1–2.
26. Neimanis, *Bodies of Water*.
27. Chatty, 'Palestinian Refugee Youth', p. 318; Khoury, *Gate of the Sun*, p. 98.

BIBLIOGRAPHY

'1 in 3 People Globally Do Not Have Access to Safe Drinking Water – UNICEF, WHO', *World Health Organization*, 18 June 2019 <https://www.who.int/news-room/detail/18-06-2019-1-in-3-people-globally-do-not-have-access-to-safe-drinking-water-unicef-who> (last accessed 28 August 2019).

'2018: Plight of Gaza Fishermen after Israel's Gradual Destruction of Their Sector', *B'Tselem*, 2019 <https://www.btselem.org/gaza_strip/20190211_gaza_fishermen_plight_due_to_israeli_restrictions> (last accessed 28 August 2019).

Abu El-Haj, Nadia, *Facts on the Ground: Archaeological Practice and Territorial Self-Fashioning in Israeli Society* (Chicago, IL: The University of Chicago Press, 2001).

Abufarha, Nasser, 'Land of Symbols: Cactus, Poppies, Orange and Olive Trees in Palestine', *Identities: Global Studies in Culture and Power*, 15.3 (2008), 343–68.

Abu-Manneh, Bashir, *The Palestinian Novel from 1948 to the Present* (Cambridge: Cambridge University Press, 2016).

Achcar, Gilbert, *The Arabs and the Holocaust: The Arab-Israeli War of Narratives* (London: Picador, 2011).

'Act of Vengeance: Israel's Bombing of the Gaza Power Plant and Its Effects', *B'Tselem*, 2006 <http://www.btselem.org/publications/summaries/200609_act_of_vengeance> (last accessed 20 August 2015).

Agamben, Giorgio, *Homo Sacer: Sovereign Power and Bare Life*, trans. by Daniel Heller-Roazen (Stanford, CA: Stanford University Press, 1998).

Agence France-Presse, 'Beach Stroll by Modi, Netanyahu Makes Internet Waves', *Times of Israel*, 6 July 2017 <https://www.timesofisrael.com/beach-stroll-by-modi-netanyahu-causes-internet-waves/> (last accessed 14 February 2020).

Agence France-Presse, 'Israel Vows to Make Hamas Pay for Alleged Murder of Three Teenagers', *The Guardian*, 1 July 2014 <http://www.theguardian.com/world/2014/jul/01/israel-vows-hamas-pay-murder-teenagers> (last accessed 20 January 2015).

Agsous, Sadia, 'Hegemonic (Israeli) Time and Minority (Palestinian) Space: Sayed Kashua's Chronotopic Approach in Let It Be Morning', *Dibur*, 6 (2018) <https://arcade.stanford.edu/dibur/hegemonic-israeli-time-and-minority-palestinian-space-sayed-kashuas-chronotopic-approach-let> (last accessed 28 August 2019).

Ahmed, Sara, *Cultural Politics of Emotion* (Edinburgh: Edinburgh University Press, 2014).

Alareer, Refaat, 'Editor's Introduction', in *Gaza Writes Back: Short Stories from Young Writers in Gaza, Palestine* (Charlottesville, VA: Just World Books, 2014), pp. 13–26.

Alatout, Samer, 'Towards a Bio-Territorial Conception of Power: Territory, Population, and Environmental Narratives in Palestine and Israel', *Political Geography*, 25.6 (2006), 601–21.

Alatout, Samer, 'From Water Abundance to Water Scarcity (1936–1959): A "Fluid" History of Jewish Subjectivity in Historic Palestine and Israel', in *Reapproaching Borders: New Perspectives on the Study of Israel-Palestine*, ed. by Mark LeVine and Sandy Sufian (Plymouth: Rowman & Littlefield Publishers, 2007), pp. 199–219.

Alatout, Samer, '"States" of Scarcity: Water, Space, and Identity Politics in Israel, 1948–59', *Environment and Planning D: Society and Space*, 26.6 (2008), 959–82.

Alatout, Samer, 'Bringing Abundance into Environmental Politics', *Social Studies of Science*, 39.3 (2009), 363–94.

Al Butmah, Abeer, Bobby Peek and Eurig Scandrett, 'Environmental Nakba: Environmental Injustice and Violations of the Israeli Occupation of Palestine', *Friends of the Earth International*, 2013 <https://www.foei.org/resources/publications/publications-by-subject/human-rights-defenders-publications/environmental-nakba> (last accessed 14 February 2020).

Allan, John Anthony, 'Hydro-Peace in the Middle East: Why No Water Wars? A Case Study of the Jordan River Basin', *SAIS Review*, 22.2 (2002), 255–72.

Allan, John Anthony, *Virtual Water: Tackling the Threat to Our Planet's Most Precious Resource* (London: I. B. Tauris, 2011).
Allan, Tony, 'IWRM/IWRAM: A New Sanctioned Discourse?' (Occasional Paper 50, SOAS Water Issues Study Group, 2003) <https://lwrg.files.wordpress.com/2014/12/iwram-a-new-sanctioned-discourse.pdf> (last accessed 28 August 2019).
'Allush, Layla, 'The Path of Affection', trans. by Salma Khadra Jayyusi and Naomi Shihab Nye, in *Anthology of Modern Palestinian Literature*, ed. by Salma Khadra Jayyusi (New York: Columbia University Press, 1994), pp. 106–7.
Almog, Oz, *The Sabra: The Creation of the New Jew* (Berkeley, CA: University of California Press, 2000).
Al-Sousi, Nour, 'Canary', in *Gaza Writes Back: Short Stories from Young Writers in Gaza, Palestine*, ed. by Refaat Alareer (Charlottesville, VA: Just World Books, 2013), pp. 53–8.
Amichai, Yehuda, 'Once I Wrote Now and in Other Days: Thus Glory Passes, Thus Pass the Psalms', in *Open Closed Open: Poems*, trans. by Chana Bloch and Chana Kronfeld (New York: Harcourt, 2000), pp. 29–36.
'Amr, Sāmī, *A Young Palestinian's Diary, 1941–1945: The Life of Sāmī 'Amr*, trans. by Kimberley Katz (Austin, TX: University of Texas Press, 2009).
Anand, Nikhil, *Hydraulic City: Water and the Infrastructures of Citizenship in Mumbai* (Durham, NC: Duke University Press, 2017).
Anderson, Mark D., *Disaster Writing: The Cultural Politics of Catastrophe in Latin America* (Charlottesville, VA: University of Virginia Press, 2011).
Andrews, Jennifer, 'Rethinking the Relevance of Magic Realism for English-Canadian Literature: Reading Ann-Marie MacDonald's Fall On Your Knees', *Studies in Canadian Literature/Études En Littérature Canadienne*, 24.1 (1999), 1–19.
Anton, Glenna, 'Blind Modernism and Zionist Waterscape', *Jerusalem Quarterly*, 35 (2008), 76–92.
Antreasyan, Anaïs, 'Gas Finds in the Eastern Mediterranean: Gaza, Israel, and Other Conflicts', *Journal of Palestine Studies*, 42.3 (2013), 29–47.
Armstrong, John A., 'Braudel's Mediterranean: Un Défi Latin', *World Politics*, 29.4 (1977), 626–36.
Arnold, David, 'Introduction: Disease, Medicine and Empire', in *Imperial Medicine and Indigenous Societies*, ed. by David Arnold (Manchester: Manchester University Press, 1988), pp. 1–26.
Aruri, Naseer, *Dishonest Broker: America's Role in Israel and Palestine* (Cambridge, MA: South End Press, 2003).

Ashly, Jaclynn, 'Drowning in the Waste of Israeli Settlers', *Al Jazeera*, 18 September 2017 <https://www.aljazeera.com/indepth/features/2017/09/drowning-waste-israeli-settlers-170916120027885.html> (last accessed 28 August 2019).

Atash (*Thirst*), film, directed by Tawfiq Abu Wael (Israel/Palestine: Axiom Films, 2004).

Avgar, Ido, *Israeli Water Sector—Key Issues*, The Knesset, Research and Information Center, 2018 <https://m.knesset.gov.il/EN/activity/mmm/mmmeng250218.pdf> (last accessed 28 August 2019).

Azaryahu, Maoz, 'Water Towers: A Study in the Cultural Geographies of Zionist Mythology', *Cultural Geographies*, 8.3 (2001), 317–39.

Azaryahu, Maoz, 'The Formation of the "Hebrew Sea" in Pre-State Israel', *Journal of Modern Jewish Studies*, 7.3 (2008), 251–67.

Bachelard, Gaston, *Water and Dreams: An Essay on the Imagination of Matter*, trans. by Edith R. Farrell (Dallas, TX: Pegasus Foundation, [1942] 1983).

Baker, Jan, 'Fears and Fantasies of Swimming and Being in Water', *Psychodynamic Practice*, 11.3 (2005), 311–24.

Bakker, Karen, *An Uncooperative Commodity: Privatizing Water in England and Wales* (Oxford: Oxford University Press, 2003).

Bakker, Karen, 'Neoliberalizing Nature? Market Environmentalism in Water Supply in England and Wales', *Annals of the Association of American Geographers*, 95.3 (2005), 542–65.

Ball, Anna, *Palestinian Literature and Film in Postcolonial Feminist Perspective* (Abingdon: Routledge, 2012).

Bardenstein, Carol, 'Threads of Memory and Discourses of Rootedness: Of Trees, Oranges, and the Prickly Pear Cactus in Israel/Palestine', *Edebiyat*, 8.1 (1998), 1–36.

Bardenstein, Carol B., 'Trees, Forests, and the Shaping of Palestinian and Israeli Collective Memory', in *Acts of Memory: Cultural Recall in the Present*, ed. by Mieke Bal, Jonathan V. Crewe and Leo Spitzer (Hanover, NH: University Press of New England, 1999), pp. 148–68.

Bar-Gal, Yoram, *Propaganda and Zionist Education: The Jewish National Fund, 1924–1947* (Rochester, NY: University of Rochester Press and University of Haifa Press, 2003).

Bar-Gal, Yoram and Shmuel Shamai, 'The Jezreel Valley Swamps—Legend and Reality', *Cathedra*, 27 (1983), 163–79.

Barghouti, Mourid, *I Saw Ramallah*, trans. by Adhaf Soueif (London: Bloomsbury, 2004).

Barghouti, Mourid, *I Was Born There, I Was Born Here*, trans. by Humphrey Davis (London: Bloomsbury, 2011).

Baroud, Ramzy, *My Father Was a Freedom Fighter: Gaza's Untold Story* (London: Pluto, 2010).

Baroud, Ramzy and Mahfouz Abu Turk, *Searching Jenin: Eyewitness Accounts of the Israeli Invasion, 2002* (Seattle, WA: Cune Press, 2003).

Barrell, John, 'The Public Prospect and the Private View: The Politics of Taste in Eighteenth-Century Britain', in *Reading Landscape: Country, City, Capital*, ed. by Simon Pugh (Manchester: Manchester University Press, 1990), pp. 19–40.

Bashir, Bashir and Amos Goldberg, *The Holocaust and the Nakba: A New Grammar of Trauma and History* (New York: Columbia University Press, 2018).

Bauman, Zygmunt, *Liquid Modernity* (Cambridge: Polity Press, 2000).

Bauman, Zygmunt, *Wasted Lives: Modernity and Its Outcasts* (Cambridge: Polity Press, 2004).

Bear, Chris and Jacob Bull, 'Water Matters: Agency, Flows, and Frictions', *Environment and Planning A*, 43.10 (2011), 2261–6.

Beaumont, Peter, 'Welcome to Shuafat, East Jerusalem: Where Water Comes Only after Dark', *The Guardian*, 14 April 2014 <http://www.theguardian.com/world/2014/apr/14/welcome-shuafat-jerusalem-camp-water-palestinians-israel> (last accessed 28 August 2019).

Beaumont, Peter, 'Israel Exonerates Itself over Gaza Beach Killings of Four Children Last Year', *The Guardian*, 11 June 2015 <http://www.theguardian.com/world/2015/jun/11/israel-clears-military-gaza-beach-children> (last accessed 28 August 2019).

Bender, Barbara, 'Time and Landscape', *Current Anthropology*, 43.S4 (2002), 103–12.

Ben-Gurion, David, 'The Navy, Israel and the Sea', in *Rebirth and Destiny of Israel*, ed. by Mordekhai Nurock (New York: Philosophical Library, 1954).

Ben-Gurion, David, *Recollections*, ed. by Thomas M. Bransten (London: Macdonald Unit 75, 1970).

Benin, Joel, 'No More Tears: Benny Morris and the Road Back from Liberal Zionism', *Middle East Report*, 34.1 (2004), 38–45.

Bennet, James, 'Police Used Excessive Force on Israeli Arabs, Panel Says', *New York Times*, 2 September 2003 <http://www.nytimes.com/2003/09/02/world/police-used-excessive-force-on-israeli-arabs-panel-says.html> (last accessed 28 August 2019).

Bennett, Jane, *Vibrant Matter: A Political Ecology of Things* (Durham, NC: Duke University Press, 2010).

Benstein, Jeremy, *The Way into Judaism and the Environment* (Woodstock, VT: Jewish Lights Publishing, 2006).

Benvenisti, Meron, *Sacred Landscape: The Buried History of the Holy Land Since 1948* (Berkeley, CA: University of California Press, 2000).

Bergquist, Daniel A., 'Sustainability and Local People's Participation in Coastal Aquaculture: Regional Differences and Historical Experiences in Sri Lanka and the Philippines', *Environmental Management*, 40.5 (2007), 787–802.

Berman, 'Falling Towers: City Life After Urbicide', in *Geography and Identity: Living and Exploring Geopolitics of Identity*, ed. by Dennis Crow (Washington, DC: Maisonneuve Press, 1996), pp. 172–92.

Bernard, Anna, '"Who Would Dare to Make It into an Abstraction": Mourid Barghouti's *I Saw Ramallah*', *Textual Practice*, 21.4 (2007), 665–86.

Bernard, Anna, 'Another Black September? Palestinian Writing after 9/11', *Journal of Postcolonial Writing*, 46.3–4 (2010), 349–58.

Bernard, Anna, 'Sayed Kashua', *The Literary Encyclopedia*, 2012 <http://www.litencyc.com/php/speople.php?rec=true&UID=13077> (last accessed 28 August 2019).

Bernard, Anna, *Rhetorics of Belonging: Nation, Narration, and Israel/Palestine* (Liverpool: Liverpool University Press, 2013).

Bernard, Anna and Ziad Elmarsafy, 'Intimacies: In Memoriam Mahmoud Darwish', *Interventions*, 14.1 (2012), 1–12.

Bernard, Anna, Ziad Elmarsafy and Stuart Murray, 'Introduction: What Postcolonial Theory Doesn't Say', in *What Postcolonial Theory Doesn't Say*, ed. by Anna Bernard, Ziad Elmarsafy and Stuart Murray (Abingdon: Routledge, 2015), pp. 1–12.

Bewell, Alan, *Romanticism and Colonial Disease* (Baltimore, MD: Johns Hopkins University Press, 1999).

Bhabha, Homi, 'Introduction: Narrating the Nation', in *Nation and Narration*, ed. by Homi Bhabha (London: Routledge, 1990), pp. 1–7.

Bhattacharyya, Gargi, 'Globalizing Racism and Myths of the Other in the "War on Terror"', in *Thinking Palestine*, ed. by Ronit Lentin (London: Zed Books, 2008), pp. 46–61.

Biger, Gideon, *The Boundaries of Modern Palestine, 1840–1947* (Abingdon and New York: RoutledgeCurzon, 2004).

Biger, Gideon, 'Ideology and the Landscape of British Palestine, 1918–1929', in *Ideology and Landscape in Historical Perspective: Essays on the Meanings of Some Places in the Past*, ed. by Alan R. H. Baker and Gideon Biger (Cambridge: Cambridge University Press, 2006), pp. 173–96.

Bishara, Azmi, 'Reflections on October 2000: A Landmark in Jewish-Arab Relations in Israel', *Journal of Palestine Studies*, 30.3 (2001), 54–67.

Bloom, Dan, *The Cli-Fi Report*, 2019 <http://cli-fi.net/> (last accessed 28 August 2019).

Blum, Hester, 'Introduction: Oceanic Studies', *Atlantic Studies*, 10.2 (2013), 151–5.

Boast, Hannah, '"Planted Over the Past": Ideology and Ecology in Israel's National Eco-Imaginary', *Green Letters*, 16.1 (2012), 46–58.

Boelens, Rutgerd, Esha Shah and Bert Bruins, 'Contested Knowledges: Large Dams and Mega-Hydraulic Development', *Water*, 11.3 (2019), 416.

Bowers, Maggie Ann, *Magic(al) Realism* (Abingdon: Routledge, 2013).

Boyarin, Daniel, *Unheroic Conduct: The Rise of Heterosexuality and the Invention of the Jewish Man* (Berkeley, CA: University of California Press, 1997).

Boym, Svetlana, *The Future of Nostalgia* (New York: Basic Books, 2001).

Braudel, Fernand, *The Mediterranean and the Mediterranean World in the Age of Philip II*, 2 vols, trans. by Siân Reynolds (Berkeley, CA: University of California Press, 1995).

Braverman, Irus, 'Silent Springs: The Nature of Water and Israel's Military Occupation', *Environment and Planning E: Nature and Space*, 2019, 1–25.

Brouillette, Sarah, *Postcolonial Writers in the Global Literary Marketplace* (Basingstoke: Palgrave Macmillan, 2007).

Buckingham, James Silk, *Travels in Palestine, Through the Countries of Basahan and Gilead East of the River Jordan: Including a Visit to the Cities of Geraza and Gamala, in the Decapolis* (London: Longman, Hurst, Rees, Orme, and Brown, 1822).

Buell, Lawrence, *The Environmental Imagination: Thoreau, Nature Writing, and the Formation of American Culture* (Cambridge, MA: Belknap Press of Harvard University Press, 1995).

Buell, Lawrence, *Writing for an Endangered World: Literature, Culture and Environment in the U.S. and Beyond* (Cambridge, MA: Belknap Press of Harvard University Press, 2001).

Buell, Lawrence, 'Wetlands Aesthetics', *Environmental History*, 10.4 (2005), 670–1.

Busbridge, Rachel, 'Israel-Palestine and the Settler Colonial "Turn": From Interpretation to Decolonization', *Theory, Culture & Society*, 35.1 (2018), 91–115.

Butler, Judith, *Precarious Life: The Powers of Mourning and Violence* (London: Verso, 2006).

Butler, Judith, *Frames of War: When Is Life Grievable?* (London: Verso, 2010).

Bystrom, Kerry and Isabel Hofmeyr, eds, 'Oceanic Routes: An ACLA Forum', *Comparative Literature*, 69.1 (2017).

Carmi, Daniella, *Izim* (Tel Aviv: Am Oved, 2011).

Carrigan, Anthony, 'Compound Disaster, Uneven Recovery: Reading the Catastrophic Legacies of 1970–71 in Bangladesh' (unpublished keynote lecture presented at Resources of Resistance: Production, Consumption, Transformation, University of York, 2014).

Carrigan, Anthony, 'Introduction: Representing Catastrophe [Pre-Publication Draft]', *Moving Worlds: A Journal of Transcultural Writings*, 14.2 (2014), 1–13.

Cascão, Ana Elisa et al., 'Why Are Water Wars Back on the Agenda?', *Undisciplined Environments*, 22 March 2018 <https://undisciplinedenvironments.org/2018/03/22/why-are-water-wars-back-on-the-agenda-and-why-we-think-its-a-bad-idea/> (last accessed 5 February 2020).

Castel-Bloom, Orly, *Human Parts*, trans. by Dalya Bilu (Boston, MA: David R. Godine, 2003).

Chakrabarty, Dipesh, 'The Climate of History: Four Theses', *Critical Inquiry*, 35.2 (2009), 197–222.

Chambers, Iain, *Mediterranean Crossings: The Politics of an Interrupted Modernity* (Durham, NC: Duke University Press, 2007).

Chatty, Dawn, 'Palestinian Refugee Youth: Agency and Aspiration', *Refugee Survey Quarterly*, 28.2–3 (2009), 318–38.

Chronicle of a Disappearance, film, directed by Elia Suleiman (Israel/Palestine: International Film Circuit, 1996).

Cleary, Joe, *Literature, Partition and the Nation-State: Culture and Conflict in Ireland, Israel and Palestine* (Cambridge: Cambridge University Press, 2002).

Cohen, Amiram, 'Eitam Prohibits Palestinians from Drilling for Water in West Bank', *Haaretz*, 22 October 2002 <https://www.haaretz.com/1.5098415> (last accessed 30 July 2019).

Cohen, Erik and Chaim Noy, 'Introduction: Backpacking as a Rite of Passage in Israel', in *Israeli Backpackers: From Tourism to Rite of Passage*, ed. by Erik Cohen and Chaim Noy (New York: State University of New York Press, 2005), pp. 1–44.

Cohen, Margaret, 'Literary Studies on the Terraqueous Globe', *PMLA*, 125.3 (2010), 657–62.

Cohen, Nir, 'Territorial Stigma Formation in the Israeli City of Bat Yam, 1950–1983: Planning, People and Practice', *Journal of Historical Geography*, 39 (2013), 113–24.

Cohen, Shaul, 'Environmentalism Deferred: Nationalisms and Israeli/Palestinian Imaginaries', in *Environmental Imaginaries of the Middle East and North Africa*, ed. by Diana K. Davis and Edmund Burke III (Pittsburgh, PA: University of Pittsburgh Press, 2011), pp. 246–64.

Connery, Christopher, 'Pacific Rim Discourse: The US Global Imaginary in the Late Cold War Years', in *Asia/Pacific as Space of Cultural Production*, ed. by Rob Wilson and Arif Dirlik (Durham, NC: Duke University Press, 1995), pp. 30–56.

Cook, Jonathan, 'The Negev's Hot Wind Blowing', *Middle East Research and Information Project*, 25 October 2011 <http://www.merip.org/mero/mero102511> (last accessed 28 August 2019).

Cooper, Marilyn, 'Meir Shalev: Israel's Dictator-in-Writing', *Moment Magazine*, 12 January 2017 <https://momentmag.com/meir-shalev-israels-dictator-writing/> (last accessed 14 February 2020).

Corbin, Alain, *The Foul and the Fragrant: Odor and the French Social Imagination*, trans. by Miriam L. Kochin (Cambridge, MA: Harvard University Press, 1986).

Cosgrove, Denis, 'Prospect, Perspective and the Evolution of the Landscape Idea', *Transactions of the Institute of British Geographers*, 10.1 (1985), 45–62.

Cosgrove, Denis, 'Landscape and the European Sense of Sight – Eyeing Nature', in *Handbook of Cultural Geography*, ed. by Kay Anderson, Mona Domosh, Steve Pile and Nigel Thrift (London: Sage, 2003), pp. 249–68.

Cowan, William Tynes, *The Slave in the Swamp: Disrupting the Plantation Narrative* (New York: Routledge, 2005).

Cronon, William, 'A Place for Stories: Nature, History, and Narrative', *The Journal of American History*, 78.4 (1992), 1347–76.

Crosby, Alfred W., *Ecological Imperialism: The Biological Expansion of Europe, 900–1900* (Cambridge: Cambridge University Press, 2004).

Crutzen, Paul J. and Eugene F. Stoermer, 'The Anthropocene', *International Geosphere-Biosphere Programme [IGBP] Newsletter*, 41 (2000), 17–18.

Cusack, Tricia, *Riverscapes and National Identities* (New York: Syracuse University Press, 2010).

Dabbagh, Selma, *Out of It* (London: Vintage Books, 2011).

Dajani, Muna, 'Drying Palestine: Israel's Systemic Water War', *Al-Shabaka*, 4 September 2014 <https://al-shabaka.org/briefs/drying-palestine-israels-systemic-water-war/> (last accessed 28 August 2019).

Dalla Costa, Mariarosa and Monica Chilese, *Our Mother Ocean: Enclosure, Commons, and the Global Fishermen's Movement*, trans. by Silvia Federici (New York: Common Notions, 2014).

Darwish, Mahmoud, *A River Dies of Thirst*, trans. by Caroline Cobham (London: Saqi, 2009).

Darwish, Mahmoud, *Unfortunately, It Was Paradise: Selected Poems* (Berkeley, CA: University of California Press, 2013).

Davidovitch, Nadav and Rakefet Zalashik, 'Pasteur in Palestine: The Politics of the Laboratory', *Science in Context*, 23.4 (2010), 401–25.

Davis, Diana K. and Edmund Burke III, 'Imperialism, Orientalism, and the Environment in the Middle East: History, Policy, Power, and Practice', in *Environmental Imaginaries of the Middle East and North Africa*, ed. by Diana K. Davis and Edmund Burke III (Athens, OH: Ohio University Press, 2011), pp. 1–22.

Davis, Heather and Zoe Todd, 'On the Importance of a Date, Or, Decolonizing the Anthropocene', *ACME: An International Journal for Critical Geographies*, 16.4 (2017), 761–80.

Davis, Mike, *Ecology of Fear* (London: Picador, 1999).

Davis, Mike, *Planet of Slums* (London: Verso, 2006).

Davis, Rochelle, *Palestinian Village Histories: Geographies of the Displaced* (Stanford, CA: Stanford University Press, 2011).

De Châtel, Francesca, 'Baptism in the Jordan River: Immersing in a Contested Transboundary Watercourse', *WIREsWATER*, 1.2 (2014), 219–27.

Deckard, Sharae, 'Water Shocks: Neoliberal Hydrofiction and the Crisis of "Cheap Water"', *Atlantic Studies*, 16.1 (2019), 108–25.

Deckard, Sharae and Stephen Shapiro, eds, *World Literature, Neoliberalism, and the Culture of Discontent* (London: Palgrave Macmillan, 2019).

Deguilhem, Randi, 'The Waqf in the City', in *The City in the Islamic World* (2 vols), ed. by Salma Khadra Jayyusi, Renata Holod, Antillio Petruccioli and André Raymond (Leiden: Brill, 2008), pp. 926–56.

Del Sarto, Raffaella A., 'Israel's Contested Identity and the Mediterranean', *Mediterranean Politics*, 8.1 (2003), 27–58.

DeLoughrey, Elizabeth, 'Toward a Critical Ocean Studies for the Anthropocene', *English Language Notes*, 57.1 (2019), 21–36.

DeLoughrey, Elizabeth and George B. Handley, 'Introduction: Towards an Aesthetics of the Earth', in *Postcolonial Ecologies: Literatures of the Environment*, ed. by Elizabeth M. DeLoughrey and George B. Handley (Oxford: Oxford University Press, 2011), pp. 3–42.

DeLoughrey, Elizabeth M., *Routes and Roots: Navigating Caribbean and Pacific Island Literatures* (Honolulu, HI: University of Hawaii Press, 2007).
Deverell, William and Douglas Flamming, 'Race, Rhetoric and Regional Identity: Boosting Los Angeles, 1880–1930', in *Power and Place in the North American West*, ed. by Richard White and John M. Findlay (Seattle, WA: University of Washington Press, 1999), pp. 117–43.
Domb, Risa, 'The Arab in Fact and Fiction – as Reflected in the Works of Moshe Smilansky', *Jewish Quarterly*, 29.4 (1981), 3–7.
Dorrian, Mark, 'Fluid and Viscous Landscapes', in *Deterritorialisations: Revisioning Landscape and Politics*, ed. by Mark Dorrian and Gillian Rose (London: Black Dog Publishing, 2003), pp. 22–3.
Douglas, Mary, *Purity and Danger: An Analysis of Concepts of Pollution and Taboo* (London: Routledge, 2003).
Dowty, Alan, 'Much Ado about Little: Ahad Ha'am's "Truth from Eretz Yisrael," Zionism, and the Arabs', *Israel Studies*, 5.2 (2000), 154–81.
Egoz, Shelley, 'The Pardess: An Israeli Symbolic Landscape', *Landscape Research*, 22.2 (1997), 175–89.
Eisenzweig, Uri, 'An Imaginary Territory: The Problematic of Space in Zionist Discourse', *Dialectical Anthropology*, 5.4 (1981), 261–85.
'Fact Sheet: Demolition and Destruction of Water, Sanitation and Hygiene (WASH) Infrastructure in the Occupied Palestinian Territory (OPT)', *EWASH Advocacy Task Force*, 2012 <https://web.archive.org/web/20140913175305/http://www.ewash.org/files/library/factsheet%2011%20-%20demolition.pdf> (last accessed 28 August 2019).
'Fact Sheet: How Gaza's Blockade Impacts on Water and Sanitation', *EWASH Advocacy Task Force*, 2011 <https://web.archive.org/web/20150403034321/http://www.ewash.org/files/library/Factsheet%201%20-%20A4.pdf> (last accessed 28 August 2019).
Farag, Joseph R., *Palestinian Literature in Exile: Gender, Aesthetics and Resistance in the Short Story* (London: I. B. Tauris, 2016).
Faris, Wendy B., *Ordinary Enchantments: Magical Realism and the Remystification of Narrative* (Nashville, TN: Vanderbilt University Press, 2004).
Farnsworth, Elizabeth 'Coping with Conflict: Israeli Author Amos Oz', *PBS Newshour*, 23 January 2002 < https://www.pbs.org/newshour/show/coping-with-conflict-israeli-author-amos-oz> (last accessed 28 August 2019).
Farrier, David, 'Washing Words: The Politics of Water in Mourid Barghouti's I Saw Ramallah', *The Journal of Commonwealth Literature*, 48.2 (2013), 187–99.

Flapan, Simha, *The Birth of Israel: Myths and Realities* (New York: Pantheon, 1987).
Flood, Alison, 'Translated Fiction Enjoys Sales Boom as UK Readers Flock to European Authors', *The Guardian*, 6 March 2019 <https://www.theguardian.com/books/2019/mar/06/translated-fiction-enjoys-sales-boom-as-uk-readers-flock-to-european-authors> (last accessed 8 August 2019).
Foucault, Michel, *The History of Sexuality Vol. 1, an Introduction* (New York: Vintage Books, 1980).
Foucault, Michel, 'On Governmentality', in *The Foucault Effect: Studies in Governmentality*, ed. by Graham Burchell, Colin Gordon and Peter Miller (Chicago, IL: University of Chicago Press, 1991), pp. 102–3.
Foucault, Michel, *Society Must Be Defended: Lectures at the Collège de France, 1975–76*, trans. by David Macey (New York: Picador, 2003).
Freedland, Jonathan, 'Cease Fire', *The Guardian*, 22 February 2001 <http://www.theguardian.com/culture/2001/feb/22/artsfeatures.israelandthepalestinians/print> (last accessed 28 August 2019).
Freud, Sigmund, *The Uncanny, with an Introduction by Hugh Haughton*, trans. by David McLintock (London: Penguin Books, 2003).
Gandy, Matthew, *Concrete and Clay: Reworking Nature in New York City* (Cambridge, MA: MIT Press, 2002).
Gandy, Matthew, *The Fabric of Space: Water, Modernity, and the Urban Imagination* (Cambridge, MA: MIT Press, 2014).
Garb, Yaakov, 'Desalination in Israel: Status, Prospects, and Contexts', in *Water Wisdom: Preparing the Groundwork for Cooperative and Sustainable Water Management in the Middle East*, ed. by Alon Tal and Rabbo (Piscataway, NJ: Rutgers University Press, 2010), pp. 238–45.
Garone, Philip, *The Fall and Rise of the Wetlands of California's Great Central Valley* (Berkeley, CA: University of California Press, 2011).
Gavron, Assaf, *Hydromania* [Synopsis, Review Quotes, Sample Translation], trans. by Assaf Gavron (unpublished manuscript, 2010).
'Gaza Emergency Humanitarian Snapshot (as of 29 August 2014, 8:00 hrs)', *United Nations Office for the Coordination of Humanitarian Affairs in the occupied Palestinian territory (UN OCHA oPt)*, 1 September 2014 < https://www.ochaopt.org/content/gaza-emergency-humanitarian-snapshot-29-august-2014-800-hrs> (last accessed 28 August 2019).
'Gaza: Initial Rapid Assessment, 27 August 2014', *United Nations Office for the Coordination of Humanitarian Affairs in the occupied Palestinian territory (UN OCHA*

oPt), 2014 < https://reliefweb.int/report/occupied-palestinian-territory/gaza-initial-rapid-assessment-27-august-2014> (last accessed 28 August 2019).

'Gaza Strip Electricity Supply', *United Nations Office for the Coordination of Humanitarian Affairs - Occupied Palestinian Territory (OCHA OPt)*, last updated 25 August 2019 <https://www.ochaopt.org/page/gaza-strip-electricity-supply> (last accessed 28 August 2019).

Ghosh, Amitav, 'Petrofiction: The Oil Encounter and the Novel', *The New Republic*, 1992, 29–33.

Giaccaria, Paolo and Claudio Minca, 'The Mediterranean Alternative', *Progress in Human Geography*, 35.3 (2011), 345–65.

Giblett, Rodney James, *Postmodern Wetlands: Culture, History, Ecology* (Edinburgh: Edinburgh University Press, 1996).

Gilbert, Emily, 'The Militarization of Climate Change', *ACME: An International Journal for Critical Geographies*, 11.1 (2012), 1–14.

Gilroy, Paul, *The Black Atlantic: Modernity and Double Consciousness* (London: Verso, 1993).

Ginsburg, Shai P., *Rhetoric and Nation: The Formation of Hebrew National Culture, 1880–1990* (Syracuse, NY: Syracuse University Press, 2014).

'Going Green: Israeli Military Chooses Solar Energy over Diesel', *Israel Defense Forces*, 4 February 2014 < https://web.archive.org/web/20140915130315/https://www.idfblog.com/blog/2014/02/05/going-green-israeli-military-chooses-solar-energy-diesel/> (last accessed 28 August 2019).

Gorney, Edna, '"Desolate" vs."Wondrous" and "Wild" vs."Rational": Representations of Nature, Native, and Self in Two Geography Books About the Hula Valley, Northern Israel', in *Palestinian and Israeli Environmental Narratives*, ed. by Stuart Schoenfeld (Toronto: Centre for International and Security Studies, York University, 2005), pp. 339–49.

Gorz, André, 'The Social Ideology of the Motorcar', in *Ecology as Politics*, trans. by Patsy Vigderman and Jonathan Cloud (Montreal and New York: Black Rose Books, 1980), pp. 69–77.

Goubert, Jean-Pierre, *The Conquest of Water: The Advent of Health in the Industrial Age*, trans. by Andrew Wilson (London: Polity Press, 1989).

Graham, Stephen, 'Constructing Urbicide by Bulldozer in the Occupied Territories', in *Cities, War, and Terrorism: Towards an Urban Geopolitics*, ed. by Stephen Graham (Oxford: Blackwell, 2004), pp. 192–213.

Graham, Stephen, *Cities Under Siege: The New Military Urbanism* (New York: Verso, 2010).

Gregory, Derek, *The Colonial Present: Afghanistan, Palestine, Iraq* (Oxford: Blackwell, 2004).

Grossman, David, *See Under: Love*, trans. by Betsy Rosenberg (London: Vintage, 1999).

Grumberg, Karen, *Place and Ideology in Contemporary Hebrew Literature* (Syracuse, NY: Syracuse University Press, 2011).

Guha, Ramachandra and Joan Martinez-Alier, *Varieties of Environmentalism: Essays North and South* (Abingdon: Earthscan, 1997).

Gundar-Goshen, Ayelet, *Waking Lions*, trans. by Sondra Silverston (London: Pushkin Press, 2016).

Habjouqa, Tanya, *Occupied Pleasures* (Brooklyn, NY: FotoEvidence, 2015).

Hall, Joseph, 'Shared Sorrow, Shared Abundance: Water-Waste Flows in Palestinian Literature', *Postcolonial Studies*, 18.3 (2015), 257–78.

Hambright, K. D. and T. Zohary, 'Lakes Hula and Agmon: Destruction and Creation of Wetland Ecosystems in Northern Israel', *Wetlands Ecology and Management*, 6.2–3 (1998), 83–9.

Hamilton, Omar Robert, 'At the Islamic University in Gaza', *LRB Blog*, 6 August 2014 <http://www.lrb.co.uk/blog/2014/08/06/omar-hamilton/at-the-islamic-university-in-gaza/> (last accessed 28 August 2019).

Handal, Nathalie, *The Lives of Rain* (Northampton, MA: Interlink Books, 2005).

Hanegbi, Haim, Moshé Machover and Akiva Orr, 'The Class Nature of Israeli Society', *New Left Review*, 1.65 (1971), 3–26.

Hanieh, Adam, 'From State-Led Growth to Globalization: The Evolution of Israeli Capitalism', *Journal of Palestine Studies*, 32.4 (2003), 5–21.

Haraway, Donna, 'Anthropocene, Capitalocene, Plantationocene, Chthulucene', *Environmental Humanities*, 6.1 (2015), 159–65.

Hartmann, Betsy, 'Converging on Disaster: Climate Security and the Malthusian Anticipatory Regime for Africa', *Geopolitics*, 19.4 (2014), 757–83.

Haviv, Ayana Sbira, 'Next Year in Kathmandu: Israeli Backpackers and the Formation of a New Israeli Identity', in *Israeli Backpackers: From Tourism to Rite of Passage*, ed. by Erik Cohen and Chaim Noy (Albany, NY: State University of New York Press, 2005), pp. 45–88.

Havrelock, Rachel, 'My Home Is over Jordan: River as Border in Israeli and Palestinian National Mythology', *National Identities*, 9.2 (2007), 105–26.

Havrelock, Rachel, *River Jordan: The Mythology of a Dividing Line* (Chicago, IL: University of Chicago Press, 2011).

Hays, James B. and Abraham E. Barrekette, *T.V.A. on the Jordan; Proposals for Irrigation and Hydro-electric Development in Palestine* (Washington, DC: Public Affairs Press, 1948).

Herbert, Gilbert, 'A View of the Sea: Jews and the Maritime Tradition', in *Jewish Topographies: Visions of Space, Traditions of Place*, ed. by Julia Brauch, Anna Lipphardt and Alexandra Nocke (Aldershot: Ashgate, 2008), pp. 181–200.

Herzfeld, Michael, 'The Horns of the Mediterraneanist Dilemma', *American Ethnologist*, 11.3 (1984), 439–54.

Herzl, Theodor, *Altneuland*, trans. by Paula Arnold (Haifa: Haifa Publishing Company, 1960).

Herzl, Theodor, *The Complete Diaries of Theodor Herzl*, ed. by Raphael Patai, trans. by Harry Zohn, 5 vols (New York: Herzl Press and Thomas Yoseloff, 1960), vol. ii.

Hever, Hannan, 'They Shall Dwell by the Haven of the Sea: Israeli Poetry, 1950–60', *Mediterranean Historical Review*, 17.1 (2002), 49–64.

Hever, Hannan, 'The Zionist Sea: Symbolism and Nationalism in Modernist Hebrew Poetry', *Jewish Culture and History*, 13.1 (2012), 25–41.

Hirsch, Dafna, '"We Are Here to Bring the West, Not Only to Ourselves": Zionist Occidentalism and the Discourse of Hygiene in Mandate Palestine', *International Journal of Middle East Studies*, 41.4 (2009), 577–94.

Hmaidan, Wael, 'Sands Are Running out for Lebanon's Ecosystem', *The Guardian*, 16 August 2006 <https://www.theguardian.com/society/2006/aug/16/guardian-societysupplement.pollution> (last accessed 28 August 2019).

Hochberg, Gil, 'To Be or Not to Be an Israeli Arab: Sayed Kashua and the Prospect of Minority Speech-Acts', *Comparative Literature*, 62.1 (2010), 68–88.

Hochberg, Gil Z., '"Permanent Immigration": Jacqueline Kahanoff, Ronit Matalon, and the Impetus of Levantinism', *Boundary 2*, 31.2 (2004), 219–43.

Hochberg, Gil Z., *In Spite of Partition: Jews, Arabs, and the Limits of Separatist Imagination* (Princeton, NJ: Princeton University Press, 2007).

Hochberg, Gil Z:, '"The Mediterranean Option": On the Politics of Regional Affiliation in Current Israeli Cultural Imagination', *Journal of Levantine Studies*, 1.1 (2011), 52.

Howarth, William L., 'Imagined Territory: The Writing of Wetlands', *New Literary History*, 30.3 (1999), 509–39.

'Hula Lake Park – Birding in Israel', *Keren Kayemeth LeIsrael – Jewish National Fund*, n.d. <http://www.kkl.org.il/eng/tourism-and-recreation/forests-and-parks/hula-lake-park.aspx> (last accessed 28 August 2019).

Institute for the Translation of Hebrew Literature, 'Meir Shalev', n.d. <http://www.ithl.org.il/page_13835> (last accessed 14 February 2020).

Intergovernmental Panel on Climate Change (IPCC) Working Group II, 'Freshwater Resources', in *Climate Change 2014: Impacts, Adaptation, and Vulnerability*, 2014, pp. 229–57 <https://www.ipcc.ch/site/assets/uploads/2018/02/WGIAR5-Chap3_FINAL.pdf> (last accessed 6 August 2019).

Interrupted Streams, film, directed by Alexandre Goetschmann and Guy Davidi (Palestine: 2010).

'Investigations', *Forensic Architecture* <https://forensic-architecture.org//> (last accessed 20 August 2019).

Iovino, Serenella, 'Introduction: Mediterranean Ecocriticism, or, A Blueprint for Cultural Amphibians', *Ecozon@*, 4.2 (2013), 1–17.

Isaac, Jad, Manal Khalil, Khaldoun Rishmawi, Ahmad Dabouqi and Ludovico Marinelli, 'The Economic Costs of the Israeli Occupation for the Occupied Palestinian Territory', *Applied Research Institute - Jerusalem (ARIJ)*, 2015 < https://www.arij.org/files/arijadmin/2016/The_Economic_Cost_of_the_Israeli_occupation_Report_upd.pdf > (last accessed 28 August 2019).

Islam, Md Saidul, *Confronting the Blue Revolution: Industrial Aquaculture and Sustainability in the Global South* (Toronto: University of Toronto Press, 2014).

'Israeli Forces Destroy UNICEF-Funded Water Pipeline in Jordan Valley', *Maan News Agency*, 20 February 2017 <https://web.archive.org/web/20170222112515/http://www.maannews.com/Content.aspx?ID=775564 > (last accessed 17 February 2020).

Ivry, Sarah and Daniel Estrin, 'Amos Oz, 74 Years Old and a National Treasure, Still Dreams of Life on the Kibbutz', *Vox Tablet*, 23 September 2013 <http://tabletmag.com/podcasts/145655/amos-oz-interview> (last accessed 28 August 2019).

Jabra, Jabra Ibrahim, *The Ship*, trans. by Adnan Haydar and Roger Allen (Washington, DC: Three Continents Press, 1985).

Jabra, Jabra Ibrahim, *The First Well*, trans. by Issa J. Boullata (Fayetteville, NC: University of Arkansas Press, 1995).

Jacobs, Gerald, 'Amos Oz: "I Was Angry with My Mother for Killing Herself"', *Jewish Chronicle*, 26 February 2009 < https://www.thejc.com/culture/interviews/interview-amos-oz-1.7825> (last accessed 28 August 2019).

Jaffa: The Orange's Clockwork, film, directed by Eyal Sivan (Israel: Momento!, 2009).

Jameson, Fredric, 'On Magic Realism in Film', *Critical Inquiry*, 12.2 (1986), 301–25.

Jayyusi, Salma Khadra, 'Introduction', in *Anthology of Modern Palestinian Literature*, ed. by Salma Khadra Jayyusi (New York: Columbia University Press, 1992), pp. 1–80.

Johnson, Penny and Eileen Kuttab, 'Where Have All the Women (and Men) Gone? Reflections on Gender and the Second Palestinian Intifada', *Feminist Review*, 69 (2001), 21–43.

Joyce, Patrick, *The Rule of Freedom: Liberalism and the Modern City* (London: Verso, 2003).

Kadman, Noga, *Erased from Space and Consciousness: Israel and the Depopulated Palestinian Villages of 1948* (Bloomington, IN: Indiana University Press, 2015).

Kaika, Maria, *City of Flows: Modernity, Nature, and the City* (London: Routledge, 2005).

Kaika, Maria and Erik Swyngedouw, 'Fetishizing the Modern City: The Phantasmagoria of Urban Technological Networks', *International Journal of Urban and Regional Research*, 24.1 (2000), 120–38.

Kanafani, Ghassan, *Men in the Sun*, trans. by Hilary Kilpatrick (Washington, DC: Three Continents Press, 1983).

Kaplan, Eran, *The Jewish Radical Right: Revisionist Zionism and Its Ideological Legacy* (Madison, WI: University of Wisconsin Press, 2005).

Kaplan, Eran, *Beyond Post-Zionism* (Albany, NY: State University of New York Press, 2015).

Kark, Ruth, and Noam Levin, 'The Environment in Palestine in the Late Ottoman Period, 1798–1918', in *Between Ruin and Restoration: An Environmental History of Israel*, ed. by Daniel E. Orenstein, Alon Tal and Char Miller (Pittsburgh, PA: University of Pittsburgh Press, 2013), pp. 1–28.

Karlinsky, Nahum, *California Dreaming: Ideology, Society, And Technology in the Citrus Industry of Palestine, 1890–1939* (Albany, NY: State University of New York Press, 2005).

Karmon, Yehuda, 'The Drainage of the Huleh Swamps', *Geographical Review*, 50.2 (1960), 169–93.

Kashua, Sayed, *Let It Be Morning*, trans. by Miriam Shlesinger (London: Atlantic Books, 2007).

Kashua, Sayed, 'Why Sayed Kashua Is Leaving Jerusalem and Never Coming Back', *Haaretz*, 4 July 2014 <https://www.haaretz.com/.premium-for-sayed-kashua-co-existence-has-failed-1.5254338> (last accessed 28 August 2019).

Katriel, Tamar, 'Sites of Memory: Discourses of the Past in Israeli Pioneering Settlement Museums', *Quarterly Journal of Speech*, 80.1 (1994), 1–20.

Katriel, Tamar, *Performing the Past: A Study of Israeli Settlement Museums* (Abingdon: Routledge, 1997).

Kausch, Kristina and Richard Youngs, 'The End of the "Euro-Mediterranean Vision"', *International Affairs*, 85.5 (2009), 963–75.

Kellerman, Aharon, 'Settlement Myth and Settlement Activity: Interrelationships in the Zionist Land of Israel', *Transactions of the Institute of British Geographers*, 21.2 (1996), 363–78.

Khalidi, Walid, *All That Remains: The Palestinian Villages Occupied and Depopulated by Israel in 1948* (Washington, DC: Institute for Palestine Studies, 1992).

Khalifeh, Sahar, *The Inheritance*, trans. by Aida Bamia (Cairo and New York: The American University in Cairo Press, 2005).

Khalifeh, Sahar, *Wild Thorns*, trans. by Trevor LeGassick and Elizabeth Fernea (London: Saqi, 2005).

Khalili, Laleh, *Heroes and Martyrs of Palestine: The Politics of National Commemoration* (Cambridge: Cambridge University Press, 2007).

Khalili, Laleh, 'A Habit of Destruction', *Society and Space - Environment and Planning D*, 25 August 2014 <https://societyandspace.org/2014/08/25/a-habit-of-destruction/> (last accessed 28 August 2019).

Khawalde, Sliman and Dan Rabinowitz, 'Race from the Bottom of the Tribe That Never Was: Segmentary Narratives amongst the Ghawarna of Galilee', *Journal of Anthropological Research*, 58.2 (2002), 225–43.

Khoury, Elias, *Gate of the Sun*, trans. by Humphrey Davies (London: Vintage, 2006).

Khoury, Jack, 'Palestinian Detainees Reach Deal to End Hunger Strike', *Haaretz*, 25 June 2014 <https://www.haaretz.com/palestinian-inmates-end-hunger-strike-1.5253242> (last accessed 28 August 2019).

Kimmerling, Baruch, *Politicide: Ariel Sharon's War Against the Palestinians* (London: Verso, 2003).

King, Tiffany Lethabo, *The Black Shoals: Offshore Formations of Black and Native Studies* (Durham, NC: Duke University Press, 2019).

Kliot, Nurit, *Water Resources and Conflict in the Middle East* (London: Routledge, 1994).

Kosmatopoulos, Nikolas, 'On the Shores of Politics: Sea, Solidarity and the Ships to Gaza', *Environment and Planning D: Society and Space* 37.4 (2019), 740–57.

Lakhani, Nina, '"People Are Dying": How the Climate Crisis Has Sparked an Exodus to the US', *The Guardian*, 29 July 2019 <https://www.theguardian.com/

global-development/2019/jul/29/guatemala-climate-crisis-migration-drought-famine> (last accessed 6 August 2019).
Langley, Tom, 'Exceptional States: The (Bio)Politics of Love in Darwish's A State of Siege', *Interventions*, 14.1 (2012), 69–82.
Langston, Nancy, *Sustaining Lake Superior: An Extraordinary Lake in a Changing World* (New Haven, CT: Yale University Press, 2017).
Laor, Yitzhak, 'It's Wild. It's New. It Turns Men On', *London Review of Books*, 23.18 (2001), 23–4.
Laor, Yitzhak, 'The Tears of Zion', *New Left Review*, 10 (2001), 47–60.
Laor, Yitzhak, *The Myths of Liberal Zionism* (London: Verso, 2009).
Latour, Bruno, *We Have Never Been Modern* (Cambridge, MA: Harvard University Press, 1993).
Lazarus, Neil, *The Postcolonial Unconscious* (Cambridge: Cambridge University Press, 2011).
Lentin, Ronit, ed., *Thinking Palestine* (London: Zed Books, 2008).
Lentin, Ronit, *Traces of Racial Exception: Racializing Israeli Settler Colonialism* (London: Bloomsbury Academic, 2018).
LeVine, Mark, 'The Discourses of Development in Mandate Palestine', *Arab Studies Quarterly*, 17.1/2 (1995), 95–124.
LeVine, Mark, *Overthrowing Geography: Jaffa, Tel Aviv, and the Struggle for Palestine, 1880–1948* (Berkeley, CA: University of California Press, 2005).
Levy, Gideon, *The Punishment of Gaza* (London: Verso, 2010).
Lidman, Melanie, 'Desalination Isn't the Magic Bullet, Water Authority Warns Israelis', *Times of Israel*, 5 June 2018 <https://www.timesofisrael.com/desalination-isnt-the-magic-bullet-water-authority-warns-israelis/> (last accessed 28 August 2019).
Liebman, Charles S. and Eliezer Don-Yehiya, *Civil Religion in Israel* (Berkeley, CA: University of California Press, 1983).
Linebaugh, Peter, and Marcus Rediker, *The Many-Headed Hydra: Sailors, Slaves, Commoners, and the Hidden History of the Revolutionary Atlantic* (Boston, MA: Beacon Press, 2000).
Linton, Jamie, *What Is Water? The History of a Modern Abstraction* (Vancouver: University of British Columbia Press, 2010).
Linton, Jamie and Jessica Budds, 'The Hydrosocial Cycle: Defining and Mobilizing a Relational-Dialectical Approach to Water', *Geoforum*, 57 (2014), 170–80.

Locke, John, *Two Treatises of Government* (Cambridge: Cambridge University Press, [1689] 2004).
Lockman, Zachary, *Comrades and Enemies: Arab and Jewish Workers in Palestine, 1906–1948* (Berkeley, CA: University of California Press, 1996).
Lowdermilk, Walter Clay, *Palestine: Land of Promise* (New York: Harper and Brothers Publishers, 1944).
McClintock, Anne, *Imperial Leather: Race, Gender, and Sexuality in the Colonial Contest* (Abingdon: Routledge, 1995).
Macdonald, Graeme, 'Oil and World Literature', *American Book Review*, 33.3 (2012), 7–31.
McKee, Emily, *Dwelling in Conflict: Negev Landscapes and the Boundaries of Belonging* (Stanford, CA: Stanford University Press, 2016).
McNeill, J. R., *Mosquito Empires: Ecology and War in the Greater Caribbean, 1620–1914* (Cambridge: Cambridge University Press, 2010).
'Made in Israel: Exploiting Palestinian Land for Treatment of Israeli Waste', *B'Tselem*, 2017 < https://www.btselem.org/publications/summaries/201712_made_in_israel> (last accessed 5 February 2020).
Malka, Inbal, 'To the Last Drop', *Haaretz*, 8 December 2008 <https://www.haaretz.com/1.5070812> (last accessed 5 February 2020).
Malkki, Liisa, 'National Geographic: The Rooting of Peoples and the Territorialization of National Identity among Scholars and Refugees', *Cultural Anthropology*, 7.1 (1992), 24–44.
Malm, Andreas, *Fossil Capital: The Rise of Steam Power and the Roots of Global Warming* (London: Verso, 2016).
Manenti, Ambrogio, Claude de Ville de Goyet, Corinna Reinicke, John Macdonald and Julian Donald, 'Report of a Field Assessment of Health Conditions in the Occupied Palestinian Territory', *World Health Organization (WHO)*, February 2016 <http://apps.who.int/gb/Statements/Report_Palestinian_territory/Report_Palestinian_territory-sp.pdf> (last accessed 28 August 2019).
Mann, Barbara, 'Modernism and the Zionist Uncanny: Reading the Old Cemetery in Tel Aviv', *Representations*, 69 (2000), 63–95.
Mann, Barbara E., *A Place in History: Modernism, Tel Aviv, and the Creation of Jewish Urban Space* (Stanford, CA: Stanford University Press, 2006).
Mann, Barbara E., *Space and Place in Jewish Studies* (New Brunswick, NJ: Rutgers University Press, 2012).
Manski, Rebecca, 'Blueprint Negev', *Middle East Research and Information Project*, 256 (2010), 2–7.

Marin, Philippe, Shimon Tal, Joshua Yeres and Klas Ringskog, 'Water Management in Israel: Key Innovations and Lessons Learned for Water-Scarce Countries', *World Bank*, 2017 <http://documents.worldbank.org/curated/en/657531504204943236/pdf/Water-management-in-Israel-key-innovations-and-lessons-learned-for-water-scarce-countries.pdf> (last accessed 23 August 2019).

Marzec, Robert, *Militarizing the Environment: Climate Change and the Security State* (Minneapolis, MN: University of Minnesota Press, 2016).

Masalha, Nur, *Imperial Israel and the Palestinians: The Politics of Expansion* (London: Pluto Press, 2000).

Masalha, Nur, *The Bible and Zionism: Invented Traditions, Archaeology and Post-Colonialism in Palestine-Israel* (London: Zed Books, 2007).

Mason, Michael, 'Climate Change, Securitisation and the Israeli-Palestinian Conflict: Climate Change, Securitisation and the Israeli-Palestinian Conflict', *The Geographical Journal*, 179.4 (2013), 298–308.

Mason, Michael, Mark Zeitoun and Ziad Mimi, 'Compounding Vulnerability: Impacts of Climate Change on Palestinians in Gaza and the West Bank', *Journal of Palestine Studies*, 41.3 (2012), 38–53.

Massad, Joseph, 'The "Post-Colonial" Colony: Time, Space, and Bodies in Palestine/Israel', in *The Persistence of the Palestinian Question: Essays on Zionism and the Palestinians* (Abingdon: Routledge, 2006), pp. 13–40.

Massalha, Manal, 'In Suspension: The Denial of the Rights of the City for Palestinians in Israel and Its Effects on Their Socio-Economic, Cultural and Political Formation: The Case of Umm Al-Fahem' (unpublished PhD thesis, London School of Economics and Political Science (LSE), 2014) <http://etheses.lse.ac.uk/3351/> (last accessed 28 August 2019).

Mattar, Karim, 'Mourid Barghouti's "Multiple Displacements": Exile and the National Checkpoint in Palestinian Literature', *Journal of Postcolonial Writing* 50.1 (2014), 103–15.

'Mediterranean Situation', *UNHCR - UN Refugee Agency*, 2019 <https://data2.unhcr.org/en/situations/mediterranean> (last accessed 25 July 2019).

Mekonnen, Mesfin M. and Arjen Y. Hoekstra, 'Four Billion People Facing Severe Water Scarcity', *Science Advances*, 2.2 (2016), e1500323.

Messerschmid, Clemens, 'Nothing New in the Middle East – Reality and Discourses of Climate Change in the Israeli-Palestinian Conflict', in *Climate Change, Human Security and Violent Conflict: Challenges for Societal Stability*, ed. by Jürgen Scheffran, Michael Brzoska, Hans Günter Brauch, Peter Michael

Link and Janpeter Schilling (Berlin, Heidelberg: Springer Berlin Heidelberg, 2012), pp. 423–59.

Messerschmid, Clemens, 'Hydro-Apartheid and Water Access in Israel-Palestine: Challenging the Myths of Cooperation and Scarcity', in *Decolonizing Palestinian Political Economy: De-development and Beyond*, ed. by Mandy Turner and Omar Shweiki (Basingstoke: Palgrave Macmillan, 2014), 53–76.

Michael, Sami, *Mayim Noshkim Le-Mayim* (Tel Aviv: Am Oved, 2005).

Mikhail, Alan, *Water on Sand: Environmental Histories of the Middle East and North Africa* (Oxford: Oxford University Press, 2013).

Mintz, Alan L., 'Tellers of the Soil', *New Republic*, 9 September 1991, pp. 39–42.

Mintz, Alan L., *Translating Israel: Contemporary Hebrew Literature and Its Reception in America* (Syracuse, NY: Syracuse University Press, 2001).

'Missing Migrants Project', *International Organisation for Migration* (*IOM*), 2019 <https://missingmigrants.iom.int/> (last accessed 25 July 2019).

Mitchell, Timothy, *Rule of Experts: Egypt, Techno-Politics, Modernity* (Berkeley, CA: University of California Press, 2002).

Mitchell, W. J. T., 'Imperial Landscape', in *Landscape and Power*, ed. by W. J. T. Mitchell (Chicago: University of Chicago Press, 2002), pp. 5–34.

Monterescu, Daniel, 'The Palestinian Trail of Fish: Artist's Graffiti Dives into Heart of Refugee Struggle', *Haaretz*, 30 November 2017 <http://pre.haaretz.com/life/.premium.MAGAZINE-trail-of-fish-graffiti-dives-into-heart-of-palestinian-struggle-1.5627199> (last accessed 28 August 2019).

Moore, Jason W., 'Ecology, Capital, and the Nature of Our Times: Accumulation and Crisis in the Capitalist World-Ecology', *Journal of World-Systems Research*, 17.1 (2011), 108–47.

Moore, Jason W., 'The Capitalocene, Part I: On the Nature and Origins of our Ecological Crisis', *The Journal of Peasant Studies*, 44.3 (2017), 594–630.

Morahg, Gilead, 'New Images of Arabs in Israeli Fiction', *Prooftexts*, 6.2 (1986), 147–62.

Morris, Benny, *The Birth of the Palestinian Refugee Problem, 1947–1949* (Cambridge: Cambridge University Press, 1987).

Mortimer-Sandilands, Catriona, 'Melancholy Natures, Queer Ecologies', in *Queer Ecologies: Sex, Nature, Politics, Desire*, ed. by Catriona Mortimer-Sandilands and Bruce Braun (Bloomington, IN: Indiana University Press, 2010).

Mosse, George L., *Fallen Soldiers: Reshaping the Memory of the World Wars* (Oxford: Oxford University Press, 1990).

Naguib, Nefissa, *Women, Water and Memory: Recasting Lives in Palestine* (Leiden: Brill, 2009).

Nash, Linda Lorraine, *Inescapable Ecologies: A History of Environment, Disease, and Knowledge* (Berkeley, CA: University of California Press, 2006).

'National Parks in East Jerusalem', *B'Tselem*, 2014, https://www.btselem.org/jerusalem/national_parks_in_planning (last accessed 28 August 2019).

Neimanis, Astrida, 'Alongside the Right to Water, a Posthumanist Feminist Imaginary', *Journal of Human Rights and the Environment*, 5.1 (2014), 5–24.

Neimanis, Astrida, *Bodies of Water: Posthuman Feminist Phenomenology* (London: Bloomsbury, 2016).

Neumann, Boaz, *Land and Desire in Early Zionism* (Lebanon, NH: Brandeis University Press, 2011).

Nitzan, Jonathan and Shimson Bichler, 'From War Profits to Peace Dividends', *Capital & Class*, 20.3 (1996), 61–94.

Nixon, Rob, *Slow Violence and the Environmentalism of the Poor* (Cambridge, MA: Harvard University Press, 2011).

Nocke, Alexandra, *The Place of the Mediterranean in Modern Israeli Identity* (Leiden: Brill, 2009).

Nofal, Mamdouh, Fawaz Turki, Haidar Abdel Shafi, Inea Bushnaq, Yezid Sayigh, Shafiq al-Hout et al., 'Reflections on Al-Nakba', *Journal of Palestine Studies*, 28.1 (1998), 5–35.

'Not Enough Water in the West Bank', *Visualizing Palestine*, 2013 <https://visualizingpalestine.org/visuals/west-bank-water> (last accessed 28 August 2019).

Nur, Ofer Nordheimer, *Eros and Tragedy: Jewish Male Fantasies and the Masculine Revolution of Zionism* (Brookline, MA: Academic Studies Press, 2014).

Ohana, David, 'Mediterranean Humanism', *Mediterranean Historical Review*, 18.1 (2003), 59–75.

Ohana, David, 'The Mediterranean Option in Israel: An Introduction to the Thought of Jacqueline Kahanoff', *Mediterranean Historical Review*, 21.2 (2006), 239–63.

Ohana, David, 'Foreword', in *The Place of the Mediterranean in Modern Israeli Identity*, by Alexandra Nocke (Leiden: Brill, 2009), pp. xiii–xviii.

Ohana, David, *Israel and Its Mediterranean Identity* (London: Palgrave Macmillan, 2011).

Ohana, David, *The Origins of Israeli Mythology: Neither Canaanites Nor Crusaders* (Cambridge: Cambridge University Press, 2012).

Omer-Sherman, Ranen, *Israel in Exile: Jewish Writing and the Desert* (Urbana, IL: University of Illinois Press, 2006).

Omer-Sherman, Ranen, *Imagining the Kibbutz: Visions of Utopia in Literature and Film* (University Park, PA: Pennsylvania State University Press, 2015).

Orlove, Ben and Steven C. Caton, 'Water Sustainability: Anthropological Approaches and Prospects', *Annual Review of Anthropology*, 39 (2010), 401–15.

Otter, Chris, 'Making Liberalism Durable: Vision and Civility in the Late Victorian City', *Social History*, 27.1 (2002), 1–15.

Oz, Amos, *In the Land of Israel*, trans. by Amos Oz (New York: Vintage, 1983).

Oz, Amos, 'The Meaning of Homeland', in *Under This Blazing Light*, trans. by Nicholas de Lange (Cambridge: Canto, 1996), pp. 77–101.

Oz, Amos, *The Same Sea*, trans. by Nicholas de Lange (London: Vintage, 2002).

Oz, Amos, 'Digging', in *Scenes from Village Life*, trans. by Nicholas de Lange (London: Chatto and Windus, 2012), pp. 55–120.

Oz, Amos, 'In a Faraway Place at Another Time', in *Scenes from Village Life*, trans. by Nicholas de Lange (London: Chatto and Windus, 2012), pp. 255–65.

Oz, Amos, 'Lost', in *Scenes from Village Life*, trans. by Nicholas de Lange (London: Chatto and Windus, 2012), pp. 121–58.

'Palestinian Obligations as Per Note for the Record of the Hebron Protocol of 15 January 1997', *Government of Israel*, 1998 <https://mfa.gov.il/MFA/ForeignPolicy/MFADocuments/Yearbook12/Pages/6%20Government%20statement%20on%20Palestinian%20Obligations.aspx> (last accessed 30 July 2019).

Pappé, Ilan, *Britain and the Arab-Israeli Conflict, 1948–51* (London: Macmillan, 1988).

Pappé, Ilan, *A History of Modern Palestine: One Land, Two Peoples* (Cambridge: Cambridge University Press, 2006).

Pappé, Ilan, *The Ethnic Cleansing of Palestine* (Oxford: Oneworld, 2007).

Pappé, Ilan, *The Forgotten Palestinians: A History of the Palestinians in Israel* (New Haven, CT: Yale University Press, 2011).

Parmenter, Barbara McKean, *Giving Voice to Stones: Place and Identity in Palestinian Literature* (Austin, TX: University of Texas Press, 1994).

Payne, R. J., 'A Longer-Term Perspective on Human Exploitation and Management of Peat Wetlands: The Hula Valley, Israel', *Mires and Peat*, 9.4 (2011), 1–9.

Peleg, Ilan and Dov Waxman, *Israel's Palestinians: The Conflict Within* (Cambridge: Cambridge University Press, 2011).

Peleg, Yaron, *Orientalism and the Hebrew Imagination* (Ithaca, NY: Cornell University Press, 2005).

Peleg, Yaron, 'Heroic Conduct: Homoeroticism and the Creation of Modern, Jewish Masculinities', *Jewish Social Studies*, 13.1 (2006), 31–58.

Peleg, Yaron, *Israeli Culture Between the Two Intifadas: A Brief Romance* (Austin, TX: University of Texas Press, 2009).

Penner, Barbara, *Bathroom* (London: Reaktion Books, 2013).

Penrose, Jan, 'Nations, States and Homelands: Territory and Territoriality in Nationalist Thought', *Nations and Nationalism*, 8.3 (2002), 277–97.

Penslar, Derek J., *Zionism and Technocracy: The Engineering of Jewish Settlement in Palestine, 1870–1918* (Bloomington, IN: Indiana University Press, 1991).

Peppard, Christiana Z., 'Troubling Waters: The Jordan River between Religious Imagination and Environmental Degradation', *Journal of Environmental Studies and Sciences*, 3.2 (2013), 109–19.

Peteet, Julie, 'Male Gender and Rituals of Resistance in the Palestinian Intifada: A Cultural Politics of Violence', *American Ethnologist*, 21.1 (1994), 31–49.

Peters, Kimberley and Jon Anderson, eds, *Water Worlds: Human Geographies of the Ocean* (Farnham: Ashgate, 2014).

Plumwood, Val, *Feminism and the Mastery of Nature* (London: Routledge, 1993).

Porter, Libby and Oren Yiftachel, 'Urbanizing Settler-Colonial Studies: Introduction to the Special Issue', *Settler Colonial Studies*, 9.2 (2017), 177–86.

Presner, Todd Samuel, *Muscular Judaism: The Jewish Body and the Politics of Regeneration* (Abingdon: Routledge, 2007).

Price, Rachel, 'Afterword: The Last Universal Commons', *Comparative Literature*, 69.1 (2017), 45–53.

'Protocol Additional to the Geneva Conventions of 12 August 1949, and Relating to the Protection of Victims of International Armed Conflicts (Protocol I), 1125 UNTS 3', *International Committee of the Red Cross*, 1977 <https://www.icrc.org/ihl/WebART/470-750073?OpenDocument> (last accessed 28 August 2019).

Puar, Jasbir, *Terrorist Assemblages: Homonationalism in Queer Times* (Durham, NC: Duke University Press, 2007).

Punter, David and Glennis Byron, *The Gothic* (Oxford: Blackwell, 2004).

Qualey, M. Lynx, '"The Book of Gaza": Short Stories from Four Decades', 26 July 2014 <https://arablit.org/2014/07/26/the-book-of-gaza-short-stories-from-four-decades/> (last accessed 14 February 2020).

Ram, Uri, *The Changing Agenda of Israeli Sociology: Theory, Ideology, and Identity* (Albany, NY: State University of New York Press, 1993).

Ram, Uri, 'From Nation-State to Nation-----State: Nation, History and Identity Struggles in Jewish Israel', in *The Challenge of Post-Zionism: Alternatives to*

Fundamentalist Politics in Israel, ed. by Ephraim Nimni (London: Zed Books, 2003), pp. 20–41.
Ramras-Rauch, Gila, *The Arab in Israeli Literature* (London: I. B. Tauris, 1989).
Raved, Ahiya, 'Case Closed: Police "Relieved, Frustrated"', *Ynet*, 18 September 2005 <http://www.ynetnews.com/articles/0,7340,L-3143845,00.html> (last accessed 28 August 2019).
Ravikovitch, Dahlia, *The Window: Poems by Dahlia Ravikovitch*, trans. by Chana Bloch and Ariel Bloch (Riverdale-on-Hudson, NY: Sheep Meadow Press, 1989).
'Reader: "Food Consumption in the Gaza Strip – Red Lines"', *Gisha – Legal Center for Freedom of Movement*, 2012 <https://www.gisha.org/UserFiles/File/publications/redlines/redlines-position-paper-eng.pdf> (last accessed 3 July 2019).
'Reflooding Hula Valley Begins, Reversing Decades of Cultivation', *Jewish Telegraphic Agency*, 6 May 1994 <http://www.jta.org/1994/05/06/archive/reflooding-hula-valley-begins-reversing-decades-of-cultivation> (last accessed 28 August 2019).
Regev, Motti and Edwin Seroussi, *Popular Music and National Culture in Israel* (Berkeley, CA: University of California Press, 2004).
Reizbaum, Marilyn, 'Max Nordau and the Generation of Jewish Muscle', *Jewish Culture and History*, 6.1 (2003), 130–51.
Relph, Sam, 'Indian Villages Lie Empty as Drought Forces Thousands to Flee', *The Guardian*, 12 June 2019 <https://www.theguardian.com/world/2019/jun/12/indian-villages-lie-empty-as-drought-forces-thousands-to-flee> (last accessed 6 August 2019).
'Report of the United Nations Fact-Finding Mission on the Gaza Conflict, A/HRC/12/48', *United Nations, General Assembly*, 29 September 2009 <https://www2.ohchr.org/english/bodies/hrcouncil/docs/12session/A-HRC-12-48.pdf> (last accessed 28 August 2019).
Ribarević-Nikolić, Ivanka and Želikjo Jurić (eds), *Mostar '92 – Urbicid* (Mostar: Hrvatsko vijece obrane opcine, 1992).
Richardson, Tanya and Gisa Weszkalnys, 'Introduction: Resource Materialities', *Anthropological Quarterly*, 87.1 (2014), 5–30.
Ricœur, Paul, *Memory, History, Forgetting*, trans. by Kathleen Blamey and David Pellauer (Chicago, IL: University of Chicago Press, 2004).
Rinat, Zafir, 'Swamps to Be Reflooded, 80 Years Later', *Haaretz*, 25 June 2009 <http://www.haaretz.com/print-edition/news/swamps-to-be-reflooded-80-years-later-1.278744> (last acccssed 28 August 2019).

Rinat, Zafir, 'Collapsing Environmental State of Gaza Poses Threat to Israel's National Security, Report Warns', *Haaretz*, 3 June 2019 <https://www.haaretz.com/israel-news/.premium-environmental-state-of-gaza-poses-threat-to-israel-s-national-security-report-warns-1.7328966> (last accessed 30 July 2019).

Robertson, Morgan M, 'The Neoliberalization of Ecosystem Services: Wetland Mitigation Banking and Problems in Environmental Governance', *Geoforum*, 35 (2004), 361–73.

Rodinson, Maxime, *Israel: A Colonial-Settler State?* (New York: Pathfinder Press, 1973).

Rotbard, Sharon, *White City/Black City: Architecture and War in Jaffa and Tel Aviv* (London: Pluto, 2015).

Rottenberg, Catherine, 'Let It Be Morning (Review)', *Journal of Middle East Women's Studies*, 4.1 (2008), 138–41.

Roy, Sara, *The Gaza Strip: The Political Economy of De-Development* (Washington, DC: Institute for Palestine Studies, 1995).

Roy, Sara, *Failing Peace: Gaza and the Palestinian-Israeli Conflict* (London: Pluto Press, 2007).

Rubenstein, Michael, *Public Works: Infrastructure, Irish Modernism, and the Postcolonial* (Notre Dame, IN: University of Notre Dame Press, 2010).

Rubenstein, Michael, 'Petro-', *ACLA State of the Discipline*, 2014 <https://stateofthediscipline.acla.org/entry/petro> (last accessed 24 August 2019).

Rubenstein, Michael, Bruce Robbins and Sophia Beal, 'Infrastructuralism: An Introduction', *MFS Modern Fiction Studies*, 61.4 (2015), 575–86.

Sa'ar, Amalia and Taghreed Yahia-Younis, 'Masculinity in Crisis: The Case of Palestinians in Israel', *British Journal of Middle Eastern Studies*, 35.3 (2008), 305–23.

Sacco, Joe, *Palestine* (London: Jonathan Cape, 2003).

Said, Edward, 'The Burdens of Interpretation and the Question of Palestine', *Journal of Palestine Studies*, 16.1 (1986), 29–37.

Said, Edward, *The Question of Palestine* (New York: Vintage Books, 1992).

Said, Edward, *After the Last Sky* (London: Vintage, 1993).

Said, Edward, 'The Morning After', *London Review of Books*, 21 October 1993, pp. 3–5.

Said, Edward, *Orientalism* (London: Vintage, 1995).

Saif, Atef Abu, 'Introduction', in *The Book of Gaza: A City in Short Fiction*, trans. by Elisabeth Jaquette (Manchester: Comma Press, 2014), pp. vii–xiii.

Saif, Atef Abu, *The Drone Eats with Me: Diaries from a City Under Fire* (Manchester: Comma Press, 2015).

Salamanca, Omar Jabary, Mezna Qato, Kareem Rabie and Sobhi Samour, 'Past Is Present: Settler Colonialism in Palestine', *Settler Colonial Studies*, 2.1 (2012), 1–8.
Saposnik, Arieh B., *Becoming Hebrew: The Creation of a Jewish National Culture in Ottoman Palestine* (Oxford: Oxford University Press, 2008).
Sayegh, Fayez A., *Zionist Colonialism in Palestine* (Beirut: Research Center Palestine Liberation Organization, 1965).
Schama, Simon, *Landscape and Memory* (London: HarperPerennial, 2004).
Schulman, Sarah, *Israel/Palestine and the Queer International* (Durham, NC: Duke University Press, 2012).
Schwartzstein, Peter, 'Biblical Waters: Can the Jordan River Be Saved?', *National Geographic*, 22 February 2014 <http://news.nationalgeographic.com/news/2014/02/140222-jordan-river-syrian-refugees-water-environment/> (last accessed 28 August 2019).
Scott, James C., *Seeing like a State: How Certain Schemes to Improve the Human Condition Have Failed* (New Haven, CT: Yale University Press, 1998).
'Seawater Pollution Raises Concerns of Waterborne Diseases and Environmental Hazards in the Gaza Strip', *United Nations Office for the Coordination of Humanitarian Affairs - Occupied Palestinian Territory (OCHA OPt)*, 9 August 2018 <https://www.ochaopt.org/content/seawater-pollution-raises-concerns-waterborne-diseases-and-environmental-hazards-gaza-strip> (last accessed 28 August 2019).
Segev, Tom, *1949: The First Israelis* (New York: The Free Press, 1986).
Sela, Maya, 'Meir Shalev Publishes New Novel and Talks Violence, the New Man and Why He Avoids Politics', *Haaretz*, 5 July 2013 <https://www.haaretz.com/.premium-author-meir-shalev-on-why-he-avoids-politics-1.5291627> (last accessed 14 February 2020).
Selby, Jan, *Water, Power and Politics in the Middle East: The Other Israeli-Palestinian Conflict* (London: I. B. Tauris, 2003).
Selby, Jan, 'Oil and Water: The Contrasting Anatomies of Resource Conflicts', *Government and Opposition*, 40.2 (2005), 200–24.
Selby, Jan, 'Cooperation, Domination and Colonisation: The Israeli-Palestinian Joint Water Committee', *Water Alternatives*, 6.1 (2013), 1–24.
Selby, Jan and Clemens Hoffmann, 'Water Scarcity, Conflict, and Migration: A Comparative Analysis and Reappraisal', *Environment and Planning C: Government and Policy*, 30.6 (2012), 997–1014.
Selby, Jan and Clemens Hoffmann, 'Rethinking Climate Change, Conflict and Security', *Geopolitics*, 19.4 (2014), 747–56.

Senor, Dan and Saul Singer, *Start-up Nation: The Story of Israel's Economic Miracle* (New York and Boston, MA: Twelve, 2009).

Seymour, Nicole, *Strange Natures: Futurity, Empathy, and the Queer Ecological Imagination* (Urbana, IL: University of Illinois Press, 2013).

Shafir, Gershon, *Land, Labor and the Origins of the Israeli-Palestinian Conflict, 1882–1914* (Berkeley, CA: University of California Press, 1996).

Shafir, Gershon, 'Capitalist Binationalism in Mandatory Palestine', *International Journal of Middle East Studies*, 43.4 (2011), 611–33.

Shaheen, Jack, *Reel Bad Arabs: How Hollywood Vilifies a People*, 2nd edn (Northampton, MA: Olive Branch Press, 2009).

Shaked, Gershon, *Modern Hebrew Fiction* (Bloomington, IN: Indiana University Press, 2000).

Shalev, Meir, *The Blue Mountain*, trans. by Hillel Halkin (Edinburgh: Canongate Books, 2004).

Shamir, Moshe, *With His Own Hands*, trans. by Joseph Shachter (Jerusalem: Institute for the Translation of Hebrew Literature and Israel Universities Press, [1951] 1970).

Shammas, Anton, *Arabesques*, trans. by Vivian Eden (Berkeley, CA: University of California Press, 2001).

Sharpe, *In the Wake: On Blackness and Being* (Durham, NC: Duke University Press, 2016).

Shavit, Ari, 'Survival of the Fittest', *Haaretz*, 8 January 2004 <https://www.haaretz.com/1.5262428> (last accessed 20 August 2019).

Shavit, Yaacov, 'The Mediterranean World and "Mediterraneanism": The Origins, Meaning, and Application of a Geo-Cultural Notion in Israel', *Mediterranean Historical Review*, 3.2 (1988), 96–117.

Shehadeh, Raja, *Strangers in the House* (London: Profile Books, 2002).

Shehadeh, Raja, *When the Bulbul Stopped Singing: A Diary of Ramallah Under Siege* (London: Profile Books, 2003).

Shehadeh, Raja, *A Rift in Time: Travels with My Ottoman Uncle* (London: Profile Books, 2010).

Shelef, Nadav G., 'From "Both Banks of the Jordan" to the "Whole Land of Israel": Ideological Change in Revisionist Zionism', *Israel Studies*, 9.1 (2004), 125–48.

Shelef, Nadav G., *Evolving Nationalism: Homeland, Identity, and Religion in Israel, 1925–2005* (Ithaca, NY: Cornell University Press, 2010).

Shewry, Theresa, *Hope at Sea: Possible Ecologies in Oceanic Literature* (Minneapolis, MN: University of Minnesota Press, 2015).

Shibli, Adania, 'This Sea Is Mohammad Al-Khatib's', *Ibraaz*, 6 October 2016 <https://www.ibraaz.org/publications/124#_edn004> (last accessed 6 August 2019).

Shimony, Batya, 'Shaping Israeli-Arab Identity in Hebrew Words—The Case of Sayed Kashua', *Israel Studies*, 18.1 (2013), 146–69.

Shlaim, Avi, *Collusion Across the Jordan: King Abdullah, the Zionist Movement and the Partition of Palestine* (Oxford: Clarendon, 1988).

Shohat, Ella, 'The Invention of the Mizrahim', *Journal of Palestine Studies*, 29.1 (1999), 5–20.

Shohat, Ella, *Israeli Cinema: East/West and the Politics of Representation* (London: I. B. Tauris, 2010).

Shpigel, Noa, 'It's No Longer That Hard to Walk on Water at the Sea of Galilee', *Haaretz*, 12 September 2018 <https://www.haaretz.com/israel-news/.premium.MAGAZINE-it-s-no-longer-that-hard-to-walk-on-water-in-the-sea-of-galilee-1.6465791> (last accessed 5 February 2020).

Siegel, Seth, *Let There Be Water: Israel's Solution for a Water-Starved World* (New York: St. Martin's Press, 2016).

Silberstein, Laurence J., *The Postzionism Debates: Knowledge and Power in Israeli Culture* (Abingdon: Routledge, 1999).

Silverstone, Roger, 'Complicity and Collusion in the Mediation of Everyday Life', *New Literary History*, 33.4 (2002), 761–80.

Slemon, Stephen, 'Magic Realism as Postcolonial Discourse', *Canadian Literature*, 116 (1988), 9–24.

Slyomovics, Susan, *The Object of Memory: Arab and Jew Narrate the Palestinian Village* (Philadelphia, PA: University of Pennsylvania Press, 1998).

Slyomovics, Susan, 'Who and What Is Native to Israel? On Marcel Janco's Settler Art and Jacqueline Shohet Kahanoff's "Levantinism"', *Settler Colonial Studies*, 4.1 (2014), 27–47.

Smilansky, Moshe, *Jewish Colonisation and the Fellah: The Effect of Jewish Land Settlement in Palestine on the Native Rural Population and on Agricultural Development in General* (Tel Aviv: Mischar w'Taasia, 1930).

Smilansky, Moshe, 'Hawaja Nazar', in *Palestine Caravan*, translator unknown (London: Methuen, 1935), pp. 145–81.

Smith, Andrew and William Hughes, *Ecogothic* (Manchester: Manchester University Press, 2013).

'State of the Mediterranean Marine and Coastal Environment', *United Nations Environment Programme/Mediterranean Action Plan (UNEP/MAP) – Barcelona*

Convention, 2012 <http://195.97.36.231/dbases/MAPpublications/SoE/SoM-MCER_ENG.pdf> (last accessed 28 August 2019).

Stein, Rebecca L., *Itineraries in Conflict: Israelis, Palestinians, and the Political Lives of Tourism* (Durham, NC: Duke University Press, 2008).

Steinberg, Philip E., 'Of Other Seas: Metaphors and Materialities in Maritime Regions', *Atlantic Studies*, 10.2 (2013), 156–69.

Steinberg, Philip and Kimberley Peters, 'Wet Ontologies, Fluid Spaces: Giving Depth to Volume through Oceanic Thinking', *Environment and Planning D: Society and Space*, 33 (2015), 247–64.

Sternhell, Zeev, *The Founding Myths of Israel: Nationalism, Socialism, and the Making of the Jewish State*, trans. by David Maisel (Princeton, NJ: Princeton University Press, 1998).

Strang, Veronica, *The Meaning of Water* (Oxford: Berg, 2004).

Sufian, Sandra M., *Healing the Land and the Nation: Malaria and the Zionist Project in Palestine, 1920–1947* (Chicago, IL: University of Chicago Press, 2007).

Sugars, Cynthia and Gerry Turcotte, eds, *Unsettled Remains: Canadian Literature and the Postcolonial Gothic* (Ontario: Wilfrid Laurier University Press, 2009).

Sultana, Farhana and Alex Loftus, 'The Right to Water: Prospects and Possibilities', in *The Right to Water: Politics, Governance and Social Struggles*, ed. by Farhana Sultana and Alex Loftus (Abingdon: Earthscan, 2012), pp. 1–19.

Swedenburg, Ted, 'The Palestinian Peasant as National Signifier', *Anthropological Quarterly*, 63.1 (1990), 18–30.

Swyngedouw, Erik, *Social Power and the Urbanization of Water: Flows of Power* (Oxford: Oxford University Press, 2004).

Swyngedouw, Erik, 'Into the Sea: Desalination as Hydro-Social Fix in Spain', *Annals of the Association of American Geographers*, 103.2 (2013), 261–70.

Swyngedouw, Erik, *Liquid Power: Contested Hydro-Modernities in Twentieth-Century Spain* (Cambridge, MA: MIT Press, 2015).

Szeman, Imre, 'Literature and Energy Futures', *PMLA*, 126.2 (2011), 323–6.

Szeman, Imre, 'Conjectures on World Energy Literature: Or, What Is Petroculture?', *Journal of Postcolonial Writing*, 53.3 (2017), pp. 277–88.

Tal, Alon, 'An Imperiled Promised Land: The Antecedents of Israel's Environmental Crises and Prospects for Progress', in *Challenging Environmental Issues: Middle Eastern Perspectives*, ed. by Joseph G. Jabbra and Nancy Walstrom Jabbra (Leiden: Brill, 1997), pp. 116–34.

Tal, Alon, *Pollution in a Promised Land: An Environmental History of Israel* (Berkeley, CA: University of California Press, 2002).

Tamari, Salim, *Mountain Against the Sea: Essays on Palestinian Society and Culture* (Berkeley, CA: University of California Press, 2009).

'Tel Aviv Gets Bus Publicity Drive in UK', *Jewish Chronicle*, 8 October 2009 <http://www.thejc.com/news/uk-news/20828/tel-aviv-gets-bus-publicity-drive-uk> (last accessed 28 August 2019).

Tessler, Mark, *A History of the Israeli-Palestinian Conflict*, 2nd edn (Bloomington, IN: Indiana University Press, 2009).

'The Hula Valley', *Tourist Israel*, 2019 <https://www.touristisrael.com/hula-valley/2540/> (last accessed 28 August 2019).

'Third Decade: 1921–1930', *Keren Kayemeth LeIsrael - Jewish National Fund*, n.d. <http://www.kkl.org.il/eng/about-kkl-jnf/our-history/third-decade-1921-1930/> (last accessed 22 April 2015).

'Troubled Waters: Palestinians Denied Fair Access to Water', *Amnesty International*, 2009 <https://www.amnestyusa.org/pdf/mde150272009en.pdf> (last accessed 28 August 2019).

Tuan, Yi-Fu, *The Hydrologic Cycle and the Wisdom of God: A Theme in Geoteleology* (Toronto: University of Toronto Press, 1968).

Tuffaha, Lena Khalaf, *Water and Salt* (Pasadena, CA: Red Hen Press, 2017).

Turner, Michael, Khaled Nasser and Nader Khateeb, 'Crossing the Jordan: Concept Document to Rehabilitate, Promote Prosperity and Help Bring Peace to the Lower Jordan Valley', ed. by Gidon Bromberg, *EcoPeace/Friends of the Earth Middle East*, 2005 <http://www.globalnature.org/bausteine.net/f/6036/crossingthejordan.pdf?fd=2> (last accessed 28 August 2019).

Tvedt, Terje and Terje Oestigaard, 'Introduction', in *A History of Water: Volume III: The World of Water*, ed. by Terje Tvedt and Terje Oestigaard (London: I. B. Tauris, 2006), pp. ix–xxii.

Twain, Mark, *The Innocents Abroad* (Hartford, CN: American Publishing Co., 1869).

Tyler, Warwick P. N., 'The Huleh Concession and Jewish Settlement of the Huleh Valley, 1934–48', *Middle Eastern Studies*, 30.4 (1994), 826–59.

Udasin, Sharon, 'Sewage Clogs Jordan River South of Baptism Site', *Jerusalem Post*, 23 December 2011 <http://www.jpost.com/Enviro-Tech/Sewage-clogs-Jordan-River-south-of-baptism-site> (last accessed 28 August 2019).

'United Nations Seminar on Assistance to Palestinian People Considers Gaza's Critical Water Crisis, Infrastructure Rehabilitation, Development', *United Nations*, 1 April 2015 <http://www.un.org/press/en/2015/gapal1330.doc.htm> (last accessed 28 August 2019).

'UNRWA Calls on Israel to Lift Book Blockade of Gaza Schools', United Nations News Service, 10 September 2009 <http://unispal.un.org/UNISPAL.NSF/0/EF3899AB900965618525762D0068D42F> (last accessed 28 August 2019).

Veracini, Lorenzo, 'Israel-Palestine Through a Settler-Colonial Studies Lens', *Interventions*, 21.2 (2018), 1–14.

'Vision', *Hydrocitizenship* <https://www.hydrocitizenship.com/vision.html> (last accessed 20 August 2019).

Warwick Research Collective (WReC), *Combined and Uneven Development: Towards a New Theory of World-Literature* (Liverpool: Liverpool University Press, 2015).

'Water and Climate Change', *UN-Water*, 2018 <https://www.unwater.org/water-facts/climate-change/> (last accessed 28 August 2019).

'Water Sector Damage Assessment Report', State of Palestine Palestinian Water Authority, 2014 <https://www.humanitarianresponse.info/sites/www.humanitarianresponse.info/files/assessments/20140819_PWA%20Water%20Sector%20Damage%20Assessment%20-%20August%202014_0.pdf> (last accessed 3 July 2019).

Weheliye, Alexander G., *Habeas Viscus: Racializing Assemblages, Biopolitics, and Black Feminist Theories of the Human* (Durham, NC: Duke University Press, 2014).

Weinthal, Erika and Jeannie Sowers, 'Targeting Infrastructure and Livelihoods in the West Bank and Gaza', *International Affairs*, 95.2 (2019), 319–40.

Weiss, Meira, 'Bereavement, Commemoration, and Collective Identity in Contemporary Israeli Society', *Anthropological Quarterly*, 70.2 (1997), 91–101.

Weiss, Meira, *The Chosen Body: The Politics of the Body in Israeli Society* (Stanford, CA: Stanford University Press, 2002).

Weizman, Eyal, 'Strategic Points, Flexible Lines, Tense Surfaces, Political Volumes: Ariel Sharon and the Geography of Occupation', *Philosophical Forum*, 35.2 (2004), 221–44.

Weizman, Eyal, *Hollow Land: Israel's Architecture of Occupation* (London: Verso, 2007).

Weizman, Eyal, *The Least of All Possible Evils: Humanitarian Violence from Arendt to Gaza* (London: Verso, 2011).

Weizman, Eyal, 'Short Cuts', *London Review of Books*, 34.23 (2012), 28.

Weizman, Eyal, *The Conflict Shoreline: Colonization as Climate Change in the Negev Desert* (Göttingen: Steidl, 2015).

Weizman, Eyal and Phillip Misselwitz, 'Military Operations as Urban Planning', *Mute*, 2003 <http://www.metamute.org/editorial/articles/military-operations-urban-planning> (last accessed 28 August 2019).
Wenzel, Jennifer, 'Amandla! Awethu!', *Interventions*, 18.6 (2016), 816–22.
Whitelam, Keith, *The Invention of Ancient Israel: The Silencing of Palestinian History* (London: Routledge, 1996).
Wiedenhöfer, Kai, *The Book of Destruction: Gaza After the 2009 War* (Göttingen: Steidl, 2010).
Williams, Patrick and Anna Ball, 'Where Is Palestine?', *Journal of Postcolonial Writing*, 50.2 (2014), 127–33.
Wilson, Anthony, *Shadow and Shelter: The Swamp in Southern Culture* (Jackson, MS: University Press of Mississippi, 2006).
Wittenberg, Hermann, 'Editorial: Coastlines and Littoral Zones in South African Ecocritical Writing', *Alternation*, 6 (2013), 1–8.
Wittfogel, Karl August, *Oriental Despotism, a Comparative Study of Total Power* (New Haven, CT: Yale University Press, 1957).
Wolf, Aaron T., *Hydropolitics along the Jordan River: Scarce Water and Its Impact on the Arab-Israeli Conflict* (New York: United Nations University Press, 1995).
Wolfe, Patrick, *Traces of History* (London: Verso, 2016).
Worster, Donald, *Rivers of Empire: Water, Aridity, and the Growth of the American West* (Oxford: Oxford University Press, 1985).
Yaeger, Patricia, 'Introduction: Dreaming of Infrastructure', *PMLA*, 122.1 (2007), 9–26.
Yaeger, Patricia, ed., 'Theories and Methodologies: Oceanic Studies', *PMLA*, 125.3 (2010).
Yaeger, Patricia, Ken Hiltner, Saree Makdisi, Vin Nardizzi, Laurie Shannon, Imre Szeman et al., 'Editor's Column: Literature in the Ages of Wood, Tallow, Coal, Whale Oil, Gasoline, Atomic Power, and Other Energy Sources', *PMLA*, 126.2 (2011), 305–26.
Young, Robert J. C., *Postcolonialism: An Historical Introduction* (Oxford: Blackwell Publishing, 2001).
Yusoff, Kathryn, *A Billion Black Anthropocenes or None* (Minneapolis, MN: University of Minnesota Press, 2019).
Yuval-Davis, Nira, 'Gender and Nation', *Ethnic and Racial Studies*, 16.4 (1993), 621–32.

Zak, David, 'From a Wasteland to a Settlement', *The Palestine Poster Project Archives*, 1955 <https://www.palestineposterproject.org/poster/from-a-wasteland-to-a-settlement> (last accessed 26 August 2019).

Zakim, Eric, 'Palimpsests of National Identity: Israeli Culture at the End of the American Century', *Shofar: An Interdisciplinary Journal of Jewish Studies*, 16.2 (1997), 48–69.

Zakim, Eric, *To Build and Be Built: Landscape, Literature, and the Construction of Zionist Identity* (Pittsburgh, PA: University of Pennsylvania Press, 2006).

Zeitoun, Mark, *Power and Water in the Middle East: The Hidden Politics of the Palestinian-Israeli Water Conflict* (London: I. B. Tauris, 2012).

Zerubavel, Yael, *Recovered Roots: Collective Memory and the Making of Israeli National Tradition* (Chicago, IL: University of Chicago Press, 1995).

Zerubavel, Yael, 'Revisiting the Pioneer Past: Continuity and Change in Hebrew Settlement Narratives', *Hebrew Studies*, 41 (2000), 209–24.

Zerubavel, Yael, 'Desert and Settlement: Space Metaphors and Symbolic Landscapes in the Yishuv and Early Israeli Culture', in *Jewish Topographies: Visions of Space, Traditions of Place*, ed. by Julia Brauch, Anna Lipphardt and Alexandra Nocke (Aldershot: Ashgate, 2008), pp. 210–22.

Zerubavel, Yael, 'The Conquest of the Desert and the Settlement Ethos', in *The Desert Experience in Israel: Communities, Arts, Science, and Education in the Negev*, ed. by A. Paul Hare and Gideon M. Kressel (Lanham, ML: University Press of America, 2009), pp. 33–44.

Zerubavel, Yael, *Desert in the Promised Land* (Chicago, IL: University of Chicago Press, 2018).

Zimmerman, Erich, *World Resources and Industries: A Functional Appraisal of the Availability of Agricultural and Industrial Resources* (New York: Harper and Row, 1933).

Zitun, Yoav, 'Israel Test Fires Target Missile in Mediterranean', *Ynet*, 9 March 2013 <http://www.ynetnews.com/articles/0,7340,L-4425797,00.html> (last accessed 28 August 2019).

INDEX

1948 Arab-Israeli War
  border changes, 13, 50
  fighting during, 43
  Israeli historiography of, 85
  see also Nakba, the

Agamben, Giorgio, 169–72, 177
agriculture (Israeli), 35–6, 72
  agricultural mystique, 78–9
  decline of, 72, 132–3
  environmental harms of, 87–8
agriculture (Palestinian), 51, 58, 86, 92
Alatout, Samer, 4, 14–15, 16, 20, 76, 176
Aliyah Bet, 117
'Allush, Layla, 9–10
Anand, Nikhil, 149, 163–4, 166, 171, 176–8, 180
animality, 48, 164, 171, 176, 177, 186n

Anthropocene, 7–8, 193
aquifers
  Israeli control of, 174
  in literature, 194
  Palestinian rights to, 14
  transboundary, 11
  see also Coastal Aquifer; Mountain Aquifer
Bachelard, Gaston, 46, 52, 56
Bakker, Karen, 16, 163
Ball, Anna, 6, 52, 54
Barghouti, Mourid, 32, 34, 55–62
bathroom, history of, 168
Bauman, Zygmunt, 57, 133–4, 137
Bedouin
  displacement, 16–17, 92, 98
  Ghawarna tribe, 81–2, 86
  water access, 13, 149
Ben-Gurion, David, 15, 16, 108, 118, 128, 131

233

Bernard, Anna, 56, 57, 60, 119, 124, 130, 157, 179
Blue Box, 8–9
Blue Humanities, 7, 27n, 111–12
Blue Revolution, 135–6
Blum, Hester, 111–12
Brand Israel, 17, 109
Braudel, Fernand, 114–15, 116
British Mandate, 20, 44, 50, 52, 74–5, 76, 170
Butler, Judith, 173, 176

Carrigan, Anthony, 157–8
cemeteries, 72–3
citrus industry, 9, 35, 36, 40, 132–3
cleanliness *see* hygiene
cli-fi, 1, 180
climate change, 1, 3, 15, 21, 98, 136, 180, 193–4
Coastal Aquifer, 11, 155; *see also* aquifers; Mountain Aquifer
Cohen, Shaul, 54–5, 56
consumerism, 131, 134, 137–8
Cusack, Tricia, 35, 43, 55

Dabbagh, Selma, 155–6
dams, 3, 15, 26n
Darwish, Mahmoud, 10–11, 32, 34, 50–5, 61–2, 164
Davis, Mike, 116–17, 187n
Dead Sea, 12, 83, 195
DeLoughrey, Elizabeth, 54, 110, 112

desalination, 2, 7, 12–13, 14, 15, 16, 118
desert
  environmental determinism and, 4, 116
  exile and, 125
  making the desert bloom, 15, 55, 118
  Palestinians and, 126–7, 128
desertification, 17, 98
Douglas, Mary, 79, 169
drought, 2, 10–11, 12, 24, 88, 180

ecocriticism
  first wave, 98
  Israeli and Palestinian literature and, 5, 6–7, 193
  water and, 5–6, 7
Energy Humanities, 21; *see also* petrofiction and petrocriticism
Environmental Humanities, 6, 193; *see also* ecocriticism
environmentalism
  colonialism and, 17, 18
  gender essentialism in, 54
  Israeli, 12, 71, 86–8, 97–9
  see also greenwashing
Eurovision, 108–9
exile (Jewish), 117, 125
exile (Palestinian), 8, 10–11, 53

Fatah, 13, 152
First Aliyah, 32–3, 35–9, 43
First Intifada, 167

Foucault, Michel, 163–4, 166, 170, 172
Freud, Sigmund, 48, 90–1, 96

Galilee, Sea of *see* Lake Kinneret
Gandy, Matthew, 155, 163, 168
Gavron, Assaf, 2–3
Gaza Strip
   blockade on, 13, 156–7, 176
   fishing industry, 138
   infrastructure, 13, 153–4
   water access, 13, 153–6, 158–9, 161, 176
   water-associated disease, 176
   water resources, 11
Ghosh, Amitav, 21
globalisation, 131, 133–8
Graham, Steven, 149, 151–2, 154, 155, 174–5, 187n
greenwashing, 13, 16, 17, 98–9
   and Israel Defense Forces, 17, 98
Grumberg, Karen, 73, 109, 150

halutzim (pioneers)
   Diaspora Judaism and, 48, 84
   draining the swamps, 69, 79–80
   erotic attachment to the land, 45–6
   literary glorification of, 33
   malaria and, 75–7
   national mythology of, 72–3, 85, 87, 89, 91, 94–7
   sacrifice, 47–8
   the sea and, 38
Handal, Nathalie, 10–11
Hamas, 13, 94, 153, 161, 176

Havrelock, Rachel, 31, 34, 40, 42, 50
Hebrew Labour, 35–6
Herzl, Theodor, 16, 69, 81, 82, 83–4, 128
high modernism *see* Scott, James C.
Hochberg, Gil Z., 128, 142n, 149–50, 159–60, 165
homeland
   Israeli, 8, 32, 42–4, 45–6
   Palestinian, 8–10, 32, 53, 54, 189
Hula Valley, 74, 86–8, 89–90, 99
humanitarianism, 152, 153, 154, 155, 176
hydraulic citizenship *see* Anand, Nikhil
hydroelectricity, 40, 76, 83
hydromodernity, 3, 4, 83, 163
hygiene, 22, 23
   hygienic landscapes, 77–8, 79
   modernity and, 163, 168–9
   racialisation and, 23, 79, 171
   under siege, 148, 154, 166, 176

Ice Bucket Challenge, 159
infrastructure, 163–4, 168
   destruction of, 150–5, 158–9, 174–5, 175–6
   see also Gaza Strip; West Bank
irrigation
   Israeli technology, 2, 12
   Palestinian, 10, 58, 81
   power and, 15, 19
   Zionist movement and, 40, 76, 91

Israel
  the beach and, 108–9, 113–14
  capitalism and, 29n, 110, 133–4, 137
  economy of, 130–5
  Europe and, 109, 113, 116, 118, 128, 121–2, 131–3
  race and, 172, 179
  the sea and, 112–14, 117–18, 121–3
  socialism and, 29n, 130–1
  see also Zionism
Israeli Arabs *see* Palestinian citizens of Israel
Israel Defense Forces (IDF), 160, 173, 175–6
  destruction of buildings, 175
  destruction of water infrastructure, 148, 153–4
  Mavi Marmara killings, 112
  military service, 124
  see also greenwashing

Jabotinsky, Ze'ev, 44–5
Jaffa, 128
Jaffa orange, 132
Jameson, Fredric, 23, 100
Jenin, Battle of, 174–5
Jerusalem, 1, 46, 120, 159–60
  East Jerusalem, 17, 149
  tourism, 108–9
  weather, 4, 180
Jewish National Fund (JNF, Keren Kayemeth LeIsrael), 69, 74, 81, 98, 99

Jezreel Valley, 40, 72
  draining the swamps, 69, 75, 80
  Indigenous inhabitants, 92
  and national mythology, 69, 86, 88–9, 96
Joint Water Committee, 14, 154
Jordan, 31, 43, 56
  Transjordan, 44
Jordan River *see* River Jordan
Jordan Valley, 40, 41, 86

Kaika, Maria, 158, 162, 163
Karlinsky, Nahum, 35, 36, 40–1, 49–50, 132
Kashua, Sayed, 149–51, 159–81
Keren Kayemeth LeIsrael *see* Jewish National Fund
kibbutzim, 8, 63, 73, 81, 118
Knowing the Land (*yediat ha'aretz*), 8, 47

Labour Zionism, 29n, 35, 80, 85, 95, 100, 132
Lake Kinneret, 11–12, 38, 87–8
Lake Tiberias *see* Lake Kinneret
landscape
  aesthetics, 47, 78, 81, 82
  agency, 91–2
  homeland and, 43, 49
  nationalism and, 35
Laor, Yitzhak, 120, 123, 129, 145n
Lentin, Ronit, 171–2
Likud, 43, 45, 85
Linton, Jamie, 3, 4, 15, 19–20, 41, 78, 127

Macdonald, Graeme, 22, 23
magical realism, 71–2, 79–80, 84, 90–3, 100
malaria, 75–7
Malthusianism, 23
maps and mapping, 8, 80
Massad, Joseph, 16
Mavi Marmara, 112
Mediterranean Sea
  ecology of, 138–9
  refugee crisis, 139
Mediterraneanism (*Yam Tikhoniut*), 109–17, 121–31
Mekorot, 11, 14, 174, 183n, 196n
Mintz, Alan, 99, 111
Mizrahi Jews, 29n, 85, 114, 129, 172
moshavim, 72
moshavot, 35, 63
Mountain Aquifer, 11, 58, 174; *see also* aquifers; Coastal Aquifer

Nakba, the
  destruction of buildings, 53, 152
  environmental Nakba, 55
  expulsion of Palestinians, 17, 50, 87, 101
  Palestinian life prior to, 59
  see also 1948 Arab-Israeli War
National Water Carrier, 11, 74, 152
nationalism
  environment and, 8–9
  gender and, 52, 54
  homoeroticism and, 39, 64
  nostalgia and, 94–7

natural disasters, 138, 157, 180
Negev Desert, 15, 16–17, 98
New Historians, 70–1, 85
Nixon, Rob, 7, 15, 70
  Slow Violence, 154, 157, 175, 176, 179
Nocke, Alexandra, 109, 110, 111, 114, 121, 122, 127

occupation, environmental harms of, 17, 18, 54–5, 98
Oceanic Studies, 111–12
Ohana, David, 109, 110, 113–14, 139
oil, 2, 21–4, 138, 139; *see also* petrofiction and petrocriticism
oranges *see* citrus industry; Jaffa orange
Oslo Accords, 14, 112, 113, 114, 126–7, 131, 134–5, 140
Ottoman Palestine, 44, 50, 52, 59, 74, 86
Oz, Amos, 93–4, 109–10, 121–41
  Mediterraneanism and, 118–21
  politics, 110, 119–20, 128
  representations of Palestinians, 126–8

Palestine
  economy, 9, 58
  environment, 9, 18n, 26, 42, 34, 54–6
  gender politics, 52, 169
  see also Gaza Strip; West Bank
Palestinian citizens of Israel, 150, 159–60, 164, 172, 173–4

Palestinian literature
  environment and, 9–10
  publishing constraints on, 156–7
  the nation and, 156
Peleg, Yaron, 33, 37, 39, 47, 70
petrofiction and petrocriticism, 21–4, 194
pinkwashing, 17, 109
pioneers *see* halutzim
postcolonial studies
  Palestine and, 6–7, 193
  water and, 7
post-Zionism, 70–1, 85, 88–9, (96), 113–14

Red-Dead Canal, 12
Redeeming the Land, 8, 15, 49, 69, 74, 81, 82–5, 95
refugees
  climate, 2–3, 10–11
  Palestinian, 20, 50, 196
Revisionist Zionism, 44–5
River Jordan
  as border, 31, 43, 44–9, 50, 52–3, 60
  overuse of, 11–12, 74
  pollution of, 31
riverscape, 34–5, 43
Roy, Sara, 14, 34, 58, 138
Rubenstein, Michael, 21, 166

Said, Edward, 50, 116, 120, 140, 157, 158
sanitation *see* hygiene

Scott, James C., 15, 20, 73, 92
Second Aliyah, 35, 69, 72–3
Second Intifada, 151, 164, 167, 192
Selby, Jan, 2, 4, 6, 14, 23, 31–2, 153–4, 194
separation wall, 54–5, 57, 140, 190
settlements, 14, 18, 151, 160, 178
settler colonialism, 26–7n, 36, 71–2
Shalev, Meir, 70–3, 76–7, 79–82, 84, 89–98, 99–100, 132
Sharon, Ariel, 13, 151, 155, 174–5
Shehadeh, Raja, 57, 66n, 98, 197n
Smilansky, Moshe, 32–4, 35–49, 95, 117
Strang, Veronica, 49, 52, 78, 166
Sufian, Sandra M., 40, 74–6, 77, 87, 89–90
sumud, 9, 18
swamps
  aesthetics, 78
  draining, 74–6, 79–82, 83–4, 94–7
  hygiene, 75, 77–8, 88
Swyngedouw, Erik, 15, 20, 153, 158, 162
Szeman, Imre, 22–3

Tal, Alon, 72, 86, 87, 88
Tel Aviv, 108–9, 128, 129
tourism, 12, 132–3
  ecotourism, 99

translation, literature in, 24, 70, 156
trees
　in Israeli and Palestinian environmental imaginaries, 8, 9–10, 32, 51
　the Nakba and, 122, 191
　Palestinian economy and, 9, 51
　swamp drainage and, 74, 91
　tree-planting, 8, 98
Tuffaha, Lena Khalaf, 194–5

United Nations Relief and Works Agency (UNRWA), 13, 159
urbicide, 152; *see also* infrastructure

war, environmental effects of, 138, 155
Warwick Research Collective (WReC), 23, 137
water
　agriculture and, 40–1, 83
　borders, 31, 43, 44–5, 50, 52–3, 60, 65n, 87, 93
　bottled, 155, 161
　Christianity and, 41, 64–5n, 125, 168
　cooperation, 14
　effect of war on, 148, 153–5, 174–5
　electricity and, 13, 14, 151, 159, 161
　health and, 154–5
　holy water, 189
　infrastructure, 13–14, 18, 83, 151–6, 158–9, 161–9, 171, 174, 178
　Islam and, 168, 185n
　Jewish immigration and, 40, 75–6
　Judaism and, 41, 168
　Palestinian economy and, 58
　pollution, 1, 11, 13, 88, 167, 171
　privatisation, 16, 163
　securitisation of, 194
　settlements and, 14, 18, 151, 160, 178
　virtual water, 12
　wastewater/sewage, 18, 161, 165, 171, 176
　water cycle, 43–4, 54, 78
　water rights, 2, 4, 14
　water/sewage intifada, 13, 17
　water towers, 96
　water wars, 2, 4, 23, 25, 31–2, 148
Weizman, Eyal, 140–1, 151, 152, 153, 158
West Bank
　agriculture, 58
　checkpoints, 56, 140, 165
　economy, 58
　infrastructure, 14, 153–4
　urban warfare, 151
　water access, 14, 151, 154, 158, 166, 172–5, 178
　water resources, 11–12

Wittfogel, Karl, 19
Worster, Donald, 15, 19

Yaeger, Patricia, 23, 150–1, 159
Yam Tikhoniut see Mediterraneanism
yediat ha'aretz see Knowing the Land

Zeitoun, Mark, 61, 148, 153
Zerubavel, Yael, 43, 47, 70, 94, 142

Zionism
   antisemitism and, 39, 48, 84, 128–9
   land and, 8–9, 45–6, 49
   masculinity and, 38–9, 64n
   myth of national sacrifice and, 47–8, 73
   Palestinians and, 36
   socialism and, 29n, 100
   water and, 14–15, 20, 83

EU representative:
Easy Access System Europe
Mustamäe tee 50, 10621 Tallinn, Estonia
Gpsr.requests@easproject.com

www.ingramcontent.com/pod-product-compliance
Lightning Source LLC
Chambersburg PA
CBHW070344240426
43671CB00013BA/2399